William Wright

The Empire of the Hittites

With Decipherment of Hittite Inscriptions. Second Edition

William Wright

The Empire of the Hittites
With Decipherment of Hittite Inscriptions. Second Edition

ISBN/EAN: 9783337121198

Printed in Europe, USA, Canada, Australia, Japan

Cover: Foto ©Andreas Hilbeck / pixelio.de

More available books at **www.hansebooks.com**

THE
EMPIRE OF THE HITTITES.

Ballantyne Press
BALLANTYNE, HANSON AND CO., EDINBURGH
CHANDOS STREET, LONDON

THE EMPIRE OF THE HITTITES.

BY

WILLIAM WRIGHT, D.D., F.R.G.S.

WITH

DECIPHERMENT OF HITTITE INSCRIPTIONS
BY PROF. A. H. SAYCE, LL.D.

A HITTITE MAP
BY COL. SIR CHARLES WILSON, K.C.B., F.R.S., AND CAPT. CONDER, R.E.

AND

A Complete Set of Hittite Inscriptions
REVISED BY MR. W. H. RYLANDS, F.S.A.

SECOND EDITION.

LONDON:
JAMES NISBET & CO., 21 BERNERS STREET.
1886.

[*All rights reserved.*]

TO

THE PRESIDENT AND MEMBERS

OF THE

Society of Biblical Archæology

BY

A MEMBER OF THE COUNCIL.

PREFACE TO SECOND EDITION.

THE second edition of this book has been much delayed by the preparation of new plates of Hittite sculptures and inscriptions. My aim has been to make the work as complete as possible, without unduly increasing its size or adding to its price. The twenty-seven plates contain reproductions of sculptures referred to in the text, and also the latest discovered inscriptions accessible. Other inscriptions have come to light in Hittite-land, but as yet they have not been copied or brought to this country; and Dr. Hayes Ward, just returned from the East, has given me a list of widely scattered Hittite monuments, which await the courageous explorer.

I think I may say that my object in compiling the Book has been attained. "The Empire of the Hittites" has been "restored to its rightful position in secular history," and "the scattered references to the Hittites in sacred history" have been confirmed. The approval which favoured my "hazardous venture" was not so much owing to the merits of the work as to the preparedness of the public to receive it, and though some would doubtless prefer a more systematic treatment of the subject, I think it better to adhere, in this issue, to the arrangement which accords best with the fragmentary character of Hittite discoveries, and which is likely to find most favour with the greatest number of readers.

The reviews of the book, with two exceptions, one English and one American, have been marked by a generous candour and honest courtesy, for which I was not altogether prepared.

Canon Taylor's review in the *British Quarterly* is a luminous summary of the whole argument. Canon Tristram's brilliant article, in the *Churchman*, covers the whole ground, and adds a graphic account of his own exploration of the Hittite country, and his personal inspection of the Hittite monuments *in situ*.

M. Claremont Ganneau introduced the book to French readers, by a paper in the *Journal Officiel*, marked by his rare and exhaustive scholarship.

The *Athenæum, Academy, Saturday Review, Standard, Telegraph, St. James's Gazette*, and the other leading papers of the secular press, discussed the subject with intelligence and favour, and such Church papers as the *Guardian* and *Record* on the one hand, and the *Tablet* on the other, dealt with the question in a thorough and scholarly fashion. All admit the chief points of my thesis, though some criticise details.

Exception has been taken to the title of the book, as if I had in view a compact homogeneous race ruled over by an Emperor—in fact, something like the late French Empire. The title lays no claim to scientific precision. By Empire, I simply mean Dominion, the one meaning given to the word by Skeat, and perhaps the best example at the present time is the Turkish Empire, a Dominion including many diverse and heterogeneous peoples, but with a voice at the seat of empire strong enough to summon warriors or allies from remote and slightly attached provinces. In the text my meaning is sufficiently clear when I speak of the King of the Hittites having under his command, at Megiddo and Kadesh, "the surrounding people, either as subjects or as allies."

Maspero and Schrader have been quoted by a few in favour of the theory that there was a Hittite people in the north, and also a tribe of Hittites in the south, but that they had no connection with each other. M. Ed. Meyer goes so far as to state that the name Hittite was erroneously applied by the Hebrews to a Canaanite tribe.¹ But these opinions were enunciated before my Book appeared, and even Wilkinson who follows Maspero² in the theory of "the two distinct tribes" declares "they both fought in cars, and used the same weapons, and we even find they lived together and garrisoned the same towns."³

Any one acquainted with history will admit that the dominant Hittites of the north who pushed the Assyrians in the east, might have sent out an enterprising colony Egyptward as far south as Hebron; and when we see the two peoples bearing the same name, fighting in great battles under the same leaders, marshalled in the same manner, using the same arms, and guarding the same towns, the conviction is irresistible that they were the same people, and this conclusion shatters the theory that the Pentateuch is a post-exilic fabrication woven and pieced together from the floating traditions of Babylonia. The story of the Hittite occupation of Hebron fits in with the contemporary history of Egypt and Assyria, and was not likely to have been written at a late period when the events referred to had faded out of history.

It has been pointed out that the Hittite name in late Assyrian inscriptions shifted west as far as Philistia;

---

¹ "Zeitschrift A. T. Wissenschaft," i. 125. 1881.
² "Histoire Ancienne," p. 192.   ³ "Ancient Egyptians," i. 258.

but we have a parallel to this in our own day when the name "Frank" is applied in Syria to Englishmen and Americans as well as to the French.

An attempt has been made to use the variations in the spelling of the word for Hittite as an argument against the oneness of the people. But this is to be explained by the fact that the Assyrians, like the Egyptians, and like people in our own day, made mistakes in spelling.

Any one who looks at Whitehouse's admirable translation of Schrader's book on "The Cuneiform Inscriptions and the Old Testament," will see that almost every proper name was spelled by the Assyrians in different ways. Hamath is spelled in a variety of ways, closely resembling the various ways in which the word for Hittite is spelled. Damascus is spelled in several ways, and so are most other names. In fact, the Queen's Inspector was not at the elbow of the Assyrian scribe.

My references to Dr. Cheyne's article in the "Encyclopædia Britannica" led to a correspondence in the *Academy*. Dr. Cheyne being the most eminent leader of a school of criticism in England, I have reproduced the correspondence in Appendix III., pp. 206–217.

As my book was just leaving the press a happy

circumstance brought me into friendly correspondence with Dr. Cheyne, and at my suggestion he has written for publication the following note, which more clearly defines his attitude to the Hittites of Genesis than anything in the correspondence :—

"I wish to express my deep respect for the labours by which Dr. Wright has added so much to our knowledge of a very obscure subject, and also my strong sympathy with him in his love for the Biblical writings. At his request, I willingly record a more deliberately worded opinion on the relation of Hittite researches to the Machpelah narration in Gen. xxiii. The nature of the composition of the great history of Israel, to which our book of Genesis belongs, justified, and still justifies, an attitude of reserve towards this narrator's implied historical theory of the settlement of the חתים so far south as Hebron, always supposing that the phrase בני חת in Gen. xiii., stands in linguistic connexion with the term חתים in Kings. But I would leave it open to future research to supply such facts as may, without constraint, render it probable that the narrator followed a tradition of the, at any rate, political influence of the חתים in the district of Hebron. I dare not close this paragraph without expressing my keen regret, as a critic to whom, perhaps, no one can deny a fundamental Christian spirit, at the haste with which many prominent speakers and writers have fostered the popular belief that archæological discoveries are altogether favourable to the ordinary English view of the dates of the historical books, including the Pentateuch. Historical criticism has its just place, not only as a branch of historical study, but as a *Hulfswissenschaft* to theology. From no point of view, is it, in my opinion, allowable to take the Bible simply as it stands, and proceed to illustrate it by archæological researches.

"T. K. CHEYNE."

I have the greater pleasure in publishing this note as it reduces to the lowest minimum the only point at issue on the Hittite question between myself and the man who, perhaps, has done most in England towards the intelligent understanding of the Hebrew Scriptures, and towards whom I have had the misfortune to be in acute antagonism.

In the study of the Hittite question, as in the wider field of Semitic literature, I gratefully acknowledge my indebtedness to Dr. Cheyne, but his theory of the historical books of the Bible does not allow of illustrating them as they stand, and hence he can only look to the facts of future research to establish the existence of a tradition of the Hittites in the district of Hebron. I join with Dr. Cheyne in keen regret at the haste with which archæological facts have sometimes been wrested to support doctrines on which they have no bearing whatever. He is no true friend of the Bible or of archæological research who founds an imposing theory on a fanciful basis of evidence. At the same time, the archæologist is justified in insisting that theories, however plausible, shall give place to the evidence of well-ascertained facts.

One critic blames me for ignoring theories antagonistic to my facts. I frankly admit that I studiously avoided giving currency to what M. Halévy so aptly speaks of as "des fadesses antibibliques." The slightest references to the wild and shifting theories of Graf, Kuenen, Wellhausen, Vatke, Stade, &c., or to the more sober views of Drs. Dillmann, Nöldeke, Schrader, &c., would have led me aside from my purpose. Their

"little systems have their day,
They have their day and cease to be."

But facts abide, and should not be trimmed or altered to accord with theories. The light shines brightly on ancient Egypt and Assyria, and the forgotten past is photographed and lives again. There is twilight in "the land of the Hittites," and the Empire in outline is fast detaching itself from the darkness. In the light of these newly-recovered Empires, facts, in the contemporary history of the Hebrews, become also visible. The increasing light from the monuments has, in my opinion, confirmed the historic character of the Pentateuch. Even Hommell treats as history the chequered life of Abraham, and identifies the Kheta with the Hittites. And it seems to me to be my clear duty to state facts as I find them, suggest inferences, and leave the reader to judge for himself.

Again I have to acknowledge my indebtedness for advice and assistance to many scholars. At my request Mr. Pinches, of the British Museum, re-examined some important Assyrian inscriptions containing references to the Hittites. The result of his investigations was laid before the Soc. Bib. Arch., and printed in the "Transactions." Prof. Sayce's reply to Mr. Pinches was also printed in the "Transactions." The discussion, which is worthy of careful study, will be found in Appendix V., pp. 220-232.

Mr. Rylands has again placed me under lasting obligation to him by drawing additional plates; and I hold with Prof. Sayce, who says that "no one can draw Hittite inscriptions like Mr. Rylands." Mr. Budge,

Canon Taylor, M. Halévy, Mr. Rylands, and many others, have pointed out errata and suggested improvements.

M. Perrot's great work on Asia Minor, one of the abiding monuments of the late Empire, has been laid under contribution for Plates XXIII. and XXIV.

To Prof. Sayce, however, my chief thanks are due. He has gone carefully over the chapter on Decipherment, correcting and improving with increasing knowledge of the character. He has added a short paper on the Babylon Bowl, which will be found at p. 198; and the following additional remarks on decipherment reach me in time to be added to the preface:—

My dear Dr. Wright,—

I do not know whether there will be room in the Preface to your new Edition for any fresh matter, or indeed, whether the Preface is not already in type, but I thought you would like to have my latest additions and corrections to the chapter on Hittite decipherment. The inscription from Merash is the first complete text of any length which we possess, and, as might be expected, therefore, it throws fresh light on the interpretation of the texts.

First of all, it gives the phonetic reading of the word for "he says." At Hamath this is expressed by the ideograph of "speaking" followed by the verbal suffix *me*, in J. I. by the ideograph and the letters *e-me*, in J. II. by the ideograph and the picture of a two-handled jar. I thought that *eme* was the phonetic complement of the full word; but as the Merash text begins with the characters *e-me* and nothing more, it is evident that *e-me* signifies "he says," the root *e* signifying "to speak." It is further evident that the two-handled jar is a phonetic character having the value of *eme*. A proper name at Tyana (line 3) is written Sandu-eme "Sandon speaks." The same name occurs at Merash (front, 2).

At Merash, between the word *eme* and the royal name, a character intervenes, which, as we have seen, interchanges with *sar-me* "he is king" on the Kouyunjik seals. A comparison of such names as Sap-lel and Sapa-lul-me, Kheta-sira and Sanda-sar-me, shows that we may read either "such and such a god rules" (*sar-me*) or "is a king" (*sar*). The character in question, therefore, which seems to denote a scourge, must be regarded as an ideograph standing as well for the substantival as for the verbal notion, and must here signify "the king" simply. The royal name, which is compounded with that of the god Sandon, is followed (as on the monuments of Carchemish) by the names of both father and grandfather, the patronymic suffix being expressed ideographically by the small semi-circle. In

b

the second case, however, it is followed by a character which I have mis-read *si*, but which really has the value of *ku*(*s*) or *eku*(*s*). This is made clear by a comparison of the last two lines of J. II.

Next comes the ideograph of "king" (the value of the animal's head being left to be determined by future research). The analogy of the other Hittite inscriptions would lead us to suppose that this was followed by the name of the country to which the king belonged, and though the ideograph of "country" does not seem to appear in the inscription on this particular lion, it does in the squeeze and photograph which Dr. Gwyther took of the inscription on another lion at Merash, and which agrees with the inscription of the cast in almost every other respect. The cuneiform monuments inform us that Merash lay within the territory of Kummukh or Komagênê, and as the Assyrian *kh* in Hittite names (like Tarkhu and Khattukhi) corresponds to a *k*, we should expect to find the territorial title of our Merash king assuming some such form as Kumukus. Now it is actually expressed by the boot followed by the characters (*e*)*ku*(*s*)-*es* or (*e*)*ku-es*, and the boot interchanges with the characters *ku-me*. The king was therefore called *Kume-kues* "the Komagenian." I may add that I was wrong in supposing that the boot had the further value of *mesi*. My error arose from my misreading the character (e)ku(s) as si. The two values of the character are really kume, and kue.

We have the same patronymic suffix in Kummukh as in Khattukhi and Tarkhu, and it is possible that Kume-ku(s) is merely a derivative from Kume or Kue "a Kuan." At all events it appears in the names of both the Moskhi and the Kaskâ or Kolkhians. Perhaps also we may see it in Kat-patú-ka (Kappadokia) and Khilak (Kilikia). The same suffix is found in Vannic. The king of Carchemish, it will be noticed, entitles himself "the god-born" (J. I. 1).

The first portion of the name of the Merash king (which is written with a variant in line 2) occurs at Hamath (H. I. 3).

Besides *beki* "a town," found in the Egyptian names of Hittite cities like Sathekh-beg and Suki-beki, Prof. Maspero has recently pointed out that Kamru or Kamlu is shown by the Egyptian determinative attached to it to have been the Hittite word for "a house." Mr. Tomkins compares the name of Sathekh-beg "the town of Sutekh" with Baal-bek, and Lenormant has shown that the same word enters into the composition of Da-bigu, mentioned in the cuneiform inscriptions as in the neighbourhood of Carchemish, as well as of Mabug, "the city of Ma," the great goddess of Komana.

I may add, by way of conclusion, that I would compare the name of Dimes with that of Dameis found in a Kilikian inscription at Selindy. Kuas, another Kilikian name met with at Hamaxia, seems to claim connection with Kue.—Yours very truly,   A. H. SAYCE.

I have been urged to add a bibliographical chapter to this edition, but I have decided not to enlarge or encumber the Book by details interesting chiefly to scholars with access to large libraries. References are given to authorities when quoted, but I have been anxious to limit them as much as possible to standard works easily consulted by English readers.

I have only now to thank several friends for assisting in proof reading, and to express my gratitude to the publishers for the excellent manner in which they have brought out this edition.

W. WRIGHT.

WOOLSTHORPF, UPPER NORWOOD,
Dec. 19, 1885.

PREFACE TO FIRST EDITION.

THE object of this book is to restore the Empire of the Hittites to its rightful position in secular history, and thus to confirm the scattered references to the Hittites in sacred history.

The Bible is not a mere compendium of history. It is a revelation of a purpose of mercy. In all its unfoldings we have sketches of peoples and things, so far as they concern the great purpose of the book. It often refers to a great people called the Hittites. From the time of Abraham to the Captivity the Hittites move on parallel lines with the chosen people.

We see them carrying out with formal courtesy a shrewd bargain with the father of the faithful. We see their serried line of chariots opposing Joshua on his entrance into the promised land, and in the decisive battle by Lake Merom. We see their soldiers of fortune leading the hosts of David and Solomon, and their women in the *hareems* of the same powerful monarchs; and finally we see the Syrian army flying in panic from the siege of Samaria for fear of the "kings of the Hittites."

Now, although the Bible is not a mere compendium of history, its veracity is deeply involved in the historic accuracy of its statements; but the Hittites had no place in classic history, and therefore it was supposed by some that the Bible references to them could not be truth.

There was a strong presumption that an important people could scarcely have dropped completely out of history, but the strong presumption did not warrant the unscientific conclusion that the Bible narrative was untrue. It was just possible that classic history might be defective regarding a people of whom sacred history had much to say.

On this subject we have reached solid ground. We can now confidently appeal from assertion to certainty. In recent years Egypt and Assyria have been yielding up their secrets to modern research. The veil has begun to lift from off dark continents of history. As soon as the key was found to the hieroglyphics of Egypt and the cuneiforms of Assyria, a mighty Hittite people began to emerge. They appeared chiefly as a nation of warriors in constant conflict with the great monarchies on their borders, but in almost every detail they corresponded to the Hittites of the Bible. Instead of at once admitting that the Bible references to the Hittites might be true after all, writers in Germany and England declared the story of the peaceful transaction at Hebron inconsistent with the warlike character of the Hittites, and pronounced the story of the panic at Samaria as "not containing a single mark of acquaintance with the contemporaneous history." These views were boldly enunciated, and have been produced in many forms. They may now be seen in survival, in an article by the Rev. T. K. Cheyne, in the current edition of the "Encyclopædia Britannica."

The arguments against the historic accuracy of the Bible, based on its references to the Hittites, are never likely to appear again in English literature. The increasing light from Egypt and Assyria reveals to us, in broad outline and in incidental detail, a series of facts, with reference to the Hittites, in perfect harmony with the narratives of the Bible.

The attempt to reinstate the Hittite Empire among the ancient monarchies of the world, is a hazardous venture; but my authority for doing so is abundant, and I have endeavoured to lay it fully in outline before the reader. I have also placed largely in evidence the conclusions of eminent scholars, who in following out different lines of investigation have found themselves confronted at many points by the great Hittite Empire. As regards the final acceptance of the views here advanced, I have no fear whatever, and I am especially encouraged by the progress of opinion on the subject hitherto. It was only in 1872 that I drew attention to the Hamah inscriptions, and pronounced them Hittite remains. My conclusions received no support at first, but they are now generally admitted.

It has been my aim to present the whole case in an intelligible form to the ordinary reader, and also to supply all the material necessary for the scholar to prosecute the study of the subject. All the copies of inscriptions thus far received are reproduced, and the chief places where they have been found are marked on the Map.

In sketching the subject from different standpoints the same facts come often into view, and in making each chapter as complete as possible some repetition has been unavoidable. I have endeavoured, however, to keep the book within reasonable limits.

I gratefully acknowledge much generous encouragement and help from many fellow-workers. Mr. W. H. Rylands, F.S.A., Secretary of the Society of Biblical Archæology, has placed me under lasting obligation, by revising, in the light of wider experience, some of the inscriptions which had been incorrectly reproduced, so that I am now able to present to the public a complete set of facsimiles as perfect as they are ever likely to be.

Captain Conder, R.E., and Colonel Sir C. W. Wilson, K.C.M.G., C.B., F.R.S., &c., kindly aided me in constructing the Map. The general outline is chiefly Captain Conder's, and Sir Charles added the names of places in Asia Minor where he had seen Hittite remains.

The Rev. Dr. Isaac Taylor generously placed at my disposal his Comparative Table of Hittite and Cypriote characters, and Mr. Theodore Pinches most obligingly re-examined for me important Assyrian texts in the British Museum.

The book has been carried through the press in the midst of incessant official duties, but the Rev. G. Wilson, M.A., F.L.S., and other friends, have lightened my labour by kindly reading the proofs.

My chief indebtedness, however, is to Professor Sayce, whose constant encouragement and unstinted and ungrudging aid I gratefully acknowledge. Mine was merely a voice crying in the wilderness until he took up the question, and it is chiefly by his unwearied labours, both as a scholar and an explorer, that so much interest has been aroused in the Hittite people. His chapter on Decipherment, written expressly for this book, is the farthest advance yet made in the study of the Hittite inscriptions, and may yet stand as an important landmark in the history of decipherment.

When this book was in type he sent me the following important communication, which finds a fitting place here. The discovery is one of the results of Professor Sayce's visit to Egypt, and completes the chain of evidence which binds the recently discovered inscriptions to the Hittites.

"When visiting the Ramesseum at Thebes with two friends one day last winter, I noticed that in the great *tableau* which represents the conquest of the Hittites at Kadesh by Ramses II., many of the Hittite warriors were depicted with boots the ends of which were turned up. Neither Rosellini, who copied the sculpture, nor the numerous visitors, including myself, who had previously examined it, had ever observed this fact before. We were unable to do more at the time than note the fact, but a week or two afterwards I returned to the spot with Mr. W. Myers, and made a careful survey of the picture. I then found that on the right-hand (or southern) side of the *tableau* all the Hittites who were clothed, or whose feet were uninjured by the weather, wore boots with turned-up ends, while this was the case with none of the figures on the left-hand side.

Either, therefore, two different artists must have been employed on the work, or else different races were intended to be represented in the Hittite army. While I was looking at the picture, Mr. Myers called me away to a smaller *tableau* of the same event carved on an inner wall of the temple. Here the Hittites were all of them provided with boots the toes of which were turned up in an exaggerated way. Evidently, therefore, it was a characteristic which had especially struck the Egyptian artist. It is curious to find that this portion of the old national costume survived among the Hittites, who had settled in the warm valley of the Orontes; such boots, or rather snow shoes, admirably adapted as they were for the snow-clad ranges of the Taurus, being wholly out of place in Syria."

I have only now to record my best thanks to the publishers for the manner in which they have brought out this book.

WILLIAM WRIGHT.

LONDON, *Sept.* 15, 1884.

TABLE OF CONTENTS,

CHAPTER I.

SECURING THE HITTITE INSCRIPTIONS.

Starting from Damascus—Burckhardt's discovery of the inscriptions—Re-discovery of the inscriptions—Various efforts to secure them—Subhi Pasha, Governor of Syria—The Pasha's cavalcade—Arrival in Hamah—Search for the inscribed stones and discovery—The Pasha's permission to take copies—The inscriptions in danger—Precautions taken to save them—Stones carried to the *Serai*—Meteoric shower—Deputation to the Pasha—Cleaning inscriptions—Finding gypsum—Taking casts—Casts sent to Palestine Exploration Fund, and British Museum. 1–12

CHAPTER II.

THE HITTITE EMPIRE FROM THE EGYPTIAN STANDPOINT.

The Kheta among the early enemies of Egypt—Brugsch identifies them with the Hittites of Scripture—Hittite palaces on the border of Egypt as early as twelfth dynasty—Thothmes I.—A five hundred years' war with the Hittites—Thothmes III. prosecutes the war—Germanicus Cæsar at Karnak and the inscriptions—Deciphering the hieroglyphics—Thirteen campaigns—Hittite confederacy against Egypt—Confederates at Megiddo—Pharaoh's march to Megiddo—Cromwellian orders—Battle and rout of the Hittites with loss of chariots—Siege of Megiddo and amnesty—Booty captured—Campaign against Carchemish—Campaign against Kadesh—Destruction of Kadesh—Additional campaigns against the Hittites—Growth of Hittite power on the death of Thothmes III.—Treaty of peace between Rameses I. and Saplel, king of the Hittites

—Seti I. at war with the Hittites—Surprises Kadesh—Conclusion of peace—Battle-scene at Karnak—Rameses II. the Pharaoh of the oppression—Great Hittite confederation—Rameses II. marches on Kadesh—Battle and peace—Pentaur's prize poem—Treaty of peace and alliance written by the Hittites on a silver plate—Egyptian copies—Kheta-Sira, the great king of the Hittites of Egypt—His daughter married to Rameses II.—Continued peace between Egypt and the Hittites—Hittite confederacy defeated by Rameses III.—Hittite king made prisoner—War with the Hittites from the twelfth to the twentieth dynasty 13–35

CHAPTER III.

THE HITTITE EMPIRE FROM THE ASSYRIAN STANDPOINT.

Assyrian inscriptions in British Museum—The world's oldest books—Hittites mentioned in nineteenth century B.C.—Perhaps much earlier—Extension of Hittite empire, east and south—Paramount from Euphrates to Lebanon in twelfth century B.C.—Tiglath-Pileser I. beats back the Hittites from his borders—His campaigns and victories—Four hundred years' struggle with the Hittites—Assur-Nasir-Pal wages war against the Hittites—Hittite resistance—Shalmaneser wages over thirty campaigns against the Hittites—War carried on by his successors—Sargon overthrows the Hittites finally in 717 B.C. 36–44

CHAPTER IV.

GEOGRAPHICAL EXTENT OF THE HITTITE EMPIRE.

Three hundred geographical Hittite names—Hittites at Hebron—The Hyksos dynasty Hittite—Capital, Zoan or Tanais—Kirjath-Sepher or Booktown—Hittites at Jerusalem according to Manetho and Ezekiel—Luz or Lûeizeh in the land of the Hittites by Lake Merom—Hittite names in Syria and Palestine—" Tahtim-Hodshi "—The "Land of the Hittites," in the promise to Joshua—Geographical references in the Egyptian inscriptions—Professor Sayce's list of Hittite names—Geographical positions of the Hittite inscriptions at Hamah, Aleppo, Jerâbis, Ibreez, &c.— The speech of Lycaonia, Hittite—Professor Sayce's discoveries—Col. Sir Charles Wilson's summary of Hittite sculptures—Dr. Isaac Taylor's statement as to extent of empire — Dr. Schliemann's discoveries at Troy 45–64

CHAPTER V.

HITTITE ART AND LEARNING.

Hittite silver plate with embossed treaty—Origin of coined money—
Hittite money, sale and conveyancing—Hittite weights—Peculiarities of Hittite art—Its origin, by Professor Sayce—Carried to Asia Minor—Alphabets and scripts of Asia Minor—Mr. Lang's discoveries in Cyprus—Views of Mr. C. T. Newton and Dr. Isaac Taylor—The Hittite origin of the numerous scripts—The Hittites a literary people—Mariette's theory and Eisenlohr's discovery—The Hittites in the art of war 65–72

CHAPTER VI.

HITTITE RELIGION.

Common origin of Hittite and Canaanite deities—Hittite deities in Asia Minor—Artemis at Ephesus—The Amazons—Position of Hittite women—Hittite ritual without morality—Numerous gods and goddesses—Guardians of the treaty of peace . . . 73–78

CHAPTER VII.

HITTITE NATIONALITY.

Who were the Hittites?—Hittite names and sculpture—Semitic names accounted for—Brugsch's opinion, Professor Sayce's, Mr. Poole's—Hittites not a Semitic people—Hamitic language—Related to the Vannic inscriptions—Alarodian—The Hittite features still seen in the land of the Hittites—What the Bible says 79–87

CHAPTER VIII.

THE HITTITES FROM THE BIBLE STANDPOINT.

Object of the chapter—Professor Newman's statement—Rev. T. K. Cheyne's statement—Both discredit the Bible statements—Bible references to the Hittites—Abraham and the Hittites—Esau's Hittite wives—Position of the Hittites among the sub-tribes—Promised hornets—Report of the spies—Promise to Joshua—Hittites at Jericho, by Lake Merom, allied with Jabin, living among the Israelites—Hittite warriors—Hittite wives—Toi of Hamah—Syrian panic for fear of the Hittites—Hittites first referred to in the

Bible and in the tablets of Sargon about the same time—Agreement between the Babylonian records and the Bible—Testimony of the inscriptions—Abraham's transactions with the Hittites, and Rev. T. K. Cheyne's criticism of the narrative—The criticism examined—Narrative not only in accord with general experience and Oriental custom, but also supported by collateral contemporary evidence—Opinions of Brugsch, Mariette, and Drs. Taylor and Schliemann—The Hyksos dynasty at Zoan, Rev. Dr. Thomson's testimony—Position of the Hittites at the Exodus — During the reign of Thothmes III.—Catalogue of Hittite names, and Brugsch's estimate of it—Hittites withdrawing northward—Hittites at Megiddo—Hittite importance during the reigns of Seti I. and Rameses II.—Estimate of Egyptian inscriptions—Treaty with Saplel, the Hittite king—Pentaur's account of the Hittite confederation, and the battle of Kadesh—Rev. T. K. Cheyne's credulity with reference to the achievements of Rameses II.—Hittite alliance with Egypt—Rameses II. marries the daughter of the Hittite king—Promise of the hornets fulfilled—Manetho's reference to Hyksos at Jerusalem—Luz in the land of the Hittites—Israel encounters the Hittites at Jericho, at Ai, and under Jabin, by Lake Merom—The Hittites the same people with whom Egypt fought—Their chariots, their discipline—Mineptah II. the Pharaoh of the Exodus—Individual Hittites in relation to the Israelites—Panic at Samaria for fear of the Hittites—Professor Newman's criticism—Criticism examined in the light of Assyrian inscriptions—Professors Sayce and Duncker—Hittite chariots—Kings of the Hittites—Final overthrow of the Hittites 88–123

CHAPTER IX.

ARE THE INSCRIPTIONS HITTITE REMAINS?

Suggested in 1872—First reception of theory—General acceptance—Professor Sayce's statement, Dr. Taylor's, George Smith's—Approaching the subject from different standpoints—Mr. Hamilton Lang's Cypriote and Phœnician inscriptions—Pre-Hellenic Alphabets—Hittite the central stock of the Asianic scripts—Hittite art —Cypriote and Hittite—Mr. Hyde Clarke's theory—Capt. Burton's—The Himyarites according to Caussin, Renan, Gesenius, and Abu El-Fida—Consul Johnson's statement—Capt. Conder's—The inscriptions bear the same relation to the Hittites as the hieroglyphics to the Egyptians—Character and use of the inscriptions—What may be expected from the inscriptions 124–136

TABLE OF CONTENTS. xxxiii

CHAPTER X.

THE HITTITE INSCRIPTIONS.

The Hamah inscriptions described—Facsimiles revised by Professor Sayce and Mr. Rylands—H. I. only a fragment of an inscription—H. III. taken from the healing stone—H. IV. has the top line defaced, and therefore begins from left to right—The originals sent to the Constantinople Museum—Aleppo inscriptions now destroyed —Mr. Rylands' account of George Smith's copies—Carchemish inscriptions described by Mr. Rylands—Ibreez inscription, Mr. Davis's description—Tyana inscription, incised and not raised like all the other inscriptions—Hittite seals—Hittite and cuneiform inscription on the silver boss of Tarkondêmos—History of the boss —Facsimile—Not a forgery—Professor Sayce's reading and analysis—Deductions compared with other inscriptions . . 137–176

CHAPTER XI.

DECIPHERMENT OF THE HITTITE INSCRIPTIONS BY PROFESSOR SAYCE.

List of characters—Dr. Isaac Taylor's Comparative Table—Historical account of the Comparative Table—Former efforts at decipherment —Comparison of characters in various inscriptions—Inferences— Tuves probably the Toi of the Bible—Value of certain ideographs —Hittite seals—People of Carchemish called Hittites by all their neighbours, Egyptian, Assyrian, Hebrew or Vannic, and probably also by themselves—Schlumberger's seals—Inscriptions begin from right to left, and proceed boustrophêdon—Hieratic forms in Hamah inscriptions—Tentative renderings of one or two inscriptions . .
177–198

APPENDICES 199–232

INDEX 233–246

LIST OF ILLUSTRATIONS.

HITTITE MAP.
THE HAMAH INSCRIPTIONS.
THE HAMAH INSCRIBED STONE-OF-HEALING.
THE JERABIS OR CARCHEMISH INSCRIPTIONS.
THE MARASH INSCRIBED LION.
THE IBREEZ INSCRIPTION.
THE TYANA INCISED INSCRIPTION.
HITTITE SEALS DISCOVERED BY SIR A. H. LAYARD.
M. SCHLUMBERGER'S HITTITE SEALS.
CARTOUCHE FROM NIOBE ON MOUNT SIPYLOS.
THE PSEUDO-SESOSTRIS.
SEVERAL PLATES WITH FRAGMENTS OF HITTITE INSCRIPTIONS, THE SECOND PSEUDO-SESOSTRIS, SEALS, ETC.
TWO-HEADED EAGLE OF EYUK.
SCULPTURES OF PTERIUM.
INSCRIBED BABYLON BOWL.
INSCRIPTION ON THE MARASH LION.
THE SILVER BOSS OF TARKONDEMOS WITH HITTITE AND CUNEIFORM INSCRIPTIONS.—See p. 165.
LIST OF HITTITE CHARACTERS, p. 177.
HITTITE AND CYPRIOTE TABLE BY DR. I. TAYLOR.—See p. 178.

THE

EMPIRE OF THE HITTITES.

CHAPTER I.

SECURING THE HITTITE INSCRIPTIONS.

On the 10th of November, 1872, I set out from Damascus intent on securing the Hamah inscriptions.

Sixty years previously, Burckhardt, in his exploration of Hamah, had discovered, in the corner of a house in one of the Bazars, a stone covered with figures and signs, which he declared to be hieroglyphics, but different from the hieroglyphics of Egypt.[1] Every one who cared to know anything of Syria, read Burckhardt's travels. All admitted his accuracy of observation and truthfulness of description, yet so little interest was taken in his discovery, even by professional explorers, that Porter, in Murray's "Handbook," so late as 1868, declares "there are no antiquities in Hamah."[2]

---

[1] Burckhardt's "Travels in Syria," &c., p. 146.
[2] Murray's "Handbook," ii. 583.

At length, in 1870, Mr. J. Augustus Johnson, the American Consul-General, and the Rev. S. Jessup, an American missionary, stumbled on the Hamah inscriptions, and from that moment a period of zealous effort to secure them succeeded the long period of apathy and neglect. The newly kindled enthusiasm with reference to the curious hieroglyphics, which had waited so long for an interpreter, seemed destined to endanger their existence, and from Damascus we watched, with almost breathless suspense, the various heroic but fruitless attempts to secure accurate copies.

The vague but much dreaded power of the American Consul, and the local knowledge and skill of an American missionary, availed not to enable them to make accurate transcripts of the re-discovered hieroglyphics.

In publishing a picture of one of the inscriptions, in the "First Quarterly Statement of the American Palestine Exploration Society," in 1871, Mr. Johnson says: "We did not succeed in getting squeeze impressions, for fanatical Moslems crowded upon us when we began to work upon the stones, and we were obliged to be content with such copies of this and other inscriptions found on stones, *over* and *near* the city gate, and *in* the ancient bridge which spans the Orontes, as could be obtained by the aid of a native painter." Mr. Johnson must have been hard pressed, for he seems to have seen only one of the stones, as he describes the positions of the others incorrectly, doubtless having been led into error by the vague reports of the people; but his efforts were not in vain, and the imperfect facsimile of one of the inscriptions, published in the "First Quarterly Statement of the American Palestine Exploration Society," did much to quicken interest in the new hieroglyphics, and stimulated others to succeed where he had partially failed.

The imperfect tracings of the "native painter" were seen by Messrs. Drake and Palmer, on their way home through Beyrout, from their wanderings in the Desert; and the Palestine Exploration Fund sent Mr. Drake back to Syria, to examine and copy the inscriptions. By his great skill in dealing with natives, Mr. Drake partly succeeded in taking photographs and squeezes of the most important, but gathering angry mobs obliged him to hasten his operations before he had effected his purpose.

Captain Burton, then Her Majesty's Consul at Damascus, also visited Hamah. He gives a good description of the stones, and points out accurately the places where they were to be found, but he also had to be content with the decipherings of one Kostatin-el-Khuri. These he published in "Unexplored Syria," with the following explanation. "The ten sheets accompanying this article had been applied to the blackened or reddened faces of the four stones, and the outlines were afterwards drawn with a reed pen. In a few cases the fancy of the copyist had been allowed to run wild," &c.[1]

[1] "Unexplored Syria," i. 335.

Captain Burton suggested that the stones should be secured "by means of a Vizerial order, intended to be obeyed," and he adds: "When at Hamah, I began to treat with the proprietor of No. 1, the Christian Jabbour, who, barbarously greedy like all his tribe, began by asking a hundred napoleons."

The publication of the rude tracings in "Unexplored Syria" increased still more the general interest in the inscriptions, and a very large sum of money was offered for the smallest stone, but the people of Hamah would not part with it at any price. Then a new and altogether different set of men began to bully and barter for the coveted curiosities, and we saw with dismay a commencement of the fussy peddling which, a short time before, had led to the destruction of the Moabite stone. At this juncture my opportunity arrived, not only of securing but of saving the precious inscriptions.

The Sublime Porte, seized by a periodic fit of reforming zeal, had appointed an honest man, Subhi Pasha, to be Governor of Syria. Subhi Pasha brought a conscience to his work, and not content with redressing wrongs that succeeded in forcing their way into his presence, resolved to visit every district of his province, in order that he might check the spoiler and discover the wants of the people. He invited me to accompany him on a tour to Hamah, and I gladly accepted the invitation. Mr. W. Kirby Green, our excellent Consul at Damascus, was also to be his guest. I thought it best to join the party in the neighbourhood of Hamah, lest familiarity should breed contempt before the critical moment had arrived for asking permission to copy the inscriptions. This I was able to do after lingering on my way among the village schools in Jebel Kalamoun.

Having spent a few days in Saidnâya, M'alûla, Yabrûd, Nebk, and Deir-Atîyeh, among the handsomest peasantry of Syria, some of them speaking a *patois* of Syriac, and all of them speaking Arabic with a Syriac accent, I struck north by Hasya, and joined the Pasha's cavalcade at Hums.

The following day we started for Hamah with an enormous following. Chiefs from all parts flocked in with their retainers to do honour to the Waly. Princelings, whose possessions had been reduced to a horse, a few arms, and a richly braided jacket, galloped over the plain, wheeling and tossing their spears in the air, and showing wonderful feats of horsemanship. Bedawîn hostages from the Desert, white-turbaned Ulema, sugarloaf-topped Dervishes, priests and peasants, made up a procession, ten deep, more than a mile long, and surrounded by a picturesque army of skirmishers, who kept up their antics for miles all round the main body during the whole journey.

On the 25th of November we arrived in Hamah, late in the afternoon. During the day the Waly had consulted Mr. Green and me as to his projects for ameliorating the condition of the people. We sat up late that night together, and I had an opportunity of asking his Excellency to aid me in getting perfect copies of the inscriptions. This he promised to do, and so gracious and kind was he, that he accompanied us to our beds to make sure that his guests were comfortable.

The next morning at an early hour Mr. Green and I sallied forth in quest of the inscriptions. None of the books or articles referring to the inscriptions had reached us in Damascus before we set out, and we had to begin our operations without any advantage from the labours of our predecessors.

Our first business was to find the inscribed stones, and this was not so easy as it might seem, for all whom we asked about them looked us steadily in the face, and swore vehemently that there were no stones such as we sought in Hamah.

In a large city of narrow crooked streets, it would have been a weary work to find the inscriptions for ourselves, and after so much disappointment we resolved to ask every person we met, in the hope that we might find some one not up to the plot of concealing the inscriptions from us. The first man we met after making this resolve proved to be Suliman-el-Kallas, in the wall of whose house was inscription H. 1. The secret being out, we had no difficulty in finding all the stones, and they were also pointed out to the Waly.

Subhi Pasha, who was known in Europe as Subhi Bey before his appointment to Damascus, was descended from a noble Greek family. He was the most learned man among the Turks, and his private collection of coins and art treasures, the greater part of which has been since sold in London, brought him into scholarly relations with many of the *savans* of Europe. Subhi Pasha, who was the creator of the Constantinople Museum, recognized at a glance the great importance of the inscriptions, and sent a telegram to the Sultan asking him to accept the inscribed stones for the Museum.

I pointed out to His Excellency that such inscriptions ought to be the common property of all, that the scholars of Europe were waiting eagerly for accurate copies of them, and that they would doubtless open a new chapter in history, which would show that a great people, called Hittites in the Bible, but never referred to in classic history,[1] had once formed a mighty empire in that region.

The Pasha not only consented to let me take copies of the inscriptions, but promised to bring the inscribed stones to the *Serai*, where I might copy them at leisure. Under other circumstances we should have experienced great difficulties in securing copies of the inscriptions, for the recent feeble attempts to get possession of the stones had brought the Hamathites to consider them of extraordinary value; and as we passed through the city to the baths with the Governor-General, we heard

[1] Mr. Gladstone has since pointed out a reference by Homer to the Hittites as the κήτειοι. ("Homeric Synchronisms," pp. 174, 182.) See Appendix No. I.

many expressions of muttered defiance, and threats of violence towards anybody that might venture to interfere with their sacred and venerable treasures.

Later in the day, when it became known that the Pasha would take the stones, we heard men vowing that they would destroy the inscriptions, as they have since done with that at Aleppo.

I saw now that a crisis was reached. For hundreds, perhaps thousands, of years these mute inscriptions had waited for some one to hear their story. Egyptian, Assyrian, Greek, Selucidæ, Roman, Saracen, Crusader and Turk had passed them by as unworthy of even a passing notice; and now that travellers from the Isles of the Sea, eager to learn their secrets, had arrived, their voice was about to be hushed for ever. A greater calamity than that of the Moabite stone tragedy was imminent. A mighty empire was about to claim its rightful position among the great nations of the ancient world, and a few fanatics were about to push it back into the outer darkness to which classic history had assigned it.

Mr. Green and I saw that we must exert ourselves if we were to gain our purpose. We visited all the men in whose grounds or walls the stones were, and assured them, on the faith of a British Consul, that Subhi Pasha was altogether different from the other Pashas whom they had known; that he would pay full value, and more, for the stones; and now that the Sultan had replied by telegram accepting them, any one who interfered with the inscriptions would be most severely punished. We thus endeavoured to enlist the cupidity and fear of the Hamathites in favour of the stones.

We also laid the matter before the Waly, who placed the inscriptions under Ibrahim Pasha for the night, and he told off a number of soldiers for their protection. Hearing from some of our people that a formidable conspiracy was on foot for the destruction of the inscriptions, and that the city guards were likely to lend assistance, we told them candidly what we had heard, and assured them that dire punishment would fall on them if any mishap befell the stones. It was an anxious and sleepless night, and on the following morning the Waly, by our advice, paid sums varying from three to fifteen napoleons each for the stones, and the work of removing them to the *Serai* began.

The removal of the stones was effected by an army of shouting men, who kept the city in an uproar during the whole day. Two of them had to be taken out of the walls of inhabited houses, and one of them was so large that it took fifty men and four oxen a whole day to drag it a mile. The other stones were split in two, and the inscribed parts were carried on the backs of camels to the *Serai*. As the shrill-voiced Moslems were summoning from the minarets the faithful to prayer at set of sun, the last stone was, to our great delight, deposited in safety.

The removal of these mysterious relics produced a great commotion in Hamah. The fact of a British Consul and a Protestant missionary being the guests of the Waly of Syria, and accompanying him to mosques and baths, seemed strange and portentous in the eyes of fanatical Moslems, but was somewhat reassuring to the cringing native Christians. Celestial portents also combined to impress the Moslem mind; for on the night following the removal of the stones to the *Serai* a meteoric shower, in Eastern splendour, was seen by the Hamathites, who beheld in every brilliant sparkling train the wrath of Heaven fulminated against Hamah in the event of their sacred stones being taken away. The wrathful stars had appeared in accordance with an ancient prophecy.

There was much shouting and invoking the name of Mohammed and Allah during the night, and in the morning an influential deputation of green and white turbaned Moslems waited on the Waly to tell him of the evil omens, and to urge a restoration of the stones.

The Waly ordered coffee and cigarettes for all the members of the deputation, who squatted in solemn dignity around him. He listened patiently to all the speakers, several of whom spoke at great length and with much animation. When they had finished, the Waly continued stroking his beard for some time. Then he asked, in a very grave manner, if the stars had hurt any one. They replied they had not. "Ah," said the Waly, brightening up and speaking with a cheery ringing voice that even the guards outside the door might hear, "the omens were good. They indicated the shining approbation of Allah on your loyalty in sending these precious stones to your beloved Khalif, the Father of the Faithful." The grave deputation rose up comforted. Each member kissed the Waly's hand and withdrew.

We had now got our hare, and we had to face the difficulty of cooking it. It was necessary to get transcriptions free from what Captain Burton called, in those which he reproduced, "the vagaries of the native painter." There was no photographer in Hamah, and we had no photographic apparatus with us, and we felt that it was of the greatest importance to secure exact facsimiles, as we knew not what might happen to the stones. I tried in vain to procure plaster of Paris in Hamah. I learned, however, that gypsum was found in the neighbourhood, and I sent two trusty men, well bribed, to search for it.

Then began the work of cleaning the inscriptions. The moss and dirt of ages had filled up the hollows between the raised characters. Lime mortar had been dashed into them, and during the lapse of ages it had grown almost as hard as the stone itself. It was a work that could be delegated to no one, and it required incessant scrubbing during the greater part of two days, with brush and water and pointed stick, to make the stones clean. Meantime the men had returned with a camel-load of gypsum in blocks. This had to be burnt, and pounded into powder.

Many attempts were made to decoy us from our labour, to shoot woodcock, or to hunt wild boars, or to stalk gazelles and bustards ; but we stuck to our task until we had two sets of perfect plaster casts of all the inscriptions. This work was fully shared in by Mr. Green, who took my place at the inscriptions when I was obliged to be elsewhere, and who managed to make up for my absence from the Pasha's parties.

As soon as the casts were firm we despatched them by a safe man to Damascus, whence Mr. Green sent one set to the Government for the British Museum, and at Mr. Tyrwhitt Drake's request I sent the other set to the Palestine Exploration Fund. We had thus succeeded in placing within the reach of scholars exact facsimiles of the Hamah inscriptions, showing the actual lengths of lines and bars and characters and blanks, perfect even to the faults of the stone.

We now propose to investigate the records of Egypt and Assyria and the Hebrew Scriptures, with reference to the Hittites, before asking the question, Are these curious inscriptions Hittite remains ?

CHAPTER II.

THE HITTITE EMPIRE FROM THE EGYPTIAN STANDPOINT.

VERY early Egyptian records point across the north-east frontiers to hereditary foes called generally *Amu*, a name which in Palestine would mean *people*, but in Egypt *herdsmen*. It was the Egyptian term for barbarians, and was doubtless used contemptuously, as the Jews spoke of Gentiles, or as the Mohammedans speak of Kaffirs.

Two of the nations or tribes composing the Amu stand out prominently. One of these is the Akharru, or Phœnicians. The other, which stands first in importance among the enemies of Egypt, are the people of the Kheta, the Khatti of the Assyrian inscriptions, and the Hittites of the Bible. According to Brugsch, "the most remarkable nations among the Amu, who appear in the course of Egyptian history, as commanding respect by their character and their deeds, are the Kheta, the Khar and the Ruten;"[1] and he further adds, with reference to the Kheta, "we believe

[1] Brugsch's "Egypt under the Pharaohs," i. 14.

we are falling into no error if we persevere in our opinion, which recognizes in these people the same Khethites—Hittites, about whom Holy Scripture has so much to tell us, from the days of the patriarch Abraham till the time of the Captivity."[1]

There is a monument in the Louvre, dating from the time of the first Pharaoh of the twelfth dynasty. Even at that early period there was a record of Hittite towns, and palaces destroyed on the border of Egypt;[2] and Mariette Bey, a very high authority, holds that one of the early Egyptian dynasties was Hittite.

It was about the middle of the seventeenth century B.C. that Thothmes I., on ascending the throne, resolved "to wash his heart" by taking vengeance on the Asiatics who had encroached on his borders. He began in his first year a war against the Hittites and their allies, which, according to Brugsch, was carried on "for nearly five hundred years by successive Pharaohs."[3]

The war was prosecuted with great vigour by Thothmes III., who came to the throne about 1600 B.C. This Pharaoh has been called the Alexander the Great of Egyptian history, and the records of his reign, one of which adorns the monument on the bank of the Thames, are exceedingly numerous, and show Egypt raised to a high position of wealth and power.

[1] Brugsch's "Egypt under the Pharaohs," ii. 2.
[2] *Idem*, ii. 405.   [3] *Idem*, i. 336.

Like Alexander, Thothmes III. made his power felt throughout the then known world. His arms were victorious from the centre of Africa to the borders of India.

In the nineteenth year of our era Germanicus Cæsar stood before the picture-writing of Karnak, and Tacitus tells us that the Thebans "read to him the tributes imposed on the nations, the weight of the silver and gold, the number of weapons and horses, and the offerings to the temples in ivory and sweet scents; also that the supplies of corn and of all utensils which each nation paid were no less immense than are now imposed by the might of the Parthians or the power of Rome."[1]

For more than 1800 years, since the time of Germanicus, the monuments have been falling into decay, and the inscriptions have been neglected; but in our day the greater part of them have been read by Dr. Samuel Birch and other Egyptologists, and they are found to contain the records of the splendid reign of Thothmes III. The outlines of thirteen campaigns are sketched, the lines of march, the rivers crossed, the cities stormed, the peoples subdued, the booty taken; and the tributes imposed in silver, gold, weapons, horses, wine, corn, spices, are all set forth in picturesque detail.

The great Pharaoh's immediate predecessor had been a queen, and during her reign the subject peoples had thrown off the yoke of Egypt, and not only refused to

[1] Tacit. "Annal." ii. 60.

pay tribute any longer, but formed dangerous confederations against the empire. Among the enemies of Egypt at that early period the Hittites occupy the most important position. The Hittite king of Kadesh had gathered together "the kings and their peoples from the water of Egypt to the river-land of Mesopotamia, and they obeyed him as their chief." He led the confederate army to the strategic and strong city Megiddo on the Kishon, the scene of many a terrible battle, and the type of the New Testament Armageddon, where the final contest between the forces of good and evil must be decided.

Pharaoh drew out against the confederates the might of Egypt. At Ihem, on his march, he held a council of war, in which he informed his army that the hostile king of Kadesh had arrived and entered Megiddo, and that he had with him the kings of all the countries from Egypt to the Euphrates, and also the Phœnicians and the people of Cyprus. The details of the march are given, and the different views expressed at the council of war.[1]

When "six hours of the day had passed" Pharaoh with his host arrived before Megiddo. "Keep yourselves ready, look to your arms, for early in the morning we shall meet this miserable enemy in battle," was the Cromwellian general order. On the following morning, the twenty-fifth anniversary[2] of the coro-

[1] Brugsch's "Egypt under the Pharaohs," i. 369.
[2] *Idem*, p. 372.

nation of the king, the battle began. The confederates were broken, and leaving their chariots behind them, fled within the city, but Pharaoh's army falling upon the rich plunder, failed to take the city before the allies barricaded it. "Oh!" exclaims the reporter, "that the warriors of the king had not yielded to their desire to plunder the goods of the enemy, for then had Megiddo been taken in that same hour." A siege followed, but "Megiddo had the might of a thousand cities," and "the king graciously pardoned the foreign princes."

The inscriptions record in detail the booty captured and the tribute imposed, and a list is added of 119 towns and nations represented by the Confederates. Of spoil there were precious stones, golden dishes, a two-handled flagon of Phœnician work; but besides these there were captured 924 chariots, and the chariot plated with gold belonging to the Hittite king. The war with the Hittites was not, however, closed. A fourth campaign was directed against Carchemish on the Euphrates, the north-eastern capital of the Hittites, and the fifth campaign had for its object Kadesh on the Orontes, their southern capital.

Seven years after the battle and siege of Megiddo, Pharaoh was engaged in his sixth campaign. He had driven the Confederates north, and "he came to the town of Kadesh and destroyed it, and cut down all the trees."[1] The destruction of the trees must have been

[1] Brugsch's "Egypt under the Pharaohs," i. 376.

oft repeated, for as I looked from the ruins of Kadesh ten years ago there was scarcely a shrub visible.

In the thirty-third year of his reign Pharaoh waged his seventh campaign in Mesopotamia. The inscriptions give lists of the spoil and tribute taken from Lebanon and the other lands through which he marched, but conspicuous among them all is "the tributes of the great land of the Hittites, in this year—301 lbs. in eight rings of silver, a great piece of white precious stone, zagu wood. . . . ."[1]

The ninth campaign closed with the storming of Kadesh once more. Thus campaign followed campaign, and though the triumphal records boast in Oriental style of Pharaoh's victories over the Hittites, and give long details as to the plunder borne back in triumph to Egypt, the Hittite resistance was not broken, and succeeding years saw new expeditions and Egyptian armies marching through the length of Syria against the hereditary foe.

On the death of Thothmes III., about 1566 B.C., the Hittite power, which he had checked and driven back, once more became formidable. Sanguinary wars were carried on by his successors, with varying fortunes but with much boasting, the result being that the Hittite power became more extended, more consolidated and more warlike. Brugsch says, "their importance grew from year to year, in such a way, that even the Egyptian inscriptions do not hesitate to mention the

[1] Brugsch's "Egypt under the Pharaohs," i. 379.

names of the kings of the Kheta in a conspicuous manner, and to speak of their gods with reverence."

The Hittites had won a respite from Egyptian invasion, and half a century after the death of the greatest of all the Pharaohs, the war between Egypt and Kheta was brought to a close by a treaty of peace concluded between Rameses I. and Saplel the Hittite king. The treaty, of which we do not possess a copy, was offensive and defensive, and for a time the two empires, having learned to respect each other, were at peace.

Seti I. came to the throne in 1366 B.C., exactly two hundred years after the death of the great Thothmes. With him the martial spirit of Egypt revived and again asserted itself. The Bedawîn and the Syrians had again begun, with impunity, to make incursions over the Egyptian border. Seti I. assembled a large army, with numerous chariots, and drove back the invaders from his frontiers, and in his two-horse chariot he led his army in pursuit of them as far as the fortress Kanaan,[1] which he stormed. Thence he pursued the retreating foe to Jamnia in Phœnicia, where he overthrew with great slaughter "the kings of the land of Phœnicia."

Seti I. had doubtless suspected the Hittites of abetting his enemies, and from the overthrow of the Phœnicians he marched against Kadesh, professedly as "the avenger of broken treaties." The city was taken by surprise. The people were engaged in their ordinary

[1] Brugsch's "Egypt under the Pharaohs," ii. 14.

pastoral pursuits when Pharaoh's chariots appeared before the city. According to the battle-scene on the north side of the great temple of Karnak, Pharaoh had thrown to the ground the Hittites and slain their princes. Then a peace was concluded, and the Egyptian army returned in triumph.

The Hittites were at this time also the central power among the enemies of Egypt. Peace with the Hittites meant peace with all the other enemies of Egypt. And so the inscriptions declare—" The great kings of the miserable land of Syria are brought by the king, in consequence of his victory over the Hittites, to fill with them the storehouse of his noble father, Amon Ra, the Lord of Thebes, because he has given him the victory over the southern world, and the subjection of the northern world."

Rameses II. was associate and successor of his father Seti I. on the throne of Egypt. He was in all probability the Pharaoh of the Oppression. He was the Sesostris of the Greeks, and in Egypt he was called the Conqueror. Many temples are adorned with the records of his achievements, the chief of which was the great battle at Kadesh on the Orontes.

War had once more broken out between Egypt and the empire of the Hittites. The king of the Hittites had brought together his forces from the remotest parts of his empire. The mighty host assembled at Kadesh to meet and roll back the tide of Egyptian invasion. There were present under the banner of the king of the Hittites his allies and satraps, from

Mesopotamia to Mysia, and from Arvad in the sea. Pharaoh set out by the old royal road along which so many Egyptian armies had marched to the land of the hereditary enemy. His route lay along the coast of Syria by the great sea, through Joppa, Tyre, Sidon, and Beyrout. Passing through the Eleutherus valley, he brought his army once more before the Hittite city, Kadesh. A great battle was fought, and the special reporters of those days have given us full details, in pen and picture sketches, of all the leading incidents of the fray.

The poet-laureate of Egypt, who accompanied the king, has celebrated the achievements of that day in a heroic poem which has come down to us in several editions. It is found on a papyrus roll, and in conjunction with splendid battle-scenes on the walls of temples at Abydos, Luksor, Karnak, and Ibsamboul.

This prize poem of Pentaur was written 3,200 years ago, and is the oldest heroic poem in the world. It may be relied upon as the earliest specimen of special war correspondence. Besides this narration, there is a simple prose account of the same battle, and this is followed by a copy of the treaty of peace which established an offensive and defensive alliance between the empire of the Hittites and Egypt.

I here insert a summary of the prize poem of Pentaur, the Theban poet, written two years after the battle of Kadesh. Reading between the lines of the boastful hieroglyphics, it is clear that the Hittites must have maintained their ground in the battle, for their king, who at the beginning of the fight is " the *vile* king of the Hittites," and "the *miserable* king of the Hittites," towards the close of the battle becomes "the *great* king of the Hittites."

It is also recorded that Pharaoh returned serenely to Egypt, but we miss the usual lists of plunder borne home by the victors. Peace sentiments also became popular towards the end of the battle, and a treaty followed, in which equals covenant for peace on mutual terms—and this is followed by mutual respect and dynastic alliances.

HEROIC POEM OF PENTAUR.[1]

Pentaur, the Theban poet, sketches the battle of Kadesh. He tells how Rameses II., in the fifth year of his reign, triumphed over the Hittites and their allies. "The miserable king of the Hittites had assembled together the people of the two rivers, the Dardanians from the shores of the Ægean Sea, the islanders from Arvad, the hardy mountaineers from Mœsius, the people of Aleppo and Carchemish and Gauzanitis, &c.

"From the remote parts of Asia Minor the mighty host converged on Kadesh on the Orontes. They left no people on the road whom they did not bring with them. They covered mountains and valleys like grasshoppers without number. No such multitude had ever been seen before. They swept all the wealth of the country before them, so that they left neither silver nor gold behind them.

[1] Literal translations may be seen in "Records of the Past," ii. 61; and in Brugsch's "Egypt under the Pharaohs," ii. 56.

"King Pharaoh was young and bold. His arms were strong, his heart courageous. He seized his weapons, and a hundred thousand sunk before his glance. He armed his people and his chariots. As he marched towards the land of the Hittites, the whole earth trembled. His warriors passed by the path of the desert, and went along the roads of the north."

At length the Egyptian army reached Kadesh on the Orontes. Arab spies were caught, and told Pharaoh that the Hittite army was in the neighbourhood of Aleppo. But "the miserable king of the Hittites" and his allies were lying in ambush to the north-west of Kadesh. The positions of the Egyptian legions are indicated, but Pharaoh was alone—no one was with him.

The Hittites rose from their ambush, and their king was in their midst. Pharaoh called on his mighty men, but they were by the lake of the Amorites. The Hittite horsemen and chariots were numberless as the sand; they stood in battle array the bravest of the Hittites, and three warriors stood in each chariot. The Hittites charged the legion of Pra-Hormakhu, which broke and fled—soldiers and chariots, When Pharaoh heard of the disaster, he was north-west of Kadesh. He grasped his weapons and put on his armour, and rushed alone into the hostile hosts of the Hittites. He looked around and found his retreat cut off, and himself surrounded by 2,500 pairs of horses, and the mightiest of the Hittites and their allies, and here Pharaoh exclaims—

"Not one of my princes, not one of my captains of the chariots, not one of my chief men, not one of my knights was there. My warriors ahd my chariots had abandoned me, not one of them was there to take part in the battle."

Deserted by his entire army, Pharaoh prayed to his father the god Amon. He recounts his own obedient and pious acts, and asks if he is to bow before the foreign people, and he thinks Amon should stand higher than the herdsmen who know not god. He reminds his god of the temples which he has builded and the offerings which he has dedicated in his honour, and then, pointing to the hosts of enemies which surrounded him, declares Amon mightier than a million warriors, a hundred thousand horses, and ten thousand brothers and sons.

The god Amon held out his hand, and Pharaoh shouted for joy. The god declared himself the lord of victory, the friend of valour. Pharaoh became like a god. He hurled darts with his right hand and fought with his left. The 2,500 horses were dashed to pieces. The hearts of the Hittites sank within them. Their limbs gave way, and they had no courage to thrust the spear. And Pharaoh swept them into the Orontes like crocodiles. He slew the Hittites at his pleasure, and no one resisted him.

The king of the Hittites sent eight of his brother kings with armed chariots against Pharaoh. With 2,500 horses they rushed on Pharaoh's flaming countenance, but he dashed them down, and killed them where they stood. Pharaoh rallied his warriors by his acts of valour. He cheered his charioteer, almost dead with fear. Six times he charged the unclean wretches who did not acknowledge his god. He killed them; none escaped. Then Pharaoh upbraids his worthless warriors, not one of whom stood by him, and calls the foreigners to witness that his own right hand had won the battle.

When the Egyptians see Pharaoh victorious, and the enemy lying like hay before his horses, weltering in their blood, they come forth one after another from the camp, and they all unite in praising his strength and courage. They extol his godlike valour for annihilating the Hittites, and for breaking their neck for ever and ever. Here Pharaoh addresses his followers, recounting their cowardice and his own mighty deeds, and promises, when at home in the palace, to see the fodder given to his pair of horses which did not leave him in the lurch. "The king returned in victory and strength, with his own hand he had smitten hundreds of thousands to the earth."

The battle is renewed on the following morning. Pharaoh and his brave warriors dash into the fight like a vulture among kids. The diadem of the royal snake on Pharaoh's head spits fire in the faces of his enemies. The Hittites tremble and fall down before him, and call for mercy. He slays them, none being able to escape.

Then the king of the Hittites sends a messenger to

tell Pharaoh that he has broken the neck of Kheta for ever and ever. He enters Pharaoh's presence with a despatch, addressed "to the great double name of the king." Pharaoh is extolled as the great in battle, and the lover of justice. He is told that the Egyptians and the Hittites ought to be brothers, that peace is better than war, that his anger weighs upon the Hittites, who ask for peace.

Then Pharaoh turned back in gentle humour, and when his warriors were assembled he permitted them to hear the message of "the GREAT king of the Hittites." The Egyptians called upon Pharaoh to accept the proffered peace. He listened to their words, and returned to Egypt in serene humour, and rested in his palace like the sun on his throne.

"Written in the seventh year of King Rameses Miamun, in the month Payni, by Pentaur, the royal scribe."

TREATY OF PEACE BETWEEN RAMESES II. AND THE HITTITES—OFFENSIVE AND DEFENSIVE ALLIANCE BETWEEN KHETA AND KEMI.[1]

1. The twenty-first year, the twenty-first day of

[1] The inscription is on the outer wall of the temple at Karnak. There are several translations. We give that of C. W. Goodwin, M.A., "Records of the Past," iv. 27 (by permission of Messrs. Bagster).

The document is the earliest diplomatic act that has come down to us. It is of special importance as showing the terms of equality on which the Hittites treated with the Egyptians in their palmiest days, and therefore we give it in full.

Tybi, in the reign of King Ra-user-ma, approved by the Sun, Son of the Sun, Ramessu-Meriamen, endowed with life eternal for ever; lover of Amen-Ra, Harmachu, Ptah of Memphis, Maut Lady of Asheru, and Chensuneferhotep; invested upon the throne of Horus, among the living, like his father Harmachu, eternally and for ever.

2. On this day, behold His Majesty was in the city of the House of Ramessu-Meriamen, making propitiations to his father Amen-Ra, to Harmachu, to Atom Lord of On, to Amen of Ramessu-Meriamen, to Ptah of Ramessu-Meriamen, to Sutech the most glorious Son of Nut; may they grant him an eternity of thirty years' festivals, an infinity of years of peace, all lands, all nations, being bowed down beneath his feet for ever.

3. There came a royal herald [nearly a whole line is erased here; the sense is, two royal heralds came, bringing a tablet of silver, which]

4. The Grand-Duke of Kheta, Kheta-sira, had sent to the king to beg for peace of King Ra-user-ma, approved of the Sun, Son of the Sun, Ramessu-Meriamen, endowed with life for ever and ever, like his father the Sun continually. Copy of the plate of silver which the Grand-Duke of Kheta, Kheta-sira, sent to the king by the hand of his herald

5. Tartisbu, and his herald Rames, to beg for peace of His Majesty Ra-user-ma, approved of the Sun, Son of the Sun, Ramessu-Meriamen, chief of rulers, whose boundaries extend to every land at his pleasure. The

covenant made by the Grand-Duke of Kheta, Kheta-sira, the puissant, Son of Marasara.

6. The Grand-Duke of Kheta, the puissant, grandson of Sapalala, the Grand-Duke of Kheta, the puissant; upon the plate of silver, with Ra-user-ma, approved of the Sun, ruler of Egypt, the puissant, Son of Ra-men-ma (Seti Meneptah I.), the great ruler of Egypt, the puissant, grandson of Ra-men-pehu (Ramessu I.).

7. The great ruler of Egypt, the puissant : The good conditions of peace and fraternity .... to eternity, which were aforetime from eternity. This was an arrangement of the great ruler of Egypt with the great prince of Kheta, by way of covenant, that God might cause no hostility to arise between them! Now it happened—

8. In the time of Mautenara, the Grand-Duke of Kheta my brother, that he fought with .... the great ruler of Egypt. But thus shall it be henceforth, even from this day—Behold, Kheta-sira, the Grand-Duke of Kheta, covenants to adhere to the arrangement made by the Sun, made by Sutech, concerning the land of Egypt,

9. With the land of Kheta, to cause no hostility to arise between them for ever. Behold, this it is—Kheta-sira, the Grand-Duke of Kheta, covenants with Ra-user-ma, approved by the Sun, the great ruler of Egypt, from this day forth, that good peace and good brotherhood shall be between us for ever.

10. He shall fraternize with me, he shall be at peace with me, and I will fraternize with him: I will be at peace with him for ever. It happened in the time of Mautenara the Grand-Duke of Kheta, my brother, after his decease, Kheta-sira sat as

11. Grand-Duke of Kheta upon the throne of his father. Behold, I am at one *in heart* with Ramessu-Meriamen, the great ruler of Egypt .... of peace, of brotherhood; it shall be better than the peace and the brotherhood which was before this. Behold, I the Grand-Duke of Kheta, with

12. Ramessu-Meriamen, the great ruler of Egypt, am in good peace, in good brotherhood; the children's children of the Grand-Duke of Kheta shall be in good brotherhood and peace with the children's children of Ramessu-Meriamen, the great ruler of Egypt. As our (treaty) of brotherhood, and our arrangements

13. (made for the land of Egypt) with the land of Kheta, so to them also shall be peace and brotherhood for ever; there shall no hostility arise between them for ever. The Grand-Duke of Kheta shall not invade the land of Egypt for ever, to carry away anything from it; nor shall Ramessu-Meriamen, the great ruler of Egypt, invade the land

14. of Kheta for ever, to carry away anything from it for ever. The treaty of alliance which was even from the time of Sapalala the Grand-Duke of Kheta, as well as the treaty of alliance which was in the time of Mautenara the Grand-Duke of Kheta, my father, if

I fulfil it, behold Ramessu-Meriamen, the great ruler of Egypt shall fulfil it

15. .... together with us, in each case, even from this day, we will fulfil it, executing the design of alliance. If any enemy shall come to the lands of Ramessu-Meriamen, the great ruler of Egypt, and he shall send to the Grand-Duke of Kheta, saying, Come and give me help against him, then shall the Grand-Duke of Kheta

16. .... the Grand-Duke of Kheta to smite the enemy; but if it be that the Grand-Duke of Kheta shall not come (himself) he shall send his infantry and his cavalry .... to smite his enemy .... of the anger of Ramessu-Meriamen

17. .... the slaves of the gates, and they shall do any damage to him, and he shall go to smite them; then shall the Grand-Duke of Kheta together with ....

18. .... to come to help to smite his enemies, if it shall please Ramessu-Meriamen, the great ruler of Egypt to go, he shall ....

19. .... to return an answer to the land of Kheta. But if the servants of the Grand-Duke of Kheta shall invade him, namely, Ramessu-Meriamen ....

(Lines 20 and 21 are nearly erased.)

22. .... from the lands of Ramessu-Meriamen, the great ruler of Egypt, and they shall come to the Grand-Duke of Kheta, then shall the Grand-Duke of

Kheta not receive them, but the Grand-Duke of Kheta shall send them to Ra-user-ma, approved of the Sun, the great ruler of Egypt . . . .

23. . . . . and they shall come to the land of Kheta to do service to any one, they shall not be added to the land of Kheta, they shall be given up to Ramessu-Meriamen, the great ruler of Egypt, or if there shall pass over . . . .

24. . . . . coming from the land of Kheta, and they shall come to Ramessu-Meriamen, the great ruler of Egypt, then shall not Ra-user-ma, approved of the Sun, the great ruler of Egypt . . . .

25. . . . . and they shall come to the land of Egypt to do service of any sort, then shall not Ra-user-ma, approved of the Sun, the great ruler of Egypt, claim them: he shall cause them to be given up to the Grand-Duke of Kheta . . . .

26. The tablet of silver, it is declared by the thousand gods, the gods male, the gods female, those which are of the land of Khita, in concert with the thousand gods, the gods male, and the gods female, those which are of the land of Egypt, those . . . .

27. . . . . Sutech of Kheta, Sutech of the city of A. . . . ., Sutech of the city of Taaranta, Sutech of the city of Pairaka, Sutech of the city of Khisasap, Sutech of the city of Sarasu, Sutech of the city of Khira(bu), Sutech . . . .

28. Sutech of the city of Sarapaina, Astarata of Kheta, the god of Taitatkherri, the god of Ka . . . .

29. . . . . the goddess of the city of . . . . . the goddess of Tain . . . . the god of . . . .

30. of the hills of the rivers of the land of Kheta, the gods of the land of Kheta, the gods of the land of Tawatana, Amen the Sun, Sutech, the gods male, the gods female, of the hills, the rivers of the land of Egypt, the . . . . the great sea, the winds, the clouds. These words

31. which are on the tablet of silver of the land of Kheta, and of the land of Egypt, whosoever shall not observe them, the thousand gods of the land of Kheta, in concert with the thousand gods of the land of Egypt, shall be (against) his house, his family, *his servants*. But whosoever shall observe these words which are in the tablet of silver, be he of Kheta . . . .

32. . . . . the thousand gods of the land of Kheta, in concert with the thousand gods of the land of Egypt, shall give health, shall give life to his (family), together with himself, together with his servants. If there shall pass over one man of the (land of Egypt) or two, or three

33. (and they shall go to the land of Kheta, then shall the Grand-Duke of Kheta cause them to be) given up again to Ra-user-ma, approved of the Sun, the great ruler of Egypt, but whosoever shall be given up to Ramessu-Meriamen, the great ruler of Egypt,

34. let not his crime be set up against him, let not . . . . himself, his wives, his children . . . . If there shall pass over a man from the land of Kheta, be it one

FROM THE EGYPTIAN STANDPOINT. 33

only, be it two, be it three, and they come to Ra-userma, approved of the Sun,

35. the great ruler of Egypt, let Ramessu-Meriamen, the great ruler of Egypt, seize (them and cause them to be) given up to the Grand-Duke of Kheta (but whosoever shall be delivered up), himself, his wives, his children, moreover let him not be smitten to death, moreover let him not (suffer?)

36. in his eyes, in his nose, in his feet, moreover let not any crime be set up against him. That which is upon the tablet of silver upon its *front side* is *the likeness* of the figure of Sutech .... of Sutech the great ruler of heaven, the *director* of the Treaty made by Khetasira the great ruler

37. of Kheta ...."[1]

"In such a form," says Brugsch, "were peace and friendship made at Ramses, the city in Lower Egypt, between the two most powerful nations of the world at that time—Kheta in the east, and Kemi in the west."[2]

Much advantage flowed to the two empires from the treaty. Fierce hate gave way to fraternal love, and it was even asserted in Egypt that Rameses II. had become a new Hittite god. A dynastic alliance followed the diplomatic. Kheta-sira, the great king of the Hittites, appeared in Egypt in Hittite costume, accompanied by

[1] "Records of the Past," iv. 32.
[2] Brugsch's "Egypt under the Pharaohs," ii. 77.

D

his beautiful daughter, Ur-ma Nofirura, and the great king of Egypt made the Hittite princess his queen in the thirty-fourth year of his reign.

A memorial tablet at Ibsamboul, dated one year after Pharaoh's marriage with the Hittite princess, preserves for us a record of the intimate relations between the Egyptian Court and the Hittites. The god Ptah addresses Rameses thus :—

"The people of Kheta are subjects of thy palace. I have placed it in their hearts to serve thee, while they humbly approach thy person with their productions, and the booty in prisoners of their king. All their property is brought to thee. His eldest daughter stands forward at their head, to soften the heart of King Rameses II.— a great inconceivable wonder. She herself knew not the impression which her beauty made on thy heart . . . . since the times of the traditions of the gods, which are hidden in the house of the rolls of writing, from the times of the sun-god Ra down to thee, history had nothing to report of the Kheta people, but that they had one heart and one soul with Egypt."[1]

The peace between Rameses II. and the Hittites lasted till the close of his long reign of sixty years. To this lasting friendship doubtless his Hittite queen contributed, and she may have been the mother of the princess (one of fifty-nine) who saved and adopted the child Moses.

Mineptah II., the Pharaoh of the Exodus, according

[1] Brugsch's "Egypt under the Pharaohs," ii. 89.

to Brugsch, succeeded his father about 1300 B.C. He also maintained the treaty of peace entered into by his father, and possibly owing to family relationship he sent "wheat in ships to preserve the lives of the Hittites."

More than a hundred years later a great confederacy had again assailed Egypt by land and sea. Rameses III. defeated the invaders in a great naval engagement near Migdol, at the Pelusiac mouth of the Nile. He then proceeded to wage a campaign of vengeance in the home lands of the invaders. He was victorious, and among the names of the conquered on the temple of Medinet Abou is that of "the miserable king of the Hittites as a living prisoner."

We thus see the Hittite kings the rivals of the Pharaohs in peace and war from the twelfth to the twentieth dynasty. The shock of Egyptian invasion exhausted itself against the frontier cities of Kadesh and Carchemish, but the mighty empire of the Hittites extended beyond, on the broad plains and highlands of Asia Minor, and so there were always fresh Hittite armies, and abundance of Hittite wealth, to enable the Hittite empire to withstand the might of Egypt for a thousand years.

CHAPTER III.

THE HITTITE EMPIRE FROM THE ASSYRIAN STANDPOINT.

IN the British Museum there are a number of inscribed objects from the library of Assurbanipal, known as the Assyrian Astronomical Tablets. These are later editions of the Clay Books which had been prepared for the ancient kings of Babylon.

Professor Sayce and others have read for us many of these tablets, and though the inscriptions are short and fragmentary, they reveal to us the existence of the Hittite power at an extremely remote period. In one of these modern editions of the world's oldest books we read—"The king of the Hittites lives and on the throne seizes."[1] And again we read—" The king of a foreign country (or the king of the Hittites) plunders and on the throne seizes."[2]

In these same records we read of a strong enemy, doubtless the Hittites, spoiling the country, and of "the king of Accad being placed under his enemy." Again there is fierce strife with a neighbouring power, and it is added—"The king of the land is not pros-

" Records of the Past," i. 159.   [2] *Idem*, p. 160.

perous : under his enemy he is : the enemy in the land campaigns."[1]

It is difficult to assign a date to these documents, but Professor Sayce, one of our greatest authorities, says— " Already in the astrological tablets of Sargon of Agané, in the nineteenth century B.C.,[2] the Hittites are regarded as a formidable power."[3] And Mr. Pinches of the British Museum has deciphered an inscription which would seem to place the reign of Sargon of Agade or Agané I. 3800 B.C. This is the most ancient date yet deciphered.

The Hittites extended their empire to the east as well as to the south, and it is the opinion of Professor Sayce that at the period when the nineteenth dynasty flourished in Egypt, the empire of Mesopotamia had been replaced by that of the Hittites. Nor was this merely a temporary or spasmodic success, for " when we come to the era of Tiglath-Pileser I., B.C. 1130, the Hittites are still paramount from the Euphrates to Lebanon."[4]

In 1857 four students of cuneiform writing succeeded simultaneously, and independently of each other, in deciphering an inscription which had been discovered at Kelah-Shergat. The result was a great triumph for Assyriologists. The inscription proved to be of Tiglath-Pileser I., and Dr. Birch says, in referring to the docu-

[1] " Records of the Past," i. 161.
[2] Mr. Theophilus G. Pinches considers that the composition of these tablets cannot be later than 2000 B.C.
[3] " Trans. of Soc. Bib. Arch.," vol. vii. part 2, p. 261. [4] *Idem*, v. 28.

ment—" On the whole, for its extent and historical information, relating to the early history of Assyria, this inscription is one of the most important, showing the gradual advance and rise of Assyria. It is nearly the oldest Assyrian text of any length which has hitherto been discovered."[1]

From this inscription we learn that the king of Assyria, on coming to the throne, immediately began to beat back the Hittites from his western borders, and during his whole reign he seems to have been engaged in a series of campaigns against that power. "While I was on this expedition," says the king, "which the Lord Ashur ordered for the enlargement of the frontiers of his territory, there were 4,000 of the Kaskaya and Hurunaya, rebellious tribes of the Kheta (Hittites), who had brought under their power the cities of Sabarta. The terror of my warlike expedition overwhelmed them. They would not fight, but submitted to my yoke. Then I took their valuables, one hundred and twenty chariots fitted to the yoke, and I gave them to the men of my country."[2]

Further on in this same inscription he says—" In the service of my Lord Ashur my chariots and warriors I assembled. I set out on my march, in front of my strong men. I went to the country of the Aramæans, the enemies of my Lord Ashur. From before Tsukha, as far as the city Carchemish, belonging to the country

[1] " Records of the Past," v. 6.
[2] Sir Henry Rawlinson, in " Records of the Past," p. 12.

FROM THE ASSYRIAN STANDPOINT. 39

of the Hittites, I smote with one blow. Their fighting men I slew. Their movables, their wealth, and their valuables in countless numbers, I carried off. The men of their armies who fled from before the face of the valiant servants of my Lord Ashur, crossed over the Euphrates; in boats covered with bitumen skins I crossed the Euphrates after them. I took six of their cities which were below the country of Bisri. I burnt them with fire, and I destroyed and overthrew them, and I brought their movables, their wealth, and their valuables to my city of Ashur."[1]

Again the king says, in the same inscription—"There fell into my hands altogether, between the commencement of my reign and my fifth year, forty-two countries with their kings, from beyond the river Zab to beyond the river Euphrates, the country of the Khatte (Hittites), and the upper ocean of the setting sun. I brought them under our government. I placed them under the Magian religion, and I imposed on them tribute and offerings."[2]

Tiglath-Pileser not only succeeded in driving back the Hittites from his borders, but in making them for a time tributaries of his empire. His successors, however, did not maintain the advantages which he had gained, and for four hundred years the struggle for supremacy between the empire of the Hittites and that of Assyria continued. Assur-Nasir-Pal, who reigned from about 883 to 858 B.C., carried the arms of Assyria as far

[1] Sir H. Rawlinson, "Records of the Past," v. 18.
[2] *Idem*, p. 20.

as Lebanon, Tyre and Sidon. The historical records of this reign are numerous. On one of these, which was found in the ruins of the temple at the foot of the pyramid at Nimroud, and which has been translated by the Rev. J. M. Rodwell, the king says—" In those days the tribute of Ahiramu, son of Yahiru, of the land of Nilaai, son of Bakhiani, of the land of the Hittites, and of the princes of the land, silver, gold, tin, kam of copper, oxen, sheep, horses, as their tribute I received."[1]

Further on he says—"To Carchemish in Syria (capital of the Hittites) I directed my steps. The tribute due from the son of Bakhiani I received; swift chariots, horses, silver, &c.,"[2] .... "I received .... The chariots and warlike engines of Carchemish I laid up in my magazines. The kings of all those lands who had come out against me received my yoke."[3] .... "From Carchemish I withdrew. To Gaza, the town of Lubarna of the Hittites, I advanced: gold and vestments of linen I received. Crossing the river Abrie, I halted, and then leaving that river approached the town of Kanulua, a royal city belonging to Lubarna of the Hittites. From before my mighty arms and my formidable onset he fled in fear, and to save his life submitted to my yoke. Twenty talents of silver, one talent of gold, one hundred talents of tin, one thousand oxen, ten

[1] "Records of the Past," iii. 52. Mr. Rodwell adds in a note—"The term Hittites is used in a large sense, as the equivalent of *Syrians*, including the northern parts of Palestine."
[2] "Records of the Past," p. 70.   [3] *Idem,* p. 72.

thousand sheep, &c., and numerous utensils of his palace, whose beauty could not be comprehended, I imposed upon him. The chariots and warlike engines of the land of the Hittites I laid up in my magazines. Their hostages I took."[1] . . . . " In those days I occupied the environs of Lebanon. To the great sea of Phœnicia I went up. Up to the great sea my arms I carried. I took tribute of Tyre, Sidon, Gebal, Maacah, &c., Phœnicia and Arvad."[2]

Making all due allowance for the boastful character of these inscriptions, we see the empire of Assyria waxing stronger and stronger, and the empire of the Hittites waxing weaker and weaker. The empire of the Hittites appears to have been split up into numerous small States under a number of kings, and the strong compact Assyrian army led by one king seems to have subdued them in detail. The records do not reveal any great Hittite confederacy, such as the Egyptians contended with in pitched battles at Megiddo and Kadesh; but city after city seems to have succumbed, after a short resistance, and to have become tributary to the conquering Assur-Nasir-Pal.

The fact, however, that the frontier towns of the Hittite empire continued their resistance to the Assyrian arms in almost yearly campaigns, throughout succeeding centuries, suggests to us that the Hittite empire was strong in resources beyond the frontier; and the existence of Hittite monuments throughout Asia Minor

[1] " Records of the Past," iii. 73. [2] *Idem*, p. 74.

explains to us how it was that the Hittite empire for more than a thousand years withstood the assaults of Egypt on the south and of Assyria on the east.

Shalmaneser succeeded his father Assur-Nasir-Pal, and reigned for thirty-five years. The campaigns of his long reign are recorded on two important monuments, one of which is known as the Black Obelisk of Nimroud, and the other as the Monolith of Kurkh. Both inscriptions have been re-translated by Professor Sayce, and both reveal the armies of Assyria at constant war with the Hittites.

Over thirty campaigns are recorded on the Black Obelisk, and the greater part of these were in the land of the Hittites.

"The Euphrates in its flood I crossed," says the king. "The city of Dabigu, a choice city of the Hittites, together with the cities dependent on it, I captured."[1]

Again he says—"The Euphrates I crossed. The city unto Assyria I restored, which the kings of the Hittites call Pethor."[2] In the sixth year of his reign the king says—"The Euphrates in its upper part I crossed. The tribute of the kings of the Hittites, all of them I received." On this campaign Shalmaneser had to encounter a confederacy, in which Benhadad of Damascus was united with the kings of the Hittites.

"In those days Benhadad[3] of Damascus, Irkhulina

[1] "Records of the Past," v. 30.
[2] *Idem*, p. 31, Pethor is the city of Balaam. [3] Rimmon-Idri.

of Hamath, and the kings of the Hittites and of the sea-coasts to the forces of each other trusted, and to make war and battle against me came. By the command of Assur, the great lord, my lord, with them I fought. A destruction of them I made. Their chariots, their war carriages, their furniture of battle, I took from them. Twenty thousand five hundred of their fighting men with arrows I slew."[1]

Year by year through succeeding centuries the same cities had to be recaptured. " In my tenth year, for the eighth time the Euphrates I crossed. The cities of Sangara and Carchemish I captured. . . . .

"In my eleventh year, for the ninth time the Euphrates I crossed, cities to a countless number I captured. To the cities of the Hittites of the land of the Hamathites I went down. Eighty-nine cities I took, Rimmon-Idri (Benhadad) of Damascus and twelve kings of the Hittites."[2]

Thus the record proceeds with weary iteration through thirty campaigns, in which the same cities had to be yearly subdued, and the same people in oriental phraseology yearly destroyed. The war continued to the close of the king's reign in 823 B.C., and was carried on by the kings who succeeded him. One hundred years later we find the Assyrians still in deadly conflict with the Hittites. The empire of the Hittites was drawing to a close. Sargon came to the throne in 721 B C., and in 717 B.C. the long wars were brought to

[1] "Records of the Past," v. 32. [2] *Idem*, p. 34.

an end by the final overthrow of the Hittites at their eastern capital, Carchemish. The important event is narrated in one of Sargon's numerous annals, translated by Dr. Julius Oppert :—

"In the fifth year of my reign, Pisiri of Carchemish sinned against the great gods, and sent against Mita the Moschian messages hostile to Assyria. He took hostages. I lifted my hands to Assur, my lord, I made him leave the town. I sent away the holy vases out of his dwelling. I made them throw him into chains of iron. I took away the gold and silver, and treasures of his palace. The Carchemish rebels who were with him, and their properties, I transplanted to Assyria. I took among them fifty cars, two hundred riders, three thousand men on foot, and I augmented the part of my kingdom. I made the Assyrians to dwell in Carchemish, and I placed them under the domination of Assur my lord."[1]

Thus ended the mighty empire of the Hittites, having maintained its existence, defying all enemies, for a period of longer duration than that of the empires of Babylon or Assyria, or Greece or Rome.

[1] "Records of the Past," vii. 31.

CHAPTER IV.

GEOGRAPHICAL EXTENT OF THE HITTITE EMPIRE.

WE may estimate the extent of the Hittite empire from the vast number of local Hittite names mentioned in the Bible and in the inscriptions, and also from the vast extent of country over which Hittite inscriptions and Hittite sculptures are scattered. In the Egyptian and Assyrian inscriptions there have already been discovered over 300 geographical Hittite names, only a few of which have as yet been identified.

The significance of so large a number of Hittite names being found in the inscriptions will appear from the following considerations. In Keith Johnston's "Physical Geography," which contains nearly 500 pages, there are only about 133 names of places in England, Ireland, and Scotland mentioned. In the "Royal History of England," which extends to over 500 pages, we find the number of places referred to in Great Britain and Ireland about 72. The inscriptions of Egypt and Assyria are comparatively few and fragmentary, and of these few which have come to light many still remain unread. They are chiefly concerned with national achievements and the glory of conquerors, and yet these stone and clay records preserve for us twice as many names of places in the Hittite empire as are to be found of English geographical names in a thousand pages of our standard geography and history combined.

In the Bible we first meet the Hittites at Hebron,[1] in southern Palestine, on the high road from Egypt to Jerusalem. They were recognized as the rightful owners of the place, and from them the mighty prince Abraham purchased a burying-ground, making sure the boundaries and the title, and weighing out as the price four hundred shekels of silver. The Hittites at Hebron were not only a commercial people, as we see them engaged in the first money transaction on record, but they were also the proprietors of the land; and we see them making out the earliest title-deeds and effecting the earliest transfer of land on record.

Four hundred years later the spies found the sons of Anak in possession of Hebron, and the Hittites dwelling in the mountains,[2] whither they had doubtless been driven; and in a parenthetical clause it is stated: "Now Hebron was built seven years before Zoan in Egypt."[3] This isolated and independent clause, which always seemed out of place in the Book of Numbers, starts now into prominence, and helps us to knit together the scattered fragments of a long-lost history. Zoan or Tanais was the capital of the Hyksos invaders

[1] Gen. xxiii.   [2] Numb. xiii. 29.   [3] Numb. xiii. 22.

and conquerors of Egypt. According to Mariette, one of the Hyksos dynasty was Hittite; and it is proved by an inscription in the Louvre, which records the destruction of Hittite palaces on the borders of Egypt, that the Hittites had once been a settled people in these regions. "The mention of this last-named people at this time," says Brugsch, "is extremely remarkable, for it appears to prove that at this time the Hittites were settled close to Egypt. In fact, in the time of Abraham the Hittites were settled in the neighbourhood of Hebron, on the range of hills in the midst of the Amorites."[1]

It would thus appear that as the Hittites bore down upon Egypt from the north they occupied the fertile plain of Mamre, and built Hebron seven years before they had secured sufficient foothold in Egypt to found their capital city Zoan. Their route from Hebron to Zoan would be the same, by Beersheba, as that by which the patriarchal family went down into Egypt, and they must have felt securely at home before erecting palaces at the entrance to Egypt.

The Hittite settlement at Hebron was not a solitary outpost, for the Hittite empire being the central power in the north of Syria, and now having seized on the throne of Egypt, the Hittites would be free to settle and occupy towns throughout southern Palestine, up to the borders of Egypt.

"Another Hittite city," says Professor Sayce, "in the

[1] Brugsch's "Egypt under the Pharaohs," ii. 405.

south of Juda, was Kirjath-sepher, or 'Booktown,' also known as Debir, the sanctuary, a title which reminds us of that of Kadesh, 'the holy city.' We may infer from its name that Kirjath-sepher contained a library stocked with Hittite books."[1]

The Hyksos were at length driven out of Egypt, and according to Manetho's statement retired to Jerusalem. This statement throws light on one of the obscure parables of the Bible, and in return it is irradiated by that passage. The passage is Ezekiel xvi. 3. Ezekiel and the nobler Jews had been carried into captivity. The baser Jews remained in Jerusalem, and assumed that because they were inhabitants of the actual holy city, they were therefore more noble, and more the people of God, than their brethren in exile.

From the river Chebar the prophet priest rebukes the pretensions of the Jerusalemites by this reference to the Hittite origin of the city. "Thus saith the Lord God unto Jerusalem: thy birth and thy nativity[2] is of the land of Canaan: thy father was an Amorite, and thy mother a Hittite." There is little doubt that the reference here is to the Hittite origin and occupation of Jerusalem.

Another obscure and incidental Scripture reference helps us in our study of Hittite geography, and receives elucidation from modern research.

[1] "Ancient Monuments," p. 111.
[2] Literally, "thy diggings and thy bringings forth."

In Judges i. 26 it is recorded that the man who had betrayed Bethel, or Luz, to the children of Joseph, "went into the land of the Hittites, and built a city, and called the name thereof Luz."

It is clear that the traitor fled for safety to a people able to protect him from Canaanite vengeance. The new Luz is spoken of as a place known, and at no great distance, and Captain Conder has identified the ruins of the city as Lûeizeh,[1] near Banias, the ancient Cæsarea Philippi. Thus in the time of the Judges the Hittites occupied the fertile region of the Ard-el-Huleh by Lake Merom. This will account for the presence of the Hittite legions and chariots in the great battle of Merom, just as the presence of the Hittites in southern Palestine and Jerusalem will account for the leading part taken by the Hittite king of Kadesh previously in the great battle of Megiddo.

The name of the Hittites still clings to places far south. "Among the names collected," says Captain Conder, " I find Tell Hetteh, which is no doubt named, as are Hatta in Philistia, and Kefr Hatta above Lydda, from the old Hittite race."[2] And to these may be added such places as Hattin at the base of the traditional Mount of Beatitudes.

Another obscure passage in the Bible throws light on Hittite geography, and is rendered intelligible by recent

---

[1] Lûeizeh signifies " little Luz," in contradistinction to a larger town of the same name.
[2] "Heth and Moab," p. 53.

research. When David sent "Joab and the captains of the host" to number the people, it is recorded that they came to Gilead, and to the land of Tahtim-hodshi."[1] The Septuagint translated the passage—"Gilead and the land of the Hittites of Kadesh;" but the translators of the Authorized Version stuck faithfully to the Hebrew words before them, which they simply transliterated by "Tahtim-hodshi." Four ancient Septuagint MSS. agree as to this rendering, and if the reading of the LXX. prove to be correct the barbarous "Tahtim-hodshi" is no other than the Hittite Kadesh on the Orontes, the southern capital of the Hittite empire.

The geographical description of "the land of the Hittites," given by divine authority in the Book of Joshua, and long looked upon as a pictorial exaggeration, may now be taken as strictly accurate.

"From the wilderness and this Lebanon, even unto the great river, the river Euphrates, all the land of the Hittites."[2] When these words were addressed to Joshua, he was within sight of the southern ends of the Lebanon ranges—namely, the Lebanon and the Ante-Lebanon. The fertile Huleh plain, at the southern base of Hermon, was then known as the land of the Hittites, and the portion of that land which was to fall to the children of Israel, and which did fall to them in the time of David and Solomon, was described thus literally—"From the wilderness and the Lebanon

[1] 2 Sam. xxiv. 6.   [2] Joshua i. 4.

this, and to the great river, the river Euphrates, all the land of the Hittites." It is clear that the words were spoken to one who had the landscape full in view. The desert extended from his feet. "The Lebanon *this*," with its snowy cone, was before him, and from the part of the land of the Hittites clearly in sight the mind took in all the land of the Hittites, up to "the great river, the river Euphrates."

We turn again to Egyptian history. "Already," says Brugsch,[1] "during the wars undertaken by Thothmes III. against the Syrian peoples and towns of that region, the Kheta or Khita had shown themselves on the scene of those yearly repeated and long-enduring struggles, under the leadership of their own kings, as a dominant race. The contemporary Egyptian inscriptions designate them as 'the great people,' or 'the great country.' . . . . We believe we are falling into no error, if we persevere in our opinion, which recognizes in these people the same Khethites (Hittites) about whom Holy Scripture has so much to tell us, from the days of the patriarch Abraham till the time of the Captivity. When Thothmes III. fought with them and conquered their towns, they were seated as an important people-in the most northern parts of the land of Syria. At the commencement of the nineteenth dynasty, the power of the Kheta had been extended over the whole of the surrounding nations. These predecessors of the Assyrian empire held the

[1] "Egypt under the Pharaohs," ii. 2.

first place in the league of the cities and kings of Western Asia. Their importance grew from year to year in such a way that even the Egyptian inscriptions do not hesitate to mention the names of the kings of Kheta in a conspicuous manner, and to speak of their gods with reverence."

In the inscriptions at Karnak, referring to the victories of Thothmes III., there is a long list of towns in the land of the Hittites. Of these Brugsch says— "It is clear that this list exhibits in their oldest orthography the greater number of these towns which are afterwards mentioned so frequently in the records of wars, in Assyrian history, in the cuneiform inscriptions which have been deciphered. They are the old allied cities of those Kheta, of unknown origin, who long before the rise of Nineveh and Babylon played the same part that at a later period the Assyrians undertook with success."[1]

The names of the Hittite towns are exceedingly numerous in the Assyrian and Egyptian inscriptions. Of these Professor Sayce has drawn up a list of nearly 300. Among them we recognize Hamah, where I secured the Hittite inscriptions. And Kadesh on the Orontes, now Tel-Neby-Mendeh, the scene of the great battle between Rameses II. and Kheta-sira, the great king of the Hittites. And Carchemish on the Euphrates, the northern capital of the Hittites, and the scene of the final overthrow of the Hittite empire

[1] Brugsch's "Egypt under the Pharaohs," ii. 7.

in 717 B.C. And Aleppo and Daphne, and Pethor the home of Balaam the soothsayer, whose Hittite name has given so much trouble to Semitic philologists.

Besides the Hittite names, known and unknown, we have the names of allied countries and towns, or satrapies and dependencies, given in conjunction with the Hittite names. These extend throughout the whole of northern Syria, and throughout Asia Minor in its length and breadth.

In the war with Rameses II., Kheta-sira, the king of the Hittites, had under his command the Dardanians and the Trojans, once brothers in arms with Æneas in the Trojan war. And Professor Sayce points out that the Paschal Chronicle, which drew some of its material from Asia Minor, declares that the Dardani were sons of Heth, or Hittites. Warriors from towns of Ilion and Pedasus of the Troad were present at the battle of Kadesh; Mysians were there from the north-west of Asia Minor, and Colchians from the north-east. The islanders from Arvad (Aradus) and Cyprus were present, and the people of Mesopotamia, and the citizens of Aleppo and Pethor and Carchemish. There were also the Syrians and their Phœnician allies. As at Megiddo in Palestine, so at Kadesh on the Orontes, the king of the Hittites had under his command all the surrounding peoples, either as subjects or allies. It is clear, however, that the mighty host was brought into the field by a voice of command that had to be obeyed.

GEOGRAPHICAL POSITION OF THE HITTITE INSCRIPTIONS.

The existence of the Hittite inscriptions and sculptures over a very large extent of country, in northern Syria and throughout Asia Minor, confirm the Egyptian and Assyrian records, and bear witness to a very extensive Hittite empire. Inscriptions, written on coins, or lamps, or such portable objects, are no certain evidences as to the existence of a people in the places where such objects are found. But it is quite different in the case of the Hittite inscriptions, and sculptures which, with few exceptions, are inscribed on rocks, or very large stones.

All the inscribed stones in Hamah must have been carved near the spot where I found them, for with the exception of the fragment No. H. I., they were all very large, and could not have been carried from a distance except at a great cost, for which there was no motive, as the art is poor, and such stones plentiful. Even the fragment was large enough to require a camel to carry it, and it had not been regarded with the slightest curiosity by the Hamathites, or as of any importance, until recent copying and re-copying, and photographing, had led the owner to look upon it as of some marketable value. The inscribed Hamah stones were built into some Hamah edifice, with the inscriptions so placed as to be read by the people. They were therefore in the language of the people, who even in the earliest times had a literary reputation.

THE HITTITE EMPIRE. 55

Hamah is the most southern point at which Hittite inscriptions have yet been discovered (unless the stone figure found at Tell es-Salahiyeh in the plain of Damascus should turn out to be Hittite), but it should not be inferred that they mark the southern limit of the empire proper, for even Kadesh, the southern capital of the empire, lay considerably further south.

It must be remembered that public opinion has only very recently been called to these curious inscriptions. It is little over ten years since I took casts of the Hamah inscriptions and declared them to be Hittite remains, and it is little more than half that time since my theory began to be accepted; and yet during these few years solitary explorers have discovered many similar inscriptions in regions wide apart. A similar inscription was discovered on a basalt stone in the wall of a ruined mosque in Aleppo. The inscription, though copied by several explorers,[1] has never been presented to the public in a satisfactory form, and it is now destroyed; but the few symbols which can be recognized with certainty are clearly of the same character as those in the Hamah inscriptions.

At Jerâbis, the ancient Carchemish on the Euphrates, a number of Hittite inscriptions have been discovered, and the inscribed stones have been secured for the British Museum. These inscriptions are richer in

[1] Mr. C. F. T. Drake, Mr. George Smith, M. Paucker, Mr. Boscawen, and General Crawford. Through the kindness of Mr. W. H. Rylands I am able to give all the extant copies.

variety of character than those of Hamah, and are accompanied by sculptures now considered peculiarly Hittite.

As long ago as 1838, Major Fisher had called attention to a curious monument at Ibreez in Cilicia, north-west of Tarsus. This monument has been re-examined, and the undefaced characters and sculptures have been published by the Society of Biblical Archæology,[1] from drawings made by the Rev. J. Davis, M.A.[2]

When Paul and Barnabas were driven from Iconium they "fled unto Lystra and Derbe, cities of Lycaonia, and unto the region that lieth round about."[3] At Lystra, Paul healed a cripple, "and when the people saw what Paul had done they lifted up their voices, saying in the speech of Lycaonia: The gods are come down to us in the likeness of men."[4]

What was the speech of Lycaonia?[5] It is clear that Paul and Barnabas did not know it, for it was only when victims and garlands were about to be presented to them as gods that they were aware of the mistake into which the simple idolatrous people had fallen. There can be little doubt that the Lycaonian *patois*, which continued to be the vernacular of the people till the days of Paul, was Hittite. They understood Paul

---

[1] "Transactions of the Society of Biblical Archæology," vol. iv. part ii.
[2] Mr. W. H. Rylands has kindly corrected the inscription for this book.
[3] Acts xiv. 7.   [4] Acts xiv. 11.
[5] Jablonski suggested in his work "De Linguâ Lycaoniâ," that the Lycaonian was corrupt Assyrian, and therefore a dialect of Semitic. Gühling supposed that it was a jargon of Greek.

addressing them in Greek, but they expressed their own excitement in their native dialect. Lystra and Derbe have not been identified with certainty, but they lay south-east of Iconium, near the Cilician gates, the public pass in the Taurus range. Derbe must have been near the town Ibreez, where stand three ancient Christian chapels now in ruins. At any rate, Ibreez was certainly in "the region that lieth round about," and we know from the inscription on the Ibreez bas-relief that the language of Ibreez was Hittite.

On the old Hittite road from Carchemish and Marash, Colonel Sir C. W. Wilson discovered two Hittite inscriptions at Gurum within the frontiers of Cappadocia. The inscriptions were on a cliff in a narrow gorge through which flows a stream to join the Euphrates. They were greatly defaced, but enough remained to show their undoubted Hittite character. He says the inscriptions are continued down to the ground, and he supposed that an undefaced part might be covered by the soil, but he was unable through lack of time to remove the earth. Similar inscriptions have also been discovered at Tyana in the south of Cappadocia, on the high road to the Cilician gates. Our copy, though imperfect, is clearly of Hittite character.

Professor Sayce has also pointed out Hittite sculptures accompanied by Hittite characters at Eyuk and Boghaz-Keui, east of the Halys, far north in Cappadocia. "These sculptures," he says, "are characteristic specimens of Hittite art, and would alone prove its derivation from the art of Babylonia. . . . ; This is important as showing that Hittite culture originated in what may be called the Babylonian period, before the rise of Assyria in the fourteenth century B.C. It is in harmony with the fact that already in the astrological tablets of Sargon of Aganè, in the nineteenth century B.C., the Hittites are regarded as a formidable power."[1]

The discovery of the Hittite character of the sculptures of Eyuk[2] and Boghaz-Keui led Professor Sayce to re-examine sculptures in the north-west of Asia Minor which had been known since the days of Herodotus. The Greek historian, in the fourth century B.C., had described two monuments in the Karabel Pass, twenty-five miles from Smyrna on the way to Ephesus and Sardis. Herodotus considered them to be figures of Rameses II., the Greek Sesostris, but he admitted that the natives of Ionia knew not in whose honour they were sculptured.

In the September of 1879 Professor Sayce visited these sculptures. He made careful *squeezes* and copies of the inscription on one of the figures, which he found to consist of the same kind of characters as those of Carchemish and Hamah. He also made drawings of the other figure, which is much defaced. All doubt was removed as to the Hittite origin of the sculptures.

[1] "Transactions of Soc. of Bib. Archæology," vol. vii. part ii. p. 261.
[2] *Vide* "Trois Monuments des Environs de Smyrne, lettre à M. G. Perrot, par A. Martin," *Revue Archéologique*, New Series, vol. xxxi. 1876, p. 322, &c.

Instead of being monuments of the great Sesostris, they were monuments of the power of his rivals the Hittites, " who," Professor Sayce says, " must have penetrated to the shores of the Ægean itself, and held the pass which commanded the rich valleys of Lydia."[1] These facts, taken with the statement of the Paschal Chronicle that the Dardanians were Hittites, as well as with the fact that the Dardanians and Trojans were in Kheta-sira's army at the battle of Kadesh, demonstrate to us the vast extent and magnitude of the Hittite empire.

Colonel Sir C. W. Wilson examined most of the Hittite inscriptions and sculptures in Asia Minor, and the following summary is of special value as coming fresh from a practised and scientific explorer:—

" The widespread influence of the Hittites may, however, be gathered from their monuments; the inscriptions on the monument at Karabel, the Sesostris of Herodotus, on the old road from Sardis to Ephesus, and near the Niobe in the valley of the Hermus, show that they penetrated to the Ægean, and there are certain indications that Sardis was once in their hands.

" The next monuments are those at Giaour-Kalessi, between Sivrihissar and Angora, and then follow the interesting remains at Boghaz-keui near Yuzgat. The ruins at Boghaz-keui, of which Herr Humann, so well known from his excavations at Pergamos, made a plan last year, are quite unlike those of an ancient Greek

[1] " Transactions of Soc. of Bib. Archæology," vol. vii. part ii. p. 267.

city; they cover a wide extent of ground, and have more in common with cities like Babylon and Nineveh than with the typical Greek city gathered round its acropolis. The walls are still standing to a considerable height, and there are underground means of exit which offer several interesting features; there are also the foundations of a large temple, constructed of massive stones jointed together in a peculiar manner, and a long inscription in which, though almost obliterated, several Hittite symbols are distinctly visible.

"The rock sculptures, of which casts were taken by Herr Humann, are a series of religious representations with Hittite symbols above the gods and goddesses; the majority of the figures are female, and amongst them are twelve of the armed Amazons who played such an important part in the religious worship of Asia Minor. In one figure can be recognized the 'effeminate character, the soft outlines, the long sweeping dress, the ornaments of the eunuch high priest of Cybele;' and in another the warlike goddess Cybele.

"Not far from Boghaz-keui are the ruins of Uyuk, with the curious sphinxes, which, though made after an Egyptian model, differ widely from the Egyptian type. Uyuk is interesting as the only instance of what may be called a Hittite mound building in Anatolia, and shows us that, contrary to the practice in Assyria, the Hittites placed their sculptures so as to face outwards. To this peculiarity of construction is probably due the almost universal selection of trachyte or basalt for the sculptures instead of a softer stone ; the only exception is, I believe, at Jerablûs, where some of the slabs are of limestone.

"In Pontus there are traces of Hittite art in two small slabs, which I found at Kaisariyeh, but which came originally from the neighbourhood of Amasia.

"At Iflatûn Bûnar, near the Lake of Beischehr, there is a large monument of Hittite origin; and at Ivriz, near Eregli, there is a well-preserved rock-hewn monument, representing a thanksgiving to the god who gives fertility to the earth. 'The god is a husbandman, marked as a giver of corn and wine by his attributes ; and the gorgeous raiment of the suppliant priest, praying for a blessing upon the country and the people, is purposely contrasted with the plain garments of the god.'

"The god wears the very dress still used by the peasantry of Anatolia ; the high-peaked cap is still in use among some of the Kurdish tribes ; the tunic fastened round the waist by a girdle is the present loose garment with its *kummerbund ;* and the tip-tilted shoes are the ordinary sandals of the country, with exactly the same bandages and mode of fastening. The sandal is very like the Canadian moccasin, and the long bandage wound round the foot and ankle is the equivalent of the blanket sock ; it is the best possible covering for the foot in a country where the cold in winter is intense, and the snow lies on the ground for a long period; and as it appears on all Hittite monuments, I think it is an evidence of the northern origin of the Hittites. It is interesting also to notice that some of the patterns on the priest's dress have not yet gone out of fashion amongst the Cappadocian peasantry.

"At Bor, between Eregli and Nigdeh, Mr. Ramsay, whilst travelling with me last year, discovered a new inscription which, unlike all Hittite texts hitherto known, is incised, and not in relief. Near the silver mines in the Bulghar Dagh is another inscription, and at the mouth of a curious gorge, close to Gurum, near the head waters of an arm of the Euphrates, I found two others; it is, however, south of the Taurus, between that range and Aleppo, and eastward to the Euphrates, that the most numerous traces of the Hittites are to be found; near the eastern extremity of the Bagtché Pass, by which Darius crossed Mount Amanus, when he came down in the rear of Alexander's army before the battle of Issus, I visited a large mound on which a long row of Hittite sculptures, representing a hunting scene with great spirit, was standing *in situ;* here, as at Uyuk, facing outwards; a few miles beyond, on the road to Aintab, I saw other sculptures taken from one of the mounds.

"The district between the Giaour Dagh (Amanus) and the Kurt Dagh contains a large number of mounds; in a small area I counted eight, which I felt sure would well repay excavation. The slabs are all small, and could be easily conveyed to the coast; but, unfortunately, the British Museum has not seen its way to excavate; and the question is now, I believe, being taken up by the Germans.

"At Marash, near the foot of the Taurus, several Hittite slabs have been found, and between Aintab and Aleppo, and towards the Euphrates, there are many large mounds, evidently of Hittite origin, including Tell Erfad, Arpad, and Azaz, the Khazaz of the Assyrian monuments. Several slabs have reached this country from Jerablûs, but the excavations at that place, owing to want of skill and experience, have not been so fruitful in their results as might have been expected. Jerablûs is generally identified with Carchemish, but unless a distinct statement is found in the Assyrian inscriptions that that city was on the Euphrates, I would place it at Membij, the ancient Hierapolis, a site which impressed me more than any other I visited west of the Euphrates.

"Hittite inscriptions have also been found at Aleppo and Hamah, and I think the slab obtained for the Palestine Exploration Fund from Tell es-Salahiyeh, near Damascus, is also Hittite."

"That their empire extended," says Dr. Isaac Taylor, "as far as the Euxine and the Ægean, is shown by hieroglyphics and sculptures in the unmistakable style of Hittite art which are scattered over Asia Minor, more especially in Lydia, Lycaonia, Cappadocia, and Cilicia." "Scholars are only just beginning to realize the vast extent of the dominion of the Hittites, and their important place in primitive history. Till the rise of Assyria they were the most powerful nation of north-western Asia. Dr. Schliemann's discoveries at Troy, and the Hittite monuments scattered over Asia, as far west as the neighbourhood of Śmyrna, prove the extent of their empire to the west; while to the south, at a time prior to the exodus of the Hebrews, their dominion extended as far as Hebron; and if Mariette is right in his belief that one of the Hyksos dynasties was Hittite, they must have established their rule over Egypt itself."[1]

[1] "The Alphabet," by Dr. Isaac Taylor, vol. ii. p. 121.

CHAPTER V.

HITTITE ART AND LEARNING.

NOTWITHSTANDING the boastful Egyptian inscriptions, the Hittites, as we have already seen, won peace and treaty rights at the battle of Kadesh. "The miserable king of the Hittites" before the battle, became "the great king of the Hittites" after the battle.

When the ambassadors of Kheta-sira, "the great king of the Hittites," went down to Egypt to make a treaty with Rameses II., they bore with them a silver plate on which the Hittite text of the treaty was engraved in the Hittite language and character. "This," says M. G. Perrot, "is the most ancient diplomatic act which has come down to us."[1]

The Hittite text has been lost, but a copy of it in hieroglyphics appears on the walls of the temples of Rameses, and is thus described: "This is the copy of the contents of the silver tablet which the great king of Kheta, Kheta-sira, had caused to be made, and which was presented to Pharaoh by the hand of his ambassador Tarthisebu and his ambassador Rames, to propose friendship to the king Ramessu-Miamun."

[1] *Revue Archéologique*, Dec. 1882.

F

In the midst of the silver tablet there were figures, thus explained in the last paragraph of the treaty :—

"That which is found in the middle of this silver tablet, and on the front side of it, represents the image of the god Sutekh, embracing the image of the great king of the land of the Hittites, and surrounded by an inscription as follows :—'This is the image of the god Sutekh, king of heaven, protector of this treaty.'"

This silver tablet seems to have resembled the silver boss of which we give an engraving.[1] In the centre there was the figure, surrounded by an inscription. Such disks are supposed to have supplied the first idea of coined money, with a figure in the centre, and an inscription running round it. The earliest coinage was attributed to the Lydians, and we now know that the Hittite influence, and perhaps empire, extended to Lydia.

The Hittites were well acquainted with silver, and Professor Sayce has frequently drawn attention to their presence in the vicinity of silver mines. Their bargain with the patriarch Abraham at Hebron involved the earliest money transaction on record, and the "shekel" referred to, "current *money* with the merchant," was doubtless the forerunner of the coin with which we are acquainted.

We here see considerable progress in commerce, law, and civil institutions among the Hittites. They used silver as the standard of value, balances for weighing it,

[1] See page 156.

and a regular recognized form of sale and conveyancing. They seem to have given standard weights to their neighbours, and Mr. Barclay Head, of the British Museum, has pointed out that the Hittite mina of Carchemish continued to be the standard weight throughout Asia Minor, and among the Greeks, long after the break-up of the Hittite empire. Besides, certain silver bars have been found by Dr. Schliemann in his excavations at Hissarlik, which served as a standard according to which certain electron coins were struck.

The Hittite inscriptions on the silver plates have a close relation to all Hittite inscriptions except one with which we are acquainted. Thin silver plates were easily beaten on the back so as to show raised characters on the front. The art still exists in the land of the Hittites. Brass plates are placed on wax, and beaten into all kinds of arabesque patterns. I have a large brass tray so ornamented by a native of Hamah, possibly a descendant of the Hittites. The characters on the silver boss are raised, having been driven out from the concave side. Hittite inscriptions, unlike those of Assyria, Phœnicia, Greece and Rome, are in cameo, or raised characters, and doubtless those who carved them on stone took as their models the embossed inscriptions on the silver plates.[1]

Professor Sayce considers that Hittite art was a modification of the art of Babylon before the rise of the

[1] Captain Conder draws my attention to the fact that the oldest Egyptian inscriptions are in relief.

Assyrian empire. This, somewhat modified[1] by that of Egypt, was borne by the Hittites throughout Asia Minor. "The art and culture, the deities and rites, which Lydia owed to Babylon, were brought by the hands of Hittites and bore upon them a Hittite stamp."[2] "This art, along with the accompanying culture and writing, was carried by them into Asia Minor, which they overran and subdued."[3]

In our engravings we give specimens of Hittite art. Professor Sayce says—"It was characterized by solidity and roundness, and work in relief. The mural crown was a Hittite invention; the animal forms, in which Hittite artists specially excelled, were frequently combined to form composite creatures, among which may be mentioned the double-headed eagle, afterwards adopted by the Seljukian sultans, and carried by the crusaders to the German States.[4] This Hittite art is the source of the peculiar art of Asia Minor, which forms a well-marked element in that of primitive Greece."[5]

He traces Hittite influence throughout Asia Minor and the islands of the Archipelago in cylinders, and sculptures, and seals, long supposed to be Phœnician, but which turn out to be after Hittite models; and he points out that "Phœnician art was but one element in the art of primitive Greece, though it was the most

[1] Sayce's "Herodotus," pp. 6, 432, &c. [2] *Idem*, p. 427. [3] *Idem*, p. 426.
[4] "The symbol first appeared on a coin struck in 1217 A.D., by Malik Salah Mahmoud. It first appeared on the arms of the German emperor in 1345."
[5] Sayce's "Herodotus," p. 432.

important; the other element being the art long supposed to be peculiar to Asia Minor, but now traceable to the Hittites."[1]

Scholars had long been perplexed by a number of alphabets which existed in the different districts of Asia Minor. They were neither Greek nor Phœnician, but they were supposed to come from the same stock as the Greek. "We may now be quite sure," says Mr. C. T. Newton, "that there were in Asia Minor several alphabets derived in the main from the same source as the Greek."[2] And Dr. Isaac Taylor recognizes five distinct alphabets: "the Lycian, the Carian, the Cappadocian, the Phrygian, and the Pamphylian," to which he thinks may be added three more—"the Lydian, the Mysian, and the Cilician."

Some of these alphabets were related to each other, and to the Greek, in a manner to be accounted for only by the supposition of common but unknown parentage. Characters which were supposed by some to be "fantastic and arbitrary" forms of Greek, vagaries of copyists, have now been shown to be lineal descendants of an ancient and important script.

Inscriptions found by Mr. Hamilton Lang, in Cyprus, supplied the key to the mysterious characters in the alphabets of Asia Minor, and proved to be distantly related even to the whorls discovered by Dr. Schliemann in the lower stratum of Hissarlik. "It was manifest,"

---

[1] Sayce's "Herodotus," p. 420.
[2] "Transactions of Soc. of Bib. Archæology," vol. iv. part ii. p 335.

says Dr. Isaac Taylor,[1] "not only that writing was practised in the Troad before the introduction of either the Phœnician or the Greek alphabet, but that the non-Hellenic characters in the Lycian, Carian and Cappadocian alphabets, as well as the Cypriote syllabics, were all derived from a common source, a syllabic writing evidently of immense antiquity, which prevailed throughout the whole of Asia Minor."

This important discovery carried the investigation farther back, and the question to be solved was what was the parent stem from which at a very remote period these various scripts had sprung? This question is fully answered by the existence throughout Asia Minor of numerous inscriptions similar to those which I copied at Hamah and pronounced Hittite in 1872.

"These monuments," says Dr. Isaac Taylor, "are those of a people who have been identified with the Hittites of the Old Testament, the Kheta of the Egyptian monuments, the Khattai of the Assyrian records, and the Keteioi of Homer.

"They were one of the most powerful peoples of the primeval world, their empire extending from the frontier of Egypt to the shores of the Ægean, and, like the Babylonians and the Egyptians, they possessed a culture, an art, and a script peculiar to themselves, and plainly of indigenous origin."[2]

That the Hittites were a literary people is abundantly proved by the inscriptions of Egypt. The

[1] "The Alphabet," ii. 115.   [2] *Idem*, p. 120.

Hittite copy of the treaty of peace, which was embossed on a silver plate, was written in Hittite characters illustrated by figures. The literary propensities of the Hittites was even a subject of ridicule with the Egyptians—as a Bedawi treats with scorn a town Arab as a *katib*, or clerk. No doubt the name Kirjath-sepher, or Booktown, the name of a Hittite town near Hebron, has some reference to Hittite literature.

We have already referred to Mariette's theory, in which he points out that one of the Hyksos dynasties was Hittite, and Professor Eisenlohr has discovered that mathematics were studied at the Court of Hyksos princes, where astronomy and applied arithmetic were also cultivated. In these branches of learning at that early period we may probably discern the genius of the Hittites. Whether or not the Hyksos astronomers and mathematicians were Hittite, we have now before us a goodly collection of Hittite inscriptions, and the number is rapidly increasing, and will increase. We may consider ourselves at the opening of a new chapter of very ancient history, and we await in hope the revelations in store for us.

It is not alone in literature that the Hittites excelled. In the Bible, and in the inscriptions of Egypt and Assyria, we read of their formidable array of chariots, and the Egyptian battle-scenes preserve for us r⋮ tures of their well-equipped and well-arrayed ꝓ " Beardless, armed in a different manner, figh⁺⋮ men on each chariot of war, arrayed in ⋮⋮

battle according to a well-considered plan previously laid down, the Hittites present a striking contrast to their Canaanite allies."

In the representations of the wars of Rameses II. against Kheta-sira, the prince of Kheta, the great foreign king appears surrounded by his generals and servants, who are mentioned by name down to the letter-writer, Khirpasar. His warriors were divided into foot soldiers and fighters in chariots, and consisted partly of native Hittites, partly of foreign mercenaries. Their hosts were led to battle by Kazans, or commanders of the fighters in chariots, by generals, and Hirpits, or captains of the foreigners. The nucleus of the army was formed of native-born Hittites, under the designation of Tuhir, or the chosen ones. In the battle of Kadesh 8,000 of these stood in the foremost rank, under the command of Kamaiz, while 9,000 others followed their king, &c."[1]

Thus we see the Hittites far ahead of their neighbours in the arts of war as well as in the arts of peace. Indeed, they were formidable in making war because they excelled in peaceful pursuits.

[1] Brugsch's " Egypt," ii. 4.

CHAPTER VI.

HITTITE RELIGION.

THE Hittites, like the Canaanites, imported their gods and goddesses from Babylonia. Nana of Babylon was the Hittite Atargatis, the Ashtoreth of the Canaanites, and the sun-god of Babylon became the Baal of the land of Canaan, the Attys of the Hittites.

The religion of the Hittites, like that of the Canaanites, was also a Babylonian importation. Each people modified and bent their gods and their religion to their own peculiar circumstances, and each people carried their gods and their religion to whatever region their fortune directed them.

Wherever the Phœnicians[1] steered their ships, and carried their art and merchandize, the rites and worship of Baal and Astartê accompanied them. In like manner, wherever the Hittites extended their empire and con-

[1] The Phœnicians carried their deities into the great cities of Egypt, as well as to the sea-coasts and islands. Brugsch says, "In mentioning the names of Baal and Astartê, which we so frequently meet in the Egyptian inscriptions, it is scarcely necessary to point out that both have their origin in the Phœnician theology. As at Sidon, so likewise at Memphis, the warlike Astartê had her own temple."—("Egypt under the Pharaohs," i. 244.)

solidated their power, there we find under some form the Atargatis of Carchemish. Thus the Hittites of the north and the Canaanites of the south, having transformed the deities and religious conceptions of Babylon to their own use, handed them on to the people beyond them. The Astartê of Phœnicia became the Aphrodite of Paphos. Borne to Cyprus by the old sea kings, she was supposed to have sprung from the froth of the sea. The Atargatis of Carchemish, carried by the Hittites to Asia Minor, becomes at Ephesus the all-fructifying Artemis. " It was in this form, and with a mural crown upon her head," says Professor Sayce, " that the Hittite settlers in Ephesus represented the divinity they had brought with them."

Professor Sayce has traced the worship of this goddess in varying forms, as it marked the extension of the Hittite empire.

" The Hittite priestesses," he says, " who accompanied the worship of the goddess as it spread through Asia Minor, were known to Greek legend as Amazons. The cities founded by Amazons—Ephesus, Smyrna, Kyme, Myrina, Priene, Pitane—were all of Hittite origin. In early art the Amazons are robed in Hittite costume, and armed with the double-headed axe; and the dances they performed with shield and bow, in honour of the goddess of war and love, gave rise to the myths which saw in them a nation of woman warriors. The Thermodon, on whose banks the poets placed them, was in the neighbourhood of the Hittite monument of

Boghaz-Keui and Eyuk, and at Komana in Cappadocia; the goddess Ma was served by 6,000 ministers."[1]

The Hittite goddess appears in conjunction with Attys or Sutekh, accompanied by the rites with which Istar and Tammuz had been honoured in Babylon. He is the Adonis, the bridegroom of the great goddess of Asia. Among the Hittites the goddess occupies a more important position than among the Canaanites, whose Baal is the great god, and Baaltis is but his reflection. This may be accounted for by the fact that the relation of the deities as they existed in Babylonia was more nearly maintained among the Hittites than among the Canaanites. In Babylonia the woman received equal honour with the man, and hence in Assyria and among the Hittites the female deities occupied an independent position.

The rites with which these goddesses were honoured should hardly be called religion. The priestesses were mere ritualists, and the business of their service was mere attention to ritual without any reference to morality. Their impure worship seems to have been mingled with the primitive nature-worship, and in the name Kadesh,[2] the capital of the Hittites, we see one of the numerous shrines where Hittite girls were devoted to wickedness in the name of religion. The worship of these deities took many repulsive forms. Devotees surrendered their children to Baal in the

[1] Sayce's "Herodotus," p. 430.
[2] Kadesh-Naphtali, Kadesh-Barnea, &c.

flames, and the children's screams were drowned by trumpet and drum; and the rites of Astarté were equally vile, though accompanied by the cooing of doves and clouds of incense.

The Baal of the Canaanites appears plural as Baalim in many forms; sometimes localized to place or expressive of quality, as Baal-Melkorth, the god of Tyre; Baal-Gad, the deity of Gad; Baal-Shemaim, the god of Heaven; Baal-Tsephon, the god of the north; Baal-Risheph, the sun-god; Baal-Berith, the god of the covenant; and Baal-Zebub, the monster fly.

In the treaty between the king of the Hittites, Kheta-sira, and Rameses II. of Egypt, we have a catalogue of Hittite gods and goddesses, and these are evidently made to appear as numerous as possible to compare favourably with the numberless deities of Egypt. At the head of the Hittite Pantheon stands the great Hittite war-god Sutekh, which was the Egyptian form of the Semitic Baal.[1] Like the Baalim of the Canaanites, the Hittite gods were localized as the gods of certain places and powers. The treaty was placed under the sanction of the gods and goddesses of the Hittites, united with those of Egypt. All were invoked as approving of the words on the silver tablet.

"This is the catalogue of the gods of the land of Khita:—

Sutekh, of the city of Tunep (Daphne).
Sutekh, of the land of the Hittites.

[1] Brugsch's "Egypt under the Pharaohs," i. 277.

Sutekh, of the city of Arnema.
Sutekh, of the city of Taranda.
Sutekh, of the city of Pilqua.
Sutekh, of the city of Khissap.
Sutekh, of the city of Sarsu.
Sutekh, of the city of Khilibu (Aleppo).
Sutekh, of the city of . . . .

* * * * * *

Sutekh, of the city of Sarpina.
Astartha, of the land of the Hittites.
The god of the land of Zaiath-Khirri.
The god of the land of Ka . . . .
The god of the land of Kher . . . .
The goddess of the city of Akh . . . .
The goddess of the land of Zaina," &c. &c.

These, and many more gods and goddesses, whose names are defaced from the inscriptions, are invoked and arrayed as guardians of the treaty. With them are associated the male and female deities "of the mountains and of the rivers of the land of the Hittites, the gods of the land of Gauzanitis—Amon, Pra, Sutekh, and the male and female gods and goddesses of the land of Egypt, of the earth, of the sea, of the winds, and of the storm ;" and they are not only called upon as witnesses to the treaty, but they are constituted avengers of its covenants on all who might transgress them. "But he who shall observe these commandments, which the silver tablet contains, whether he be

Hittite or Egyptian, because he has not neglected them, the company of the gods of the land of the Hittites, and the company of the gods of the land of Egypt shall secure his reward, and preserve his life, and his servants of those that are with him, and who are with his servants."

In this transaction the Hittite deities, whom we have seen as the patrons of lewd and hideous rites, are joined with the Egyptian deities as the guardians of international morality and good faith. The rewards, however, seem to be only temporal; nevertheless, the treaty was faithfully and scrupulously kept for a long time, and secured the blessings of peace and friendship to Egypt and the Hittites.

CHAPTER VII.

HITTITE NATIONALITY.

WHO were the Hittites? To what race or people did they belong?

Outside the Bible our two sources of information on this subject are Hittite names and Hittite sculptures.

It is now pretty generally conceded that the language of the Hittites was not Semitic—that is, it was not of the same family as the language spoken in varying dialects by the Jews and other Semitic people.[1]

The Egyptian inscriptions preserve for us a great many names of Hittite towns, kings, princes and princesses, generals, scribes, &c. Some of these names are Semitic. The gods and goddesses which were derived from Babylon, their sacred shrines dedicated to the Kedeshoth, or sacred women, and certain terms of rank, are clearly Semitic. Nor is it to be wondered at that the Hittites adopted names from their Semitic neighbours with whom they were in close intercourse for a thousand years.

Mr. Reginald S. Poole, referring to the names of the

[1] Mr. George Grove says, in Smith's "Dictionary of the Bible," the Hittites were a Hamitic race, neither of the country nor kindred of Abraham.

Hittites found in the Bible, remarks that "the language of the Hittites was nearer to the Hebrew than to the Chaldee."[1] A Hittite, however, who had thrown in his fortune with King David might be called Ahimelech, "brother," or friend of the king, without being of Semitic origin; and a Hittite residing among the Canaanites might be called Beeri, or "Fontanus," from some special circumstances connected with a well or fountain.

And this view is confirmed by the fact that Berri and his daughter are mentioned by their original names in another passage in the Bible. In Gen. xxvi. 35, it is recorded that Esau "took to wife Judith, the daughter of Beeri the Hittite, and Bashemath, the daughter of Elon the Hittite." In this passage we have the Semitic names of Esau's wives and their fathers. Judith, "the praised," Beeri, "Fontanus" or "Weller," Bashemath, "fragrant," and Elon, the "strong hero." But in Gen. xxxvi. 2, Judith is called Aholibamah, and her father Beeri is called Anah, which are probably their old Hittite names Semiticized; and this may explain the fact, which has so much puzzled commentators, that Esau's wives had double names.

The Semitic word Sar was used by the Hittites for prince, or king, but this does not prove that the Hittites were Semitic, any more than the use of the Persian name Khedive for the ruler of Egypt proves that he is Persian. Afghans, Persians, Armenians,

[1] Kitto's "Biblical Literature," ii. 314. See Appendix No. II.

Kurds, and others settling among the Semitic Syrians at the present day, are uniformly in the habit of adopting the names and terms in common use.

Besides, foreigners writing Hittite names would write them to a certain extent in their own way. Take for instance the Egyptian Mazor, which was called by the Hebrews Mizraim, a dual form, by the Persians Mudraya, by the Assyrians Muzur, and by the Arabs Misr, each fitting the name into the groove of his own language. In like manner, the name of Carchemish, the northern Hittite capital, began with a G in Assyrian, a K in Egyptian, and a C in Hebrew, each people dealing with the guttural in their own way.

The Egyptians, from their constant intercourse with Semitic-speaking people, adopted and incorporated into their vocabulary a very large number of words of purely Semitic origin. In the same manner, the Hittites not only borrowed Semitic gods and a Semitic ritual, but also a large number of words from their southern and eastern neighbours.

The great mass of the Hittite names that have come down to us are clearly of a non-Semitic origin. Brugsch after quoting such names as Thargathazas, Zauazas, Tarthisebu, adds—" It is evident at once that these names do not bear a Semitic stamp, or at any rate not a pure Semitic stamp."[1] And Professor Sayce says—"The Hittite proper names preserved on the Egyptian and

[1] "Egypt under the Pharaohs," ii. 5.

Assyrian monuments show that the Hittites did not speak a Semitic language."[1]

Those Hittite names which are compounded with Semitic names show from their structure that the genius of the language was not Semitic. The Hittites wrote Kheta-sira for king of the Hittites, and Kaui-sira, king of the Kuans. Had they been a Semitic people they would have placed the defining word last, as in the case of Melchizedek—Malki-sedek, Prince of Peace—Sar-Shalôm, Prince of Persia—Sar-Faras.[2]

This point has been strengthened by Professor Sayce from the inscriptions. He has pointed out that grammatical suffixes are invariably affixed and not prefixed to the ideographs to which they are attached; "and this," he says, "by itself would be enough to show that the language of the Hittites was not Semitic, since Semitic flectional suffixes as often precede as follow the root."[3]

Several links of a linguistic chain have been discovered which seem to connect the Hittites with the Georgians, whose language belongs to the family of speech called Alarodian. M. Lenormant drew attention to the fact that the inscriptions at Van in Asia Minor belonged to the Alarodian family, and Professor Sayce has pointed out the affinity between the Hittite and the ideographs in the Vannic inscriptions: "So far as it

[1] "Transactions of Soc. Bib. Archæology," vii. 251.
[2] See also Gen. xii. 15, xxii. 8, 30; Judges vii. 25, viii. 6, &c.
[3] "Transactions of Soc. Bib. Archæology," vii. 276.

is possible to infer from proper names, the language of the Hittites belonged to the same family of speech as the languages spoken by the Patiani (between the Orontes and the bay of Antioch), the Kilikians, Kuai, Samahlai, Gamgumai, Komagenians, Moschi and Tibareni, the proto-Armenians, and other tribes who occupied the country between the Caspian and the Halys on the one side, and Mesopotamia on the other. This family of speech has been conveniently termed Alarodian."[1] This view, which in itself is reasonable, is confirmed by the similarity of the Hittite nominative and genitive to that of the other languages referred to.

There are several eminent linguists, whose opinions are entitled to deferential consideration, who believe that the Hittite language was Semitic. There should be no dogmatism where our certain knowledge is so limited, but with the most careful balancing of all the facts, we are compelled to the conclusion that the weight of evidence is on the side of the non-Semitic character of the Hittite language.

This conclusion as to the language is backed up by the Hittite, and also by the Egyptian, sculptures.

On the great temple at Ibsamboul there is a picture of the battle of Kadesh, nineteen yards long by more than eight yards deep. In this great battle-scene there are eleven hundred figures, and among these there is no difficulty in recognizing the slim Egyptians

[1] "Transactions of Soc. Bib. Archæology," vii. 235.

and their Sardonian allies, with horned and crested helmets, and long swords, shields, and spears. "The host also of the Hittites and of their allies are represented," says Brugsch, "with a lively pictorial expression, for the artist has been guided by the intention of bringing before the eyes of the beholder the orderly masses of the Hittite warriors, and the less regular and warlike troops of the allied peoples according to their costume and arms. The Canaanites are distinguished in the most striking manner from the allies, of races unknown to us, who are attired with turban-like coverings for the head, or with high caps such as are worn at the present day by the Persians."[1]

Captain Conder also draws attention to the distinct characteristics of the Hittites and their allies as pictured on the temple at Ibsamboul: "In this picture the Hittites and their allies are represented as distinct races with different kinds of weapons. The one race is bearded, the other beardless, and in the Ibsamboul picture the Chinese-like appearance of the Hittites, who have long pigtails, is very remarkable."[2] This would seem to point to a Tartar or Mongolian people.

Professor Sayce feels very confident that the Hittite sculptures as well as their language stamps them as a non-Semitic people. "The Hittite proper names," he says, "preserved on the Egyptian and Assyrian monu-

---

[1] Brugsch's "Egypt under the Pharaohs," ii. 50.
[2] "Heth and Moab," p. 22.

ments, show that the Hittites did not speak a Semitic language. The Hittite sculptures further show that they did not belong to a Semitic race. Their features and physical type are those of a northern people, and their northern origin is confirmed by their use of boots, which is at least as old as their writing, since the boot is one of the commonest of the Hittite hieroglyphics The boots are always represented with turned-up toes, like the mountaineers of Asia Minor and Greece at the present day."[1]

On this subject the words of Colonel Sir Charles Wilson, who has recently returned from Asia Minor, will be considered of great weight: "I fully agree with Professor Sayce in considering that the Hittites of northern Syria and Palestine were intruders, and that they came from the Anatolian plateau east of the Halys, which was occupied by Hittite tribes from the Black Sea to the Mediterranean. This view of their northern origin is supported by their physical appearance as depicted on the monuments, by the moccasin sandal already noticed, and by the fingerless glove,[2] which is still commonly used by the peasantry, and is found in all cold countries. The sculptures show that the Hittites did not belong to a Semitic race. The features are rather those of a northern people, and on the temple of Ibsamboul the Hittites have a very Scythic character, with shaven head and a single lock from the crown. This peculiarity in the mode of dressing the

[1] "Transactions of Soc. Bib. Archæology," vii. 252.   [2] Cf. page 166.

hair is not seen on the Hittite monuments, but at Karnak and Thebes I noticed figures with the same type of feature as those on the monuments in Anatolia."[1]

Captain Conder thought he saw Hittites and Canaanites still side by side on the plain of Kadesh, in the land of the Hittites: "It was interesting to contrast the Semitic agriculturists with their Turkoman neighbours; for in the mixture of races—the Semitic tillers of the plains, and the Turanian shepherds on the downs—we find a condition of society precisely parallel to that which existed in this very region when Rameses the Great attacked the Turanian Hittites and their bearded Syrian allies."[2]

Sir Charles Wilson recognized in the Cappadocian troglodytes the Hittite type of countenance as portrayed on sculptures. "The type," he says, "which is not a beautiful one, is still found in some parts of Cappadocia, especially amongst the people living in the extraordinary subterranean towns which I discovered last year beneath the great plain north-west of Nigdeh."[3] He adds, in referring to the Hittite priest sculptured at Ibreez, a sketch of whom we reproduce: " It is interesting to notice that some of the patterns on the priest's dress have not yet gone out of fashion amongst the Cappadocian peasantry."

[1] "Quarterly Statement of Palestine Exp. Fund," for Jan. 1884.
[2] "Heth and Moab," p. 16.
[3] "Quarterly Statement of Palestine Exp. Fund" for Jan. 1884.

It would thus appear that the testimony of the sculptures as well as of the proper names of the Hittites seems to prove that the Hittites were a non-Semitic people. And this conclusion is in accordance with the genealogies in the Book of Genesis, where Heth is declared to be the grandson of Ham. In Gen. x. 6, Canaan is the fourth son of Ham; and in verse 15, Heth is the second son of Canaan; and in verse 18, it is stated that "the families of the Canaanites spread abroad." We have thus not only the Hamitic and non-Semitic origin of the "sons of Heth" indicated, but also the fact of their wide dispersion.

CHAPTER VIII.

THE HITTITES FROM THE BIBLE STANDPOINT.

MY object in this chapter is to show that the statements of the Bible with reference to the Hittites are fully confirmed by the cumulative evidence of modern discovery, and that the light of the nineteenth century A.D. reveals to us the existence of a Hittite power in the nineteenth century B.C., and enables us to follow the fortunes of that power down to 717 B.C., when the Hittite empire was finally crushed on the fatal field of Carchemish. I hope not only to prove the Bible true by contemporary and corroborative evidence, but also to show that a great empire, forgotten by ancient and modern historians, must be restored to the ancient kingdoms of the world. By confirming the Bible we shall discover a lost empire.

It is desirable that this investigation should be undertaken, because the casual references to the Hittites in the Bible have been used by scholars, of repute as critics, to discredit the historical accuracy of the book, and some of the weak defenders of the Bible have begun to propagate doubt where they cannot disprove.

For example, in 1857, Professor F. W. Newman, Fellow of Balliol College, Oxford, in his "History of the Hebrew

Monarchy,"[1] speaks of the Bible references to the Hittites as "unhistorical," and as "not exhibiting the writer's acquaintance with the times in a very favourable light;" and the Rev. T. K. Cheyne, Fellow of the same College, writing on the Hittites in the new edition of "The Encyclopædia Britannica,"[2] treats the Bible statements regarding the Hittites as unhistorical and unworthy of credence. Referring to the mention of the Hittites in the Book of Genesis, he says: "The lists of these pre-Israelitish populations cannot be taken as strictly historical documents," "they cannot be taken as of equal authority with Egyptian and Assyrian inscriptions;" and, carrying out his comparison, he adds: "Not less unfavourable to the accuracy of the Old Testament references to the Hittites is the evidence deducible from proper names."

The insinuation in this passage clearly is that the Bible assumed, by the use of Semitic names, that the Hittites were of Semitic origin. Mr. Cheyne mentions Ephron, Ahimelech, and Uriah, and he asks, "Is it unnatural to infer that these three names are no less fictitious than the Semitic names ascribed in the Old Testament to the non-Semitic Philistines?" The Bible is therefore wrong, and the names—Hittite and Philistine—are fictitious. But what saith the Bible itself? It says without any reservation that the Hittites were Canaanites (Gen. x. 15): "And Canaan begat Sidon his firstborn, and Heth."

It must be borne in mind that Oriental names are to a

[1] Pages 178, 179. [2] Vol. xii. Art. Hittites.

large extent *significates*. Men receive names according to some personal peculiarity or striking circumstances.

I knew a youth in Syria called "the father of two blue eyes" until he grew up, and then he was called "the father of a red beard." His firstborn was named Youseph, and then he was called Abu Youseph. My landlord in Damascus was called "the father of a nose;" Moses was his name, and in my house his *sobriquet* was translated into " Mozambique."

With a Semitic people there was nothing more natural than that a Hittite, with an unpronounceable name, on attaching himself to King David when an outlaw, should be called Ahimelech, the brother or friend of the king. I have already drawn attention, however, to the fact that some of the Hittites had duplicate names, one Semitic and the other probably Hittite. The statements by Professor Newman and Mr. Cheyne with reference to the Bible are typical of a class of statements.

I shall examine them in the light of Egyptian and Assyrian inscriptions when I come to the passages referred to. It is enough here to draw attention to the manner and progress of unbelief. Professor Newman, writing before Egypt and Assyria had given up their secrets, discredits what he does not understand; and Mr. Cheyne, writing in the full light of recent discovery, mistakes the confidence of scepticism for disproved facts, and accepts his predecessor's conclusions, and gives them the wider currency of his own credit.[1]

[1] See Appendix No. III.

BIBLE REFERENCES TO THE HITTITES.

We find the Hittites among the settled inhabitants of Canaan while as yet Abraham was only a wandering sheikh. By peaceful pastoral pursuits, and by skill and valour in war, Abraham had attained to a high position of wealth and influence. He finds himself, however, in the land of the stranger, with no sons to support or succeed him, and the only heir to his wealth and fame, Eliezer, a Damascene ; and when, in presence of the uncertain future, he begins to despond, the Lord appears to him and renews His former promises, and in addition makes with him a new covenant, that his own children shall possess the land then occupied by the Hittites and other heathen tribes, from the river of Egypt to the river Euphrates (Gen. xv. 20).[1]

Fifty years later, Abraham secures his first possession in Canaan by purchasing a grave for Sarah from the sons of Heth. The Hittites are in possession and power at Hebron, and Abraham, as he stands up before them, declares himself "a stranger and a sojourner" (Gen. xxiii. 4). The Hittites call Abraham a mighty prince, and in the phrases and customs stereotyped in Syria to this day, sell to the patriarch the field with the cave of Machpelah.

"The stranger and sojourner" purchased his field

[1] This event is placed by Usher about 1913 B.C. I do not, however, rest any part of my case on the exact accuracy of any system of chronology sacred or secular. I simply take the common dates as useful approximations more or less correct.

from the Hittites of Hebron, secured his title, and buried his wife in the cave where, nearly forty years later, Isaac and Ishmael laid his own body by the side of his faithful companion,[1] "in the cave of Machpelah, in the field of Ephron the son of Zohar the Hittite" (Gen. xxv. 9).

The family of the patriarch and the Hittite people continued to live side by side in the land, and Esau, the grandson of Abraham, took to wife several Hittite women, who were a bitterness of spirit to Isaac and Rebekah (Gen. xxvi. 35).

During the weary years spent in Egypt the discouraged Israelites were often cheered by the renewed promise of a return to the land of the Hittites. From the bush on Horeb the Lord declared to Moses that He had heard the cry of the Israelites, and had come down to deliver them from their taskmasters, and to bring them "unto the place of the Canaanites, and the Hittites, and the Amorites, and the Perizzites, and the Hivites, and the Jebusites" (Exod. iii. 8), thus enumerating the nations then in possession of the promised land.

The Canaanites probably included all the Hamite races of the land, and the Hittites stand generally first in order and first in importance of the sub-tribes. Later the Lord not only promised to send His angel to lead them to the land of the Hittites, but He declared that He would send before them hornets to drive out the Hittites before them (Exod. xxiii. 28).

[1] 1822 B.C.

On their return to Moses, the spies described in a general way the regions occupied by the different peoples (Numb. xiii. 29). "The Amalekites," they said, "dwell in the land of the south; and the Hittites, and the Jebusites, and the Amorites, dwell in the mountains; and the Canaanites dwell by the sea and by the coast of Jordan."

After the death of Moses, the Israelitish host, having received many commands to destroy utterly the Hittites, reach the border of the promised land, ready, with Joshua as their leader, to cross the Jordan. Then the Lord spake unto Joshua, assuring him of the fulfilment of former promises, and defining the limits of the land of promise viewed from the speaker's standpoint: "From the wilderness and this Lebanon even unto the great river, the river Euphrates, all the land of the Hittites, and unto the great sea toward the going down of the sun, shall be your coast" (Josh. i. 4).

The Israelites crossed the Jordan, and in the taking of Jericho (Josh. xxiv. 11) first met the Hittites with the Amorites. In the various confederacies formed against the invaders (Josh. ix. 1) the Hittites seem to have taken a part; but especially in the battle by lake Merom we recognize the Hittite allies of Jabin by the multitude of their horses and chariots (Josh. xi. 3).

The Hittite power in Palestine was crushed, but some of the people continued to dwell in the land (Judg. iii. 5), and the Israelites dwelt among them, and intermarried with them, and served their gods. King David had among his mighty men Hittite warriors, and

Bathsheba, the mother of Solomon, and ancestress of our Lord, was the wife of Uriah the Hittite. Solomon also had among his foreign wives women of the Hittites (1 Kings xi. 1), and he caused the people of the Hittites to pay tribute.

When King David went to establish his frontier on the Euphrates, he took from King Hadadezer a thousand chariots, and seven hundred horsemen, and twenty thousand footmen; and Toi king of Hamah sent to him vessels of silver and gold (2 Sam. viii.). We have pointed out that the correct reading in 2 Sam. xxiv. 6, is not *Tahtim-hodshi*, but *Kadesh of the Hittites*, thus showing that the southern capital of the Hittites was within the borders of King David's empire.[1]

The Hittites, however, must have enjoyed an independent national existence, for in the time of Solomon horses and chariots were brought up out of Egypt for the kings of the Hittites (1 Kings x. 29), and the very price is mentioned. In later years the Syrians fled panic-stricken from the siege of Samaria on hearing what they supposed to be a noise of chariots and horses. They said, "The king of Israel hath hired against us the kings of the Hittites . . . . wherefore they arose and fled in the twilight" (2 Kings vii. 6).

We have thus summarized the chief Bible references to the Hittites during a period of a thousand years. We now turn to the contemporary records of Assyria and Egypt to see what light they throw on these references.

[1] See page 50.

THE BIBLE REFERENCES TO THE HITTITES IN THE LIGHT OF THE INSCRIPTIONS OF ASSYRIA AND EGYPT.

The labours of a few men in recent years have drawn floods of historic light from the records of Egypt and Assyria; and the nineteenth century before Christ is yielding up its secrets to the nineteenth century of our era.

At that early period the Hittites are recognized among existing peoples. "In the astrological tablets," says Prof. Sayce, "compiled for the library of Sargon of Aganè (about B.C. 1900),[1] the Hittites are already spoken of as formidable rivals of the Babylonians in the northwest, at a time when the kingdom of Assyria did not exist."[2] The astrological tablets chronicled events in relation to omens. They are chiefly later editions from the libraries of Babylonian kings. Thus we meet the Hittites, for the first time in the national history of Babylon, just about the time, according to Usher's chronology, when they are mentioned as a people in the Book of Genesis (xv. 20).

The divine promise, in which Abraham's posterity receives the land of the Hittites, points to a people stretching to the river Euphrates—"unto the great river, the river Euphrates"—and the Babylonian records, read

[1] This date is only thirteen years earlier than the date of Abraham's transactions with the Hittites at Hebron, according to Usher's chronology.
[2] "Transactions of Soc. of Bib. Archæology," vol. vii. part ii.

in our day for the first time in two millenniums, point to the Hittites firmly established in the neighbourhood of Carchemish 1900 B.C., and show that they had already adopted the elements of Babylonian art and civilization.

The two chief cities of the Hittites were Kadesh on the Orontes, the modern Tell-Neby-Mendeh, and Carchemish on the upper Euphrates, now called Jerabîs, and between these two cities lies the region from south of Hamah unto the great river Euphrates. Surely such a marvellous coincidence as this between the Bible and the Babylonian inscriptions, with reference to events on the very outer horizon of history, should compel any candid scholar to accord the same credence at least to the book of Genesis as to the tablets of Sargon. The Rev. T. K. Cheyne, however, referring to the Bible statements regarding the Hittites, declares they "cannot be taken as of equal authority with Egyptian and Assyrian inscriptions."[1] Yet we find the Assyrian chronology by Professor Sayce, and the Bible chronology by Usher, practically agreeing as to a state of facts over 3,780 years ago. If the tablets of Sargon are correct in this instance, the Tôrah of Moses must also be correct, for they are in perfect accord. If the king of Aganè's astrological records are strictly historical, the statement in the Pentateuch must also be strictly historical. Those who accept the record of this inscription must also accept the record of the Bible

[1] "Encyclopædia Britannica," vol. xii. Art. Hittites.

They appeal from the Bible to ancient inscriptions, and the stony records of forgotten ages condemn them and confirm the historic accuracy of the Bible.

Half a century later the Bible reveals to us Abraham engaged in purchasing a burial-place from a Hittite people in the south of Palestine. The whole account is so true to Oriental ways that we should not have paused to draw special attention to this passage had not the Rev. T. K. Cheyne used it as a proof of his assertion that the narrative of the Bible "cannot be taken as of equal authority with Egyptian and Assyrian inscriptions."[1] "How meagre," he says, "the tradition respecting the Hittites was in the time of the great Elohistic narrator is shown by the picture of Hittite life in Genesis xxiii."[2] But is there anything contrary to universal experience in a great people stretching out branches on different sides? The Phœnicians, the Greeks, the Romans, the Spaniards, the Dutch, the English, have all sent out colonists on the lines of their commerce. The Hittites drew most important resources from Egypt, and it would have been contrary to all experience had Hittite merchants not been found in the direction of Egypt. It would also be contrary to common experience if we found a strong warlike people firmly established in northern

---

[1] In his article on the Canaanites, in the "Encyclopædia Britannica," he says of the Bible record: "The Hittites seem to have been included among the Canaanites by mistake. Historical evidence, both Biblical and extra-Biblical, prove convincingly that they dwelt beyond the borders of Canaan"!

[2] "Encycl. Brit.," vol. xii., Art. Hittites.

Syria and not sending forth in half a century peaceful colonists towards Southern Palestine. Mr. Cheyne, referring to this amicable transaction between Abraham and the Hittites, says, "the undoubted authentic inscriptions of Egypt and Assyria reveal the Hittites in far different guise, as pre-eminently a warlike, conquering race." No doubt the inscriptions of Egypt and Assyria represent the Hittites for the most part in the attitude of war, but the inscriptions are at best meagre, and in great part pictorial representations of campaigns and victories executed in honour of the victors. No one, however, who reflects will infer that because the Hittites appear among the pictorial representations of campaigns as pre-eminently warlike, that therefore a Hittite colony was incapable of a simple business transaction. Many of our own English histories are little more than a record of wars and victories, and yet the English people might be discovered in as peaceful transactions sometimes as that which took place between Abraham and Ephron the Hittite. The German nation was a terrible instrument of war a few years ago, and yet the Germans are industrious at home, and enormous numbers of them are now flying away to peaceful pursuits in other lands. The Turks are " pre-eminently a warlike race," and yet the writer of these pages had once some peaceful transactions with them in regard to the making more secure a Christian cemetery by the fanatical city of Damascus.

Not only is the transaction between Abraham and

the Hittites at Hebron so entirely in accord with general experience and local usage as to require no collateral corroboration, but there seems to be some evidence from Egyptian inscriptions as to the existence of the Hittites on the borders of Egypt at a very remote period. The stone now in the Louvre, of the time of Amenemhat, of the twelfth dynasty, contains an inscription which refers to the overthrow of Hittite palaces in that region; and Brugsch Bey, referring to the record of the Hittites in this inscription, says: "The mention of the last-named people at this time is extremely remarkable, for it appears to prove that at this time the Hittites were close to Egypt."[1] And this view, as we have seen, is supported by Mariette Bey's theory, that one of the Hyksos dynasties was Hittite.

Dr. Isaac Taylor, referring to the extent of the Hittite empire, says: "Dr. Schliemann's discoveries at Troy and the Hittite monuments scattered over Asia Minor, as far west as the neighbourhood of Smyrna, prove the extent of their empire to the west; while to the south, at a time prior to the Exodus of the Hebrews, their dominion extended as far as Hebron; and if Mariette is right in his belief, that one of the Hyksos dynasties was Hittite, they must have established their rule over Egypt itself."[2]

The capital of the Hyksos Dynasty was Zoan or Tanais, and the Bible informs us that "Hebron was

[1] Brugsch's "Egypt under the Pharaohs," ii. 405
[2] "The Alphabet," ii. 121.

built seven years before Zoan in Egypt."[1] The reference seems to indicate the order in which the Hittites consolidated their power. The wave of northern invasion had reached Hebron, and made a lodgment there before it swept over the border into the Land of Goshen. Supposing that the Hittites possessed the throne of Egypt, we can more easily understand how their settlements would extend up to and over the Egyptian border.

The story as told in Genesis is true in all the formal details which embellish the framework of a shrewd Oriental bargain. It is in accordance with all that we know of such nations as the Hittites to push out their surplus and enterprising population along the highways of their commerce. As Damascus and Aleppo now encourage the Bedawîn to encamp under their walls and exchange the produce of the desert for the merchandise of the settled populations, so a Hittite colony established at Hebron would in their own interest encourage the great nomadic chieftain Abraham, with his surplus lambs, wool, and cheese, to linger in their neighbourhood, and purchase the produce of the looms of Egypt and the workshops of Phœnicia. And it is quite in accordance with the known instincts of such a colony to sell as a favour for a large sum a useless field with a useless cave.[2] We think the accuracy of the Bible has never been challenged on more frivolous

[1] Numb. xiii. 22.
[2] The Rev. Dr. Thomson, who lived nearly half a century amidst the scenes and scenery described in the new edition of his "Land and the Book," shows that every item of this transaction between Abraham and

grounds. The argument that because the Hittites in Northern Syria were often at war, therefore a Hittite colony in Southern Palestine was not likely to be engaged in a peaceful transaction, does not rest on a profound view of things. We think rather that the Hittites could never have sustained the shocks of war from Babylon, Egypt, and Assyria for a thousand years if they had not been industrious and commercial in times of peace as well as skilful and valiant in the time of war.

In the Book of Exodus the Hittites have grown in importance. The promised land is described by an enumeration of the peoples who inhabit it, and the Hittites, who are never absent from that enumeration, occupy the place of distinction (Exod. iii. 8, 17 ; xiii. 5; xxiii. 23, 28).

What testimony do the Egyptian hieroglyphics bear to this growth of Hittite power?

We have seen that Thothmes III., the Egyptian Alexander, began his splendid reign of over half a century[1] in 1600 B.C. According to Usher, this was about six years after Jacob went down into Egypt, and thirty-five years before the death of Joseph. The hieroglyphics of Thothmes are numerous and important. They have been read by Dr. Birch, Professor Ebers,

the sons of Heth is in strict accordance with unchanged Oriental ways. "In fact," he adds, "up to this present day, in this very city of Hebron, a purchase thus witnessed is legal; while the best drawn deeds of a modern lawyer, though signed, sealed, and attested, would be of no avail without such living witnesses" (p. 249).

[1] Reckoned from the accession of Queen Hashop, with whom he became associated on the throne.

M. de Rougé, Mariette Bey, and others, and they recount numerous campaigns undertaken by Egypt in which the Hittites play an important part. In the Egyptian hieroglyphics the Hittites occupy exactly the same position as is assigned to them in the Book of Exodus. They are first in order and first in importance among the peoples of the promised land.[1]

There still stands at Karnak the splendid temple known as "the Hall of Pillars," erected by Thothmes III., in which Egyptian art reached its highest point. The walls and pillars are covered by pictures and names of the peoples and places which he had conquered. A few years ago the sand was removed from the wall of a lower story, and revealed a catalogue of 119 conquered places. The first place mentioned on this list is Kadesh on the Orontes, the capital of the Hittites. Brugsch Bey, in referring to this list of names, says :—

"What gives its highest value to this catalogue is the indisputable fact that, more than three hundred years before the entrance of the Israelites into the land of Canaan, a great confederacy of tribes of a common race existed in Palestine under petty kings, who dwelt in the very same towns and fortresses which for the most part, in later times, fell by conquest into the hands of the Jewish immigrants. Among them the king of Kadesh on the Orontes, in the land of the Amorites, as

[1] Professor Rawlinson, in his "History of Ancient Egypt," vol. i. p. 111, referring to the enemies of Egypt in Syria and Palestine, says, "the most important tribes were those of the Khita (children of Heth or Hittites)."

the inscriptions expressly testify, played the first part, for the kings and their peoples, from the water of Egypt to the land of Naharaim, obeyed him as their chief leader."[1]

During the sojourn of Israel in Egypt, the Bible references not only show the Hittites growing in power, but they point to that power becoming localized more and more in the north. The Hittites, whom we first meet at important stations on the way to Egypt, such as Hebron and Beersheba, become the great northern people: "From the wilderness and this Lebanon even unto the great river, the river Euphrates, all the land of the Hittites, and unto the great sea toward the going down of the sun" (Josh. i. 4).

Do the inscriptions give any countenance to this Bible representation of the Hittites? The Egyptian hieroglyphics and Assyrian inscriptions confirm this Bible reference fully and irresistibly.

Thothmes III. first encounters the king of the Hittites at Megiddo in Palestine. Ample details of the march and the battle are given. The king marched out of Egypt to meet the confederacy under the king of the Hittites. He passed through Gaza, "full of power to conquer the miserable enemy, and to extend the boundaries of Egypt." At Ihem he held a council of war, and addressed his followers in a speech preserved on the temple of Karnak :—

"That hostile king of Kadesh (king of the Hittites)

[1] Brugsch's "Egypt under the Pharaohs," i. 394.

has arrived. He has entered into Megiddo. He has assembled with him the kings of the tribes over against the water of Egypt, as far as the land of Naharaim (Mesopotamia)."[1]

In the battle the Egyptian king fought in a copper chariot. He was like Hor the Smiter. "The enemy fled head over heels to Megiddo, and left behind them their horses, and their gold and silver chariots, and were drawn up by their clothes, as by ropes, into that town . . . . for the miserable king of Kadesh (king of the Hittites) had gone up together with the miserable king of that town. The enemy lay kicking in heaps like fishes on the ground."[2]

In his subsequent campaigns Thothmes III. encounters the Hittites in the neighbourhood of Kadesh on the Orontes, between the river Euphrates and the Great Sea. He had followed them up towards the centre of their power.

The Hittites continued to grow in power in that region, and in the time of Seti I. and Rameses II. they had become formidable adversaries of the power of Egypt. Brugsch Bey says: "At the commencement of the nineteenth dynasty, the power of the Kheta," whom he recognizes as the Hittites, "had been extended over the whole of the surrounding nations. Their importance grew from year to year in such a way that even the Egyptian inscriptions do not hesitate

---

[1] Brugsch's "Egypt under the Pharaohs," i. 369.
[2] *Idem*, p. 372; and Dr. Birch in "Records of the Past," ii. 38.

to mention the names of the kings of the Kheta in a conspicuous manner, and to speak of their gods with reverence."[1]

Rameses I., B.C. *cir.* 1400, had been engaged in war with the Hittites, and had concluded a treaty of peace with Saplel their king. The treaty had been broken by the Hittites, and Seti I., successor of Rameses, marched northward with a mighty army. His march and victories are traced in inscriptions and pictures on the north wall of the great national temple at Karnak. He first overthrows the encroaching Bedawin in Southern Palestine, and then the Bedawin and Phœnicians in Southern Phœnicia, "where Pharaoh annihilated the kings of the land of the Phœnicians." Then the people of Central Canaan, and, finally, as the avenger of broken treaties, he falls on Kadesh. The Hittites were taken unawares, which shows that they had withdrawn from their southern allies to the north, and, after a gallant resistance, they succumb to the onslaught of the Egyptians. In the words of the inscription, "Seti has struck down the Asiatics, he has thrown to the ground the Kheta; he has slain their princes." A peace was concluded with the Hittites, "He returns home in triumph, he has annihilated the people, he has struck to the ground the Kheta. He has made an end of his adversaries. The enmity of all people is turned into friendship."[2]

Rameses II. the Conqueror, the Sesostris of the

[1] Brugsch's "Egypt under the Pharaohs," ii. 3. [2] *Idem*, p. 17.

Greek historians, succeeded, and in his day the Hittites probably reached the zenith of their power.

In his fifth year he marched forth against the Hittites, between whom and the Egyptians war had again broken out.

We possess very complete records of this campaign. Painters and sculptors have exaggerated every detail, and the poet Pentaur, who accompanied the king, sings his praises in the heroic poem, which not only adorns the walls of the temples of Abydos, Luksor, Karnak, and the Rammesseum at Ibsamboul, but has come down to us on a roll of papyrus now in the British Museum. I have given a summary, at page 22, of this most important inscription.

On the testimony of prose and poetry, of picture and papyrus, the king was triumphantly victorious.

According to the Theban poet: "The king of the hostile Kheta had assembled with him all the people from the uttermost ends of the sea to the people of the Kheta. They had arrived in great numbers—the people of Naharaim, the people of Arathu, of the Dardani,[1] the Masu, the Pidasa, the Malunna, the Karkish, the Leka, Qazuadana, Kirkamish, Akerith, Kati, the whole people of Anaugas every one of them, Mushanath and Kadesh. He had left no people on his road without bringing them with him. Their number was endless. Nothing like it had ever been

[1] M. De Rougé recognized in this list the Dardani of Asia Minor, the Mysians, the Lysians, &c.

before. They covered mountains and valleys like grasshoppers for their number. He had not left silver nor gold with his people; he had taken away all their goods and possessions to give it to the people who accompanied him in war."[1]

Such was the host of the Hittites assembled at Kadesh. Pharaoh hearing from Arab spies that the king of the Hittites was at Aleppo, approached Kadesh on the north-west. Suddenly he finds that the Hittites, who had been in ambush, are issuing forth to attack him, "and Pharaoh called together all the chief men of his warriors. Behold, they were at the lake of the land of the Amorites."[2]

"Then the king arose, like his father Month: he grasped his weapon, and put on his armour, just like Baal in his time. And the noble pair of horses which carried Pharaoh, and whose name was 'Victory in Thebes,' they were from the Court of King Rameses Miamun. When the king had quickened his course he rushed into the midst of the hostile hosts of Kheta all alone, no other was with him. When Pharaoh had done this he looked behind him, and found himself surrounded by 2,500 pairs of horses, and his retreat was beset by the bravest heroes of the king of the miserable Kheta, and by all the numerous people that were with him, of Arathu, of Masu, of Pidasa, of Keshkesh, of Malunna, of Qazuadana, or Khilibu, of

---

[1] Poem of Pentaur, Brugsch's "Egypt under the Pharaohs," ii. 57.
[2] *Idem.*

Akerith, of Kadesh, and of Leka. And there were three men on each chariot, and they were all gathered together. And not one of my princes, not one of my captains of the chariot, not one of my chief men, not one of my knights was there. My warriors and my chariots had abandoned me, not one of them was there to take part in the battle."[1]

In his straits Pharaoh addressed himself in a long prayer to the god Amon, recounting the temples and altars and offerings which he had dedicated to him. The god Amon, under a sense of gratitude, replied promising aid, and declaring himself "worth more than hundreds of thousands united in one place." The king thus encouraged fell single-handed upon the whole army of the Hittites; but the heroics of Pentaur are so extravagant that we turn to the simple prose of the temple inscription:

"He was alone. He rushed into the midst of the hostile hosts of the king of the Kheta, and the much people that were with him. And Pharaoh, like the god Sutekh, the Glorious, cast them down and slew them. And I the king flung them down head over heels one after another into the water of the Orontes. I subdued all the people, and yet I was alone, for my warriors and my charioteers had left me in the lurch. None of them stood by me. Then the king of the Hittites raised his hands to pray before me. I swear it as truly as the sun-god loved me, as truly as my

[1] Poem of Pentaur.

father the god Tum blesses me, that all the deeds which I the king have related, these I truly performed before my army and my charioteers."[1]

The Rev. T. K. Cheyne, who places the inscriptions of Egypt before the Bible records in veracity, receives as authentic this representation of the battle. "Rameses," he says, "was indeed victorious, but he owed his life, and consequently his victory, to his personal bravery, and, as Pentaur represents it, to his child-like faith in his god." I am inclined to agree with Brugsch Bey "that Rameses came out of the battle a doubtful conqueror." And I am the more inclined to think so because an immediate peace followed the battle. "The miserable king of the Hittites" became "the great king of the Hittites," and the borders of the Hittites were spared. Besides, we do not find any enumeration of booty such as followed other conquests, and one of the results of the battle was an offensive and defensive alliance, with extradition clauses, drawn up between Kheta-sira, the great king of the Hittites, and the prince of Egypt in terms of perfect equality,[2] and not as between the

[1] Brugsch's "Egypt under the Pharaohs," ii. 54.

The inscription relating to this treaty, translated by Mr. C. W. Goodwin ("Records of the Past," iv. 25), is given at page 26; there is also a translation in Brugsch's "Egypt," ii. 71. It is called "offensive and defensive alliance between Kheta and Kemi." The Hittite stands before the Egyptian. "This is the copy of the contents of the silver tablet, which the great King of Kheta, Kheta-sira, had caused to be made, and which was presented to the Pharaoh, &c. . . . . The treaty which had been prepared by the great King of Kheta, Kheta-sira, the powerful, the son of Maro-sir, the great King of Kheta, &c., to Ramessu Miamun, the great Prince of Egypt," &c.

subduer and subdued. And a memorial tablet in the temple of Ibsamboul declares that the Egyptian married the daughter of the king of the Hittites, and that the prince of Kheta, clad in the dress of his country, conducted his daughter as a bride to his son-in-law.[1]

We have thus brought the light of the Egyptian inscriptions to bear upon the Bible references to the Hittites, as regards their existence in the south, their gradual withdrawal from the south, and the greatness of their power in the north,[2] and in each case the ample records of Egypt more than confirm the sacred narrative. And even the willingness of the Hittites to provide wives for the Hebrew chiefs and kings, has a parallel in the Court of Egypt.

The promise to the Israelites to send hornets before them to drive out the Hittites (Deut. vii. 20; Josh. xxiv. 12; Exod. xxiii. 28),[3] seems to have been largely fulfilled by the devastating border wars between the Pharaohs and the people of Southern Palestine, who

[1] "The subsequent battles, and the treaty of Rameses II. with the Kheta, proved how slight were the successes so highly extolled in the inscriptions."—(Professor Max Duncker's "History of Antiquity," i. 155.)

[2] Professor Sayce says: "That from the seventeenth to the twelfth century B.C., the Hittites were the leading people of Western Asia, holding the balance of power between Egypt on the one side, and Assyria on the other, and that their two centres of power were Kadesh on the Orontes, and Carchemish, now Jerabis, on the Euphrates. About this period the Semitic Aramaeans seem to have begun to push the Hittites further and further to the north."—("Transactions of Soc. Bib. Arch." vol. vii. part ii. p. 251.)

[3] According to the "Speaker's Commentary," referring to Exodus xxiii. 28, "There seems to be no reasonable doubt that the word is used figuratively for a cause of terror and discouragement."

were always the first to feel the shock of the Egyptian arms. We can trace the march of Seti I., on his first campaign, from Khetam, the Etham of the Bible (Numb. xxxiii. 6), past Rehoboth, south of Beersheba, to the fortress of Kanaan which he stormed, and became subduer of the whole of Edomitish Negeb. On the northern side of the great temple of Karnak this conquest is recorded thus : " In the first year of King Seti, there took place by the strong arm of Pharaoh the annihilation of the hostile Shasu, from the fortress of Khetam, of the land of Zalu as far as Kanaan ; the king was against them like a fierce lion. They were turned into a heap of corpses. They lay there in blood."[1]

In such fierce border encounters the hand of Pharaoh would press heavy on any Hittite colonies as being advanced branches of the great national enemy. Hence Joshua found the Anakim at Hebron, and the spies found the Amalekites dwelling in the south, and the Hittites driven back to the mountains (Numb. xiii. 29).[2]

We have already drawn attention to Manetho's statement that the Hyksos on withdrawing from Egypt retired to Jerusalem, and this may account for the reproach uttered by Ezekiel against Jerusalem, when he rebuked the pretensions of the Jerusalem Jews by a reference to the Hittite origin of the material city.

[1] Brugsch's " Egypt under the Pharaohs," ii. 14.
[2] Professor Max Duucker represents the Amorites as driving the Hittites northward about the middle of the thirteenth century B.C.: "The Amorites pressed forward against the Hittites, and took possession of their land as far as lake Merom."— (" Hist. Antiq." i. 349.)

"Thus saith the Lord God unto Jerusalem : thy birth and thy nativity is of the land of Canaan ; thy father was an Amorite, and thy mother an Hittite."[1]

We are also able to follow the Hittites on their slow withdrawal north, from a very incidental reference to the Hittites in the Book of Judges.[2]

The man by whose assistance the Israelites effected their entrance into Luz or Bethel "went into the land of the Hittites, and built a city, and called the name thereof Luz." Through the exploration of the Palestine Exploration Fund, we now know that this city stood near the sources of the Jordan, in the great fertile plain of Merom, which was the land of the Hittites in the time of Joshua.

On their entrance into the promised land the Israelites encountered the Hittites and the other hill tribes ; and no doubt the Hittites, as being skilful and valiant warriors, directed the less disciplined hosts of the land. The great northern people, who had secured peace with the Pharaohs, would naturally give a helping hand to stem the tide of invasion (Josh. ix. 1). And hence we find that the kings in the hills, and in the valleys, and in all the coasts of the great sea over against Lebanon—the Hittite, and the Amorite, and other tribes—gathered themselves together to fight with Joshua and with Israel with one accord.

At Jericho and Ai (Josh. xxiv. 11) Joshua seems to have overcome the opposition in detail. But King

[1] Ezek. xvi. 3.   [2] Judges i. 26.

Jabin, seeing the approaching danger, sent far and near to all the kings and peoples of the land (Josh. xi. 1). The common danger drew the people together from north and south of Hermon and from Lebanon, and south of Chinnereth, and from the Phœnician coast, and they assembled by the lake Huleh on the upper Jordan: "Much people, even as the sand that is upon the sea-shore in multitude, with horses and chariots very many."

It was the supreme and united effort of the doomed people. They were there in their strength, the disciplined hosts of the Hittites. In the Egyptian hieroglyphics their well-ordered armies form a striking contrast to the Canaanitish crowd. The beardless light-red Hittites, on horse and foot, march in battle array with well-drilled precision; but they were especially distinguished by their chariots, each of which carried three warriors. In the battle-song of Pentaur, Rameses II., whom Brugsch Bey considers the oppressor of Israel,[1] seems to have taken little note of any branch of the Hittite army except that of the chariots. Twice he refers to the 2,500 pairs of horses by which Pharaoh was surrounded: "they stood three men on each chariot, and they were assembled in one spot, the best heroes of the army of Kheta, well appointed with all weapons for the fight." Such

[1] Brugsch's "Egypt under the Pharaohs," ii. 103. "Rameses II. is the Pharaoh of the oppression, and the father of that unnamed princess who found the child Moses exposed in the bulrushes on the bank of the river."

was the army of the Hittites which secured from the proudest and most boastful of the Pharaohs a formal treaty and dynastic alliance. Such the chisel of the sculptor and the brush of the painter portrayed them on abiding stone, and such was the chief force of that mighty host by the waters of Merom on which Joshua fell suddenly, and by a great overthrow became possessor of the land of promise from Mount Halak on the south to Baal-gad on the north (Josh. xi. 17). We recognize in the Hittites by the Huleh lake the same people who fought with Rameses by the water of Kadesh, and whose pictures still adorn the temples of Egypt.

During the long reign of Rameses II., the treaty of peace seems to have been observed between the Egyptians and the Hittites, and we find his successor, Mineptah II., whom Brugsch Bey considers the Pharaoh of the Exodus, actually supplying "wheat in ships, to preserve the lives of the people of Kheta."[1] Later we meet the Hittites among the enemies of Egypt, and Rameses III. again carried the Egyptian arms as far as the northern capital of the Kheta. Referring to a hostile movement against Egypt, the inscription declares of the invaders, "they came leaping from their coasts and islands, and spread themselves all

---

[1] Brugsch's "Egypt under the Pharaohs," ii. 124. My friend, Dr. Delitzsch, who kindly read the *revise* of this chapter, reminds me that the son of Rameses II., "Mineptah (beloved of Ptah), is the Pharaoh of the Exodus, according to Lepsius, Ebers, and almost all Egyptologists."

over the lands. No people stood before their arms, beginning with the people of Kheta."[1] Rameses III. was victorious over these enemies of Egypt, and in his palace at Medinet Abou he caused to be sculptured portraits of kings and leaders whom he had subdued, and among these there is one whom the accompanying inscription calls "The miserable King of Kheta taken alive."[2] Pharaoh not only subdued the Hittites, but he returned laden with spoil and accompanied by a Hittite princess, whom he associated with himself on the throne of Egypt.[3]

In the Bible, also, we have frequent reference to individual Hittites. Two of King David's most faithful warriors were Hittites—Ahimelech (1 Sam. xxvi. 6) and Uriah the Hittite (2 Sam. xi. 21)—and we see King David and King Solomon, like Rameses II. and III., allying themselves with Hittite wives (1 Kings xi. 1). We also see King David pushing his conquests and consolidating his empire among the towns of the Hittites. And King Solomon, like Mineptah II., appears to have supplied the Hittites with the commodities which they needed (1 Kings x. 29).

Thus we find that even obscure and incidental references to the Hittites in the Bible have their counterpart in the stony handwriting of Egypt.

In connection with the siege of Samaria, as recorded in 2 Kings vii., we have an important reference to the

---

[1] Brugsch's "Egypt under the Pharaohs," ii. 154.   [2] *Idem*, p. 158.
[3] *Idem*, p. 173.

Hittites. The Israelites under Jehoram son of Ahab were hard pressed in their capital by the army of Benhadad of Damascus. The besieged were in sore straits, and must soon have surrendered or perished. Then, according to Elisha's prophecy, deliverance came (ver. 6): "For the Lord had made the host of the Syrians to hear a noise of chariots, and a noise of horses, even the noise of a great host : and they said one to another, Lo, the king of Israel hath hired against us the kings of the Hittites, and the kings of the Egyptians, to come upon us. Wherefore they arose and fled in the twilight, and left their tents, and their horses, and their asses, even the camp as it was, and fled for their life" (2 Kings vii. 6, 7).

Professor F.W. Newman, in speaking of this narrative, says, "The unhistorical tone is too manifest to allow of our easy belief in it." He thinks "there was a real event at bottom," for Xenophon in his Anabasis speaks of dangerous night panics in the Greek and Persian hosts, and therefore the Syrian army may have fled in a sudden panic. "But," he adds of the Bible account, "the particular ground of alarm attributed to them does not exhibit the writer's acquaintance with the times in very favourable light." "No Hittite kings can have compared in power with the king of Judah, the real and near ally, who is not named at all." "Nor is there a single mark of acquaintance with the contemporaneous history."[1]

[1] "History of the Hebrew Monarchy," pp. 178, 179.

Professor F. W. Newman casts discredit on the incident because he thinks the Hittites were too insignificant to have caused alarm to the Syrian hosts. Let us see what light the inscriptions throw on this point. We have seen the important position occupied by the Hittites in the Egyptian inscriptions, let us now turn to the rising power of Assyria, and examine their records, that we may learn from contemporary documents the position of the Hittites at the period referred to.

According to Professor Sayce, the empire of Naharaim had been replaced by that of the Hittites about the period of the nineteenth dynasty, and he adds, "when we come to the era of Tiglath-Pileser I., B.C. 1130, the Hittites are still paramount from the Euphrates to Lebanon."[1] This king of Assyria undertook several campaigns against the Hittites which remained without results. Duncker declares that the position which Tiglath-Pileser had won on the Euphrates was not maintained by his successors in any one instance.[2]

Usher places the siege of Samaria about 892 B.C., and Assyriologists agree in fixing the reign of Assur-Nasir-Pal about 883–858 B.C. Of this monarch, who added new vigour to the wars against the people of northern Syria, there are very ample records. An inscription, discovered in the ruins of a temple near the pyramid at Nimroud, was published among the "Cuneiform Inscriptions of Western Asia,"[3] and a translation by the Rev.

[1] "Transactions Soc. Bib. Arch.," v. 28.
[2] "Hist. Antiq.," ii. 308.   [3] Vol. i. plates 17–27.

J. M. Rodwell is printed in "Records of the Past."[1] From this inscription Assur-Nasir-Pal appears to have carried the Assyrian arms not only to Carchemish and Lebanon, but as far as Tyre and Sidon. " Ahiramu, son of Yahiru, son of Bahiani of the land of the Hittites," was then at the head of the Hittites, a term, according to Mr. Rodwell, used in a large sense at that time, as including the inhabitants of Northern Palestine. At that period the Hittites were still a strong people, especially were they formidable on account of their chariots, the dread of which struck terror into the hearts of the hosts which were besieging Samaria.

Assur-Nasir-Pal levied tribute on the conquered Hittites. "To Carchemish in Syria I directed my steps. The tribute due from the son of Bahiani, swift chariots, horses, silver, tin, copper, khami of copper, I received. The chariots and warlike engines of the officer of the son of Bahiani I added to my magazines."[2]

The inscriptions here refer to the chariots of the Hittites before even referring to their gold and silver. Farther on in the inscription he refers again and again to the Hittite chariots. "The chariots and warlike engines of the general of Carchemish I laid up in my magazines."

He passed from Carchemish "to Hazazi, the town of Lubarna of the Khatti," and levied tribute. Then he proceeded to the royal city Kanulua of the Hittites, and imposed upon the chief or king a tribute of an

[1] Vol. iii. p. 37.   [2] "Records of the Past," iii. 70.

enormous quantity of precious metals and stones, and also cattle; and he adds, "the chariots and warlike engines of the land of the Khatti I laid up in magazines. Their hostages I took."[1] Again he marched to the fortified city belonging to Lubarna of the land of the Khatti."[2]

From these inscriptions, then, it is clear that about the time of the siege of Samaria the Hittites were still a mighty people, spread over the north of Syria from Carchemish to Lebanon, that they had numerous chieftains or kings, who ruled over independent districts or strongholds, and that as in the days of Rameses II., so in the time of the siege of Samaria, the Hittite chiefs were distinguished among the nations for "their swift chariots, their horses, and their engines of war." We are thus led to the conclusion that the sacred writer was thoroughly acquainted with the times in which he wrote, and with the facts which he narrated, and that it was Professor Newman's acquaintance with the times of which he wrote that does not appear in a very favourable light.

The confirmation of the sacred narrative does not depend on the necessary accuracy of Biblical or Assyrian chronology, nor on mere isolated or obscure hints found

---

[1] "Records of the Past," iii. 72, 73.
[2] Professor Max Duncker, after reviewing these campaigns, adds: "According to the evidence of the inscriptions, Assur-Nasir-Pal established the supremacy of Assyria in the region of the sources of the Tigris: but even he does not seem to have gone much farther than Tiglath-Pileser before him."—("Hist. Antiq.," ii. 310.)

in the cuneiform inscriptions. Nor can it be said that the power of the Hittites was broken before the siege of Samaria. The Assyrian records represent the Khatti as a martial people strong in war chariots, during a space which must of necessity have included the time when Samaria was besieged, whatever be the true period for that event in Biblical chronology.

Shalmaneser, the son of Assur-Nasir-Pal, who reigned for thirty-five years, the contemporary of Ahab, Jehu, and Hazael, set up a large stone at Kurkh, on the river Tigris, covered with a long inscription. The stone is now in the British Museum, and the whole inscription has been translated by Professor Sayce. This inscription represents the Hittites of Carchemish marshalling "with others for battle." "With them I fought," says Shalmaneser. "Their corpses like chaff through the country I scattered. Multitudes of chariots and horses trained to the yoke I seized."[1]

Again, he says he approached Carchemish, and the kings of the country fled at the sight of his weapons. Farther on he records that he passed through a city "which the men of the Hittites the city of Pethor have called,"[2] and from Hamah, a town of the Hittites, he carried away seven hundred war chariots and seven hundred magazines. The inscriptions end with a reference to the Hittite chariots: "The river Orontes I reached. Their chariots, their magazines,

---

[1] "Records of the Past," iii. 88.
[2] The native place of Balaam by the river (Numb. xxii. 5).

and their horses trained to the yoke I took away from them."¹

In the British Museum there is another important inscription of the same king, inscribed on what is known as the Black Obelisk. It was found by Sir H. Layard in the mound at Nimroud, and was one of the first read by Rawlinson and Hincks. The very language of this inscription is strikingly in accord with the language of the Bible. "The Euphrates in its flood I crossed. The city of Dabigu, a choice city of the Hittites, together with the cities which were dependent on it I captured." Then he refers to a city on the further side of the Euphrates, upon the river "Sagurni, which *the kings of the Hittites* call Pitra, for myself I took." "The Euphrates in its upper part I crossed. The tribute of *the kings of the Hittites* all of them I received." . . . . Their chariots, their war carriages, their war material I took from them."²

Ceaseless wars seem, from this inscription, to have been waged by Assyria against the Hittites and their neighbours. "In my eleventh year, for the ninth time, the Euphrates I crossed. Cities to a countless number I captured. To the cities of the Hittites of the Hamathites I went down. Eighty-nine cities I took. Rimmon Idri³ of Damascus, and *twelve of the kings of the Hittites.*" "The tribute of *the kings of the Hittites* all of them I received."⁴ Duncker says Shalmaneser "crossed the Euphrates for the twenty-first time," but he does not say

¹ "Records of the Past," iii. 99, 100.   ² *Idem*, v. 31, 32.
³ Benhadad.   ⁴ "Records of the Past," v. 34-36.

he reduced the Hittites. He only asserts that he received tribute of Tyre, Sidon, and Byblus, and then assures us, quite briefly, in the account of his twenty-fifth campaign (835 B.C.), that he received "the tribute of all the princes of Syria of the land of the Khatti."[1]

Shalmaneser died in 823 B.C., but the wars between the Assyrians and the Hittites seem to have been carried on to the time of Sargon. In the annals of Sargon, translated by Dr. Julius Oppert, we find two facts with important bearings on our argument recorded. "In the beginning of my reign," says Sargon (B.C. 721), "with the help of the Sun, who aided me to vanquish my enemies, I besieged, I occupied the town of Samaria, and I brought into captivity 27,800 persons." Four years later, in 717 B.C., Sargon finally overthrew the Hittite kingdom by the defeat of Pisiri, and the capture of Carchemish. "In the fifth year of my reign, Pisiri of Carchemish sinned against the gods."[2] In the sequel, the Hittites were carried into captivity, and Assyrians were placed in their cities.

Thus the Hittites, who appear for the first time in the inscriptions[3] of Sargon I., king of Agané,[4] cir. 1900 B.C.,[5]

[1] "Hist. Antiq.," ii. 319. See also Rawlinson, "Ancient Monarchies," ii. 363.   [2] "Records of the Past," vii. 28-30.

[3] The late George Smith surmises that we owe the preservation of the inscriptions of Sargon I. to Sargon, king of Assyria, who named himself after the earlier monarch ("Records of the Past," v. 57).

[4] Dr. Delitzsch reminds me that this word should be written *Agade*. In the unsettled orthography of such words I have followed the authors quoted.

[5] Mr. Pinches, of the British Museum, by means of a cylinder of Nabonidus, has placed the date of Sargon as early as 3800 B.C.

disappear from history in the inscriptions of Sargon B.C. 717. They were a people before Abraham went forth from Ur of the Chaldees, and they only yielded to the arms of Assyria after the Israelites had been swept from Samaria. During the history of the chosen people, from the time of Abraham to the captivity, the Hittites are often referred to in the Bible. These references have been discredited by professed assailants and by weak apologists of the historic accuracy of the Bible. We have examined the contemporary records of Babylon, Assyria, and Egypt, and we find not only collateral evidence, which creates a probability in favour of the authenticity of the sacred narrative, but side lights, which shine so clearly on the incidents that unbelief is impossible.[1]

[1] "The veracity of the Old Testament account of the Hittite princes contemporary with Solomon had been deemed as presenting insuperable difficulties, but the indisputable testimony of the granite records of Thothmes and Rameses has left no doubt as to the contemporary rule of this powerful race in Northern Syria in the times of the Hebrew Judges and Kings."—(Lieutenant Conder, "Quarterly Statement of Palestine Exploration Fund," January, 1881.)

CHAPTER IX.

ARE THE INSCRIPTIONS HITTITE REMAINS?

IN 1872, when sending casts of the Hamah inscriptions to England, I suggested that they were Hittite remains. As Captain Burton says, my theory was received, when "first suggested, *magno cum risu*."[1]

The theory is now accepted by most scholars who have a claim to be heard on such subjects. Professor Sayce, who has devoted his life to the study of such questions, not only in his library at home, but by a minute examination of the Oriental lands referred to, arrived subsequently at the same conclusion without having seen my article. He says—"We may now consider the Hittite origin of the peculiar system of writing first noticed by modern travellers on the site of Hamath, to be among the ascertained facts of science;"[2] and Dr. Isaac Taylor, in his learned book, "The Alphabet," refers to these hieroglyphics and sculptures "as in the unmistakable style of Hittite art."[3]

[1] Besant's "Memoir of C. F. T. Drake," p. 19.
[2] "Transactions Soc. Bib. Arch.," vol. vii. part ii. p. 248.
[3] Vol. ii. p. 120.

Professor Sayce, Dr. Taylor, and other scholars seem to have come to identify the Hamah inscriptions with the Hittites as astronomers have sometimes been led to the discovery of new planets by the existence of certain phenomena which could only be accounted for by the presence of some commanding influence.

The late George Smith "believed that the real connection between the traditions of Babylonia and Palestine would never be cleared until the literature of the Syrian population which intervened was recovered."[1] The Hittite inscriptions and peculiar sculptures supplied the missing link looked for by Professor Sayce, Dr. Taylor, Mr. George Smith, Dr. Duncker, and others. A number of curious inscriptions on rocks and coins were discovered throughout Asia Minor. The characters on some of these inscriptions were remotely related to the Greek, but others had no affinity to either Greek or Phœnician.

By means of a Cypriote and Phœnician inscription discovered at Idalion, by Mr. Hamilton Lang, and read by the late George Smith, the key was found to the mysterious Asianic scripts. "There could be little doubt," says Dr. Isaac Taylor, "that the Cypriote syllabary, thus curiously recovered, was no arbitrary invention, but the survival of an extremely ancient script, which must have prevailed in Cyprus prior to the introduction of alphabetic writing."[2] "It was manifest not only that writing was practised in the Troad before

[1] George Smith's " Chaldean Account of Genesis," p. 311.
[2] "The Alphabet," ii. 114.

the introduction of either the Phœnician or the Greek alphabet, but that the non-Hellenic characters in the Lycian, Carian, and Cappadocian alphabets, as well as the Cypriote syllabics, were all derived from a common source." [1]

"To complete the solution of the problem offered by the Asianic alphabets, one step only was required —namely, the discovery of the source from which the Cypriote syllabary was itself obtained. It had no recognizable affinities with the graphic systems of the Greeks, the Phœnicians, the Egyptians, or the Assyrians; but the analogy of other scripts made it probable that it was the ultimate survival of some extremely ancient mode of picture-writing." [2] The central stock, of which the Cypriote, and the other mysterious scripts of Asia Minor, are branches, is represented by the Hamah and kindred inscriptions of which we supply copies. "These monuments," says Dr. Isaac Taylor, "are those of a people who have been identified with the Hittites of the Old Testament, the Kheta of the Egyptian monuments, the Khatti of Assyrian records, and the κήτειοι of Homer [3] (Od. xi. 521). They were one of the most powerful peoples of the primeval world, their empire extending from the frontier of Egypt to the shores of the Ægean, and, like the Babylonians and the Egyptians, they possessed a culture, an art, and a script peculiar to themselves, and plainly of indigenous origin." [4]

[1] "The Alphabet," ii. 115.   [2] *Idem*, p. 119.
[3] Gladstone's "Homeric Synchronisms," pp. 174, 182.
[4] "The Alphabet," ii. 120.

"It is now admitted that the primitive art, the mythology, and the metrical standards of Asia Minor, were to a great extent obtained from the Hittites, and the independent system of picture-writing which they possess, offers an obvious source from which the Asianic syllabary might have been obtained."[1]

Dr. Taylor gives in a tabular form some of the Hittite and Cypriote characters,[2] which have been identified by Professor Sayce as agreeing in appearance and value; and while he considers the decipherment provisional, he thinks it suffices to show that the true origin of the Cypriote syllabary has at last been discovered.[3]

The above conclusions have been reached chiefly under the guidance of Professor Sayce. In an Appendix to Dr. Schliemann's work on his excavations at Hissarlik, he declared that the Cypriote characters were but a local form of a syllabary once in use throughout Asia Minor before the introduction of the simpler Greek alphabet, and he adds, after comparing the Cyprus script with the scripts of Asia Minor, "that we must seek the origin of the syllabary, not in Cyprus, but in Asia Minor, and compare the Hittite characters rather with those of the syllabary of the mainland than with those of the syllabary of the island."[4]

Professor Sayce, however, takes in a wider field in his generalization. He reviews the curious monuments

[1] "The Alphabet," ii. 122.   [2] See page 169.
[3] "The Alphabet," ii. 123.
[4] "Transactions Soc. Bib. Arch.," vol. vii. part ii. p. 279.

scattered throughout Asia Minor, and while he considers them related to early Babylonian[1] art, and not altogether unaffected by Egyptian,[2] he unhesitatingly pronounces them "characteristic specimens of Hittite art." " On the whole," he says, " I am inclined to think that they are memorials of the Hittites themselves, partly because no other people in that part of the world seem to have had either the power or the culture needful for their creation, partly because the monuments found in Lykaonia and Lydia are plainly the monuments of a successful invasion, and the Hittites were the only people in Western Asia strong enough to undertake distant conquests."[3]

It seems to me that the Hamah inscriptions, and others of similar character since discovered, are Hittite remains, from the consideration that none of the other theories advanced as to their origin appear satisfactory. I shall first examine the most plausible of these theories, and then give my reasons for believing that the inscriptions scattered throughout the land of the Hittites are nothing less than Hittite remains.

At first, as Mr. Hyde Clarke said, "they were pronounced by men of high authority not to be inscriptions at all, but vagaries of ornamentation."[4] But a glance at the sharply cut figures showed that they were in great part ideographic characters, and more closely resembling phonetic writing than the hieroglyphics of

[1] "Transactions Soc. Bib. Arch.," vol. vii. pp. 250 and 261.
[2] *Idem*, p. 273.   *Idem*, p. 253.
[4] "Unexplored Syria," i. 341.

Egypt. Comparisons show that the characters resemble the Cypriote syllabary, to which they doubtless stand in parental relation. The discovery of additional inscriptions of the same kind has removed all doubt on this point.

Captain Burton thought the key to the inscriptions was to be found in the Bedawi tribe-marks. "I would suggest," he says, "that the most feasible way of deciphering them would be by comparing them with the *Wusûm* of the several Bedawi families, tribes, and clans." But the location of these inscriptions in great cities, and on mountains far from Bedawi influence, and the neat appearance and good finish of the characters, show that they were executed by a settled people, with good instruments, and that they are not likely to have any affinity to the scratchy tribe-marks of the Bedawîn.

Mr. Hyde Clarke considered the inscriptions allied with the Himyaritic, and through it with the Libyan. "We obtain," he says, "out of the Hamah characters at least sixteen identifications of form with the Himyaritic and Libyan, leaving no reasonable doubt that the Hamah characters are partly related to one alphabet, in its origin allied to another."[1]

The geographical position of the Himyarites, as well as their position in history, make it impossible to accept this theory. Mr. H. Clarke takes strange liberties with the history of the Himyarites in favour of his views. He says, "as to the age of the inscriptions,

[1] "Unexplored Syria," i. 354.

they can hardly be lower than the latest date assigned to the Himyarites—namely, 100 of the common era, but they may be as old as the oldest Himyaritic are supposed to be, 600 before the common era."[1] So far from these being the assigned dates to the Himyarites, M. Caussin places the foundation of the Himyaritic kingdom one century before our era, and M. Renan declares, "La date des inscriptions Himyarites semble être le 3me et le 4me siècle après Jésus Christ."[2] Gesenius also fixes the date of the Himyaritic inscriptions in the fourth century of the Christian era, a period very remote from the time when the inscribed clay seals found by Layard were used in Sennacherib's palace.

The location of the Hittites is equally unfavourable to Mr. H. Clarke's theory.

According to Abu el-Fida, the great Arab historian of Hamah, "Himyar was the son of Saba, who built the city Ma'rib, and the famous Ma'rib dyke, into which flowed seventy rivers, and the sons of Himyar were the kings of Yemen."[3] The Himyaritic as a written language seems to have had its earliest home in Yemen, and M. Renan says, "it still exists as a living dialect in the adjacent regions, under the name Akhkili."[4] There is no proof that the Himyaritic ever existed in any force far from the shores of the Red Sea. It is clear, then, both as regards space and time, that the

[1] "Unexplored Syria," i. 359.   [2] "Langues Sémitiques," p. 315.
[3] "Abu el-Fida," i. 105. Ed. Constantinople, A. H. 1286.
[4] "Langues Sémitiques," p. 303.

Himyaritic lies outside the circle of kinship with the Hamathite; and what is true of the Himyaritic is still more true of the Libyan, which Mr. H. Clarke supposed to be related to the Hamah inscriptions.

In 1877 Mr. H. Clarke published a pamphlet setting forth a Khita-Peruvian theory. The pamphlet shows wide and patient research, but the central hypothesis requires support.

The theories that would connect the inscriptions with the Aztec, Corean and Japanese, are so devoid of plausibility that we need not consider them.

Mr. J. A. Johnson, in drawing attention to the inscriptions in the "First Statement of the American Palestine Exploration Society,"[1] suggested that they were the work of Assyrians, or Egyptians, or Hebrews. "We should naturally," he says, "expect to find in this vicinity some trace of the Assyrian and Egyptian conquerors, who ravaged the valley of the Orontes, and of their struggles with the Hittites on this ancient field, and of Solomon who built stone cities in Hamah. The arrow-headed characters are suggestive of Assur-Nasir-Pal."

Captain Conder also draws "attention to the similarities of the Hittite and the earliest Egyptian hieroglyphics," and he has drawn up a list of sixty symbols for which parallels may be found in Egyptian inscriptions of all ages.[2] He also among other guesses

---

[1] July, 1871.
[2] "Quarterly Statement of Palestine Explor. Fund," October, 1883.

suggests " that the Hamathite texts represent the earliest Phœnician inscriptions."[1] Perhaps it is sufficient to state at once that the Egyptians, the Assyrians, and the Phœnicians and Hebrews had their own peculiar styles of writing, and that these inscriptions are neither Egyptian, nor Assyrian, nor Hebrew. The busts and birds and feet and animals' heads, and other symbolic forms in the inscriptions, are suggestive of the hieroglyphics, while the spear-heads have a resemblance to the cuneiform ; but Assyriologists and Egyptologists are agreed that the Hamah and kindred inscriptions are neither Assyrian nor Egyptian.

Is it not more reasonable to suppose that the inscriptions are not monuments of the invaders, who boasted so often that they had "utterly destroyed the Hittites," but rather that they are the records of that great Hittite people themselves, who for more than a thousand years held their own against the might of Assyria and Egypt ?

We have seen that the Egyptians inscribed the records of their victories over the Hittites very conspicuously on their temples, and that the Assyrians minutely chronicled on stones and bricks their triumphs in the same region ; but we cannot reasonably conclude from this that therefore they wrote them up in the streets of Hamah and Carchemish for the edification of the vanquished Hittites.

The inscribed Hamah stones, as we have seen, were

[1] " Heth and Moab," p. 425.

dressed narrow towards the parts on which the inscriptions were carved, and the bases were undressed for several feet. The stones were built into walls, with the dressed and inscribed parts standing out. They were intended to be publicly read, and were doubtless in the vernacular of the people.

Nor is it at all likely that the Hittites would live surrounded by such literary nations as the Egyptians, the Assyrians, the Jews, and the Phœnicians, occupying so large a place in their estimation, and maintaining their ground so well in war and in peace, without having a literature of their own, or at least a written language.

The relations of the Hittites with Assyria were very extensive. They seem to have been often in alliance with the Phœnicians, who were doubtless their carriers by sea. Hittite warriors were among King David's mighty men at the time he wrote his Psalms, and both he and Solomon extended Israelitish influence among the Hittites (2 Sam. viii. 10 ; 1 Kings xi. 1 ; 2 Chron. viii. 4). In addition to waging wars, and concluding treaties and forming dynastic alliances with the Egyptians, the Hittites had commercial transactions with them.

When Kheta-sira went down into Egypt he would see on the great temples of the land the pictures and records of victories gained over his ancestors. Every Hittite who went down into Egypt for horses, or chariots, or fine linen, would see wherever he went abroad, pictures of the captive Kheta accompanying the boastful Egyptian records, and it is impossible to conceive that anything but lack of a written language would prevent so patriotic a people as the Hittites from writing up their own achievements. But we know that the Hittites had a written language, and that the "Offensive and Defensive Alliance between Kheta and Kemi," which Kheta-sira took with him to Egypt, and the translation of which was inscribed on the temples, was written in the language of the Hittites on a silver tablet. There is even a contemptuous reference in one of the inscriptions to the literary propensities of the Hittites.

From all the evidence before me, internal and external, I am led to conclude that the Hamah ·inscriptions are in the language of the inhabitants, by whom they were intended to be publicly read, and that these inhabitants were the Kheta or Hittites. Had they been inscribed by the invaders who so often ravaged the Orontes valley, they would doubtless have been destroyed as soon as the hereditary enemy turned his back.

We have thus tried to clear our way by showing what these inscriptions are not, and we believe we have pointed out what they are. Up to the present time we have known the Hittites only on the testimony of their neighbours and rivals. In these inscriptions the Hittites, I believe, have something to say for themselves, and they have doubtless something in return to say of their neighbours. They are beginning to find a tongue, and we await their story with intense impatience. Other similar inscriptions besides those of Hamah are being brought to light, and many more await the careful explorer among the great mounds in the land of the Hittites, where the spoiler has been at work for so many years.

We have full confidence that the inscriptions will not long remain mute now that Professor Sayce has given a clue to their secrets. When they do speak out clearly they may simply duplicate the Egyptian and Assyrian records of blood-shedding. But we may have some additional confirmation of Bible story; of Joshua's wondrous conquest by the waters of Merom; of the relations of King David and King Toi (2 Sam. viii. 10); of Solomon's alliance with a Hittite wife; of his building stone cities in Hamath, &c. (2 Chron. viii. 4); and at least they will assist in restoring the Hittite kingdom to its position in history as one of the mightiest empires of the ancient world.[1]

We must, however, labour to unloose the dumb tongue of these inscriptions, and to unlock their mysteries, not with the view of finding something

[1] Mr. Cheyne closes his article with these words: "If the Hittites be really the inventors of the Hamathite hieroglyphics, this wonderful nation steps into a position hardly surpassed by any of the nations of the distant East."—("Encl. Brit.," Art. Hittites.)

sensational in them, or for the purpose of advancing some theory, but from a love of knowing what they really contain ; and I doubt not that, proceeding in the right method of investigation, we shall reach results satisfactory to the Oriental scholar, and confirmatory of Divine truth.

CHAPTER X.

THE HITTITE INSCRIPTIONS.

THE COPIES TAKEN AT HAMAH.

THE Hamah inscribed stones were four in number, and these contained five inscriptions, one of the large stones being inscribed on the side and on the end. All the stones were close-grained basalt (fully ripe, as the Arabs say), doubtless brought from the basaltic region east of the city. Many similar stones were lying about or built into the walls, some of them with Greek and Arabic inscriptions, and some of them having the figures of animals carved upon them.

The Hittite inscriptions differ from the inscriptions of Babylon, Egypt, Assyria, Greece and Rome, in that they are all except that of Tyana and the Babylon Vase in raised character. The lines of inscriptions and their boundaries are clearly defined by raised bars about four inches apart. The interstices between the bars and characters have been cut away. The faces of the stones had been dressed smooth before the inscriptions were carved upon them, and the stones, as I have already pointed out, were dressed narrow towards the inscribed parts, their bases being left undressed for several feet. They were clearly intended to be inserted in masonry with the inscribed parts standing out, so that the inscriptions might be publicly read, and these were doubtless in the language of the people of Hamah. The inscriptions begin at the top on the right side, and read along the line between the bars to the left. The next line is read from left to right, and thus the reader proceeds from right to left and left to right, *boustrophedon* style, or as an ox ploughs. The flow of the line is always in the opposite direction from that in which the speaking figures in the inscriptions look.

We owe it to the accomplished Secretary of the Society of Biblical Archæology, Mr. W. H. Rylands, that we are able to present the Hittite inscriptions so complete and perfect. It is only fair, however, to remember when we compare these facsimiles of the inscriptions with those published by Captain Burton, in "Unexplored Syria," that he had to trust to the "native painter," against whose artistic fancies he puts us on our guard.

Mr. Rylands, with skill and leisure, reproduced the inscriptions for the Society of Biblical Archæology, and by the assistance of Professor Sayce, who has since gone over the casts with him, they have been revised and corrected for the present work. Except in the case of a few defaced characters, we have now before us the Hamah and other inscriptions in as perfect a form as that in which the old Hittites first read them.

THE HITTITE INSCRIPTIONS. 139

In referring to the Hamah stones, I shall follow the order in which I first announced them to the Palestine Exploration Fund,[1] and I shall follow Mr. Rylands' convenient system of notation, giving on the different plates the first letter of the name of the place where the inscription was found followed by a number. Thus H. V. means Hamah No. five, and J. I. means Jerabis No. one.

PLATE I.

H. I. consists of three lines, commencing at the top to the right, by a speaking figure with hand raised to the mouth. The stone bearing this inscription was built into the wall of a house in Harat ed-Dahan (the painters' quarter), belonging to M. Kallas, and numbered 23. The stone, which lay on its side about five feet from the ground, had four spaces prepared and smoothed for inscriptions, but only three lines were written in. When taken from the wall, the stone proved to be only a thin fragment cut off a larger one. The inscription is complete at the right side, but at the left side it is broken off, and will therefore be found incomplete. The second half of this inscription is yet to be found.

H. II. This inscription consists of three lines; beginning with a speaking figure at the top to the right, and coming to an end before filling the lower

[1] "Quarterly Statement" for April, 1873, p. 77.

line to the left. The stone containing this inscription was built into a wall in the garden of Sayyid 'Amr, son of Sheik Hassan, west of the gate at the southern end of Bab ej-Jisr.

PLATE II.

H. III. This inscription[1] consists of two lines which were inscribed on the end of a large long stone that lay in the Darb Tak et-Tahun. We were told that a great many rheumatic people had been cured by stretching themselves on this stone. And our informants assured us that it was equally efficacious to the true believer calling on the name of Mohammed, and to the unbelieving Nasara muttering the names of St. George and the Virgin Mary. The inscribed part was simply cut off the stone and carried to the Serai. It would be interesting to know if the remaining part lost its healing virtue when the inscription was cut off.

I add a sketch of the stone as it lay on the darb or path.

PLATE III.

H. IV. This inscription,[2] which consists of four lines, was on the northern end of a very large stone in the

---

[1] The inscription is numbered H. IV. in the "Transactions of the Soc. Bib. Arch.," but as the next two inscriptions were taken from the same stone it is necessary to follow the order in which I originally described them in the "Quarterly Statement of the Palestine Exploration Fund," April, 1873.

[2] This inscription is numbered H. III. in "Transactions Soc. Bib. Arch."

THE HITTITE INSCRIPTIONS. 141

north-west corner of a little shop belonging to Mohammed Ali, in a little street near the western end of the Tayyarah Bridge. It was under the very nose of the French Vice-Consul. Above the four lines there was a plain space more than sufficient for another line, but it did not contain any trace of an inscription. As this is the only one of the inscriptions that does not begin with the speaking figure, and as the reading begins at the left side instead of the right, unlike the others, I am inclined to believe that a top line has been carefully removed, probably owing to the name of some obnoxious king, or to the record of some disagreeable fact.

MARASH INSCRIPTION.

In the first edition I added to Plate III. the picture of an inscribed lion on the Castle of Marash. The picture was made from a photograph taken by Dr. Gwyther. I am now able to give on Plates XXVI. and XXVII. a photograph of the inscription.

PLATE IV.

H. V. This inscription consists of five lines, and was on the broad side of the stone which had H. IV. on its end. The inscribed end and side of the stone were carefully dressed for the inscription, but the part of the stone most remote from the inscriptions was undressed. It had doubtless been built into the corner of some large square structure. This was the stone which took fifty men and four oxen a whole day to bring it to the Serai. Some of the characters in the upper and lower lines of this inscription have been effaced.

All the stones containing the above inscriptions were sent by Subhi Pasha to the Constantinople Museum, where they now lie.

PLATES V. VI. VII.

HITTITE INSCRIPTION AT ALEPPO.

In 1872, Mr. C. F. Tyrwhitt Drake published, in "Unexplored Syria,"[1] the facsimile of an inscription which he had copied in Aleppo.

In the following year, M. Claremont-Ganneau published, in the "Quarterly Statement of the Palestine Exploration Fund,"[2] a copy of the same inscription which had been made for him by M. Paucker. Both copies were evidently very imperfect, and scholars were waiting for a cast of the stone, when the news arrived that the Moslems had destroyed it, and that not a fragment of it remained.

The monument is completely lost, and Mr. Rylands did the best thing that could be done under the circumstances. He collected all the published and unpublished copies he could find and reproduced them in the "Proceedings of the Society of Biblical Archæology."[3] We reproduce the different copies, as it is better to

[1] Vol. ii. 186.   [2] 1873, p. 73.   [3] June 5, 1883.

have mutilated fragments than nothing at all, and even they may aid in the decipherment of other inscriptions when the knowledge of the characters is in a more advanced state.

It is necessary to give the following explanation, by Mr. Rylands, of the copy taken from the note-book of the late George Smith: "It appears from the fact that the inscription has always been printed wrong way up, that the stone was so placed in the wall. George Smith probably guessed this, and endeavoured, in the portion of the inscription copied at the head of the page, to correct it in his drawing. Doubtless he found it difficult to do so, broke off suddenly without completing his first copy, turned his sketch-book round, as is proved by the reversal of the (?) marks attached to some doubtful characters, and in this manner made his final copy."

The stone was basalt, and Mr. Boscawen says the characters were in low relief, and that the stone was worn away by the people rubbing their eyes against it in order that they might be cured of ophthalmia.

PLATE VIII.

JERABIS, OR CARCHEMISH INSCRIPTIONS.

These inscriptions, which are among the best specimens, may now be seen in the British Museum as they were originally cut out in the basalt. We are indebted to the late George Smith and Mr. Consul Henderson for these inscribed stones. The following description is by Mr. W. H. Rylands, and taken from the "Transactions of the Society of Biblical Archæology."[1]

"J. I. is a large piece of basalt, 39½ inches in height, it is cut in vertical steps,[2] and for this reason, in the facsimile the columns are not placed in their proper sequence. Letters are added at the foot of each column, which, with the assistance of the annexed diagram, will make the arrangement quite clear. The

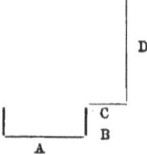

stone is flat at the top, and I believe that we have the inscription complete in the columns A, B, and C. A vertical division will be noticed in the angles where the columns B and C meet, with bands of flat stone of the same level as the horizontal dividing lines, possibly, as I have before suggested, denoting a separation."

PLATE IX.

"J. II. is also of basalt, and apparently complete as to height and width, although the figure is much damaged. The stone is 3 feet 10¾ inches in height, and 2 feet 1¾ inches in width. The figure is clothed

[1] Vol. vii. part iii.
[2] The following are the widths of the different columns: A is 8¾ inches; B, 8½ inches; C, 7 inches; and D, at the greatest width, 22 inches.

in a long robe reaching to the ankles; what remains of the shoes shows that the toes were slightly turned up; an armlet of three or four rings encircles the arm, which is bare, near the elbow; and in the left hand, the only one now remaining, is held a bâton or mace: it has been thought by some to be one or more arrows."

PLATE X.

" J. III. appears to have been first noticed and copied by the late George Smith; copies have also been made by various travellers who visited the mound. Like the other stones, it is of basalt, now about 5 feet 5 inches in height and 2 feet 6½ inches broad on the flat side.

"The stone, as it at present exists, represents in section a segment of a circle, 3 feet 5 inches on the curve. On the flat side, cut in low relief, is the full-face figure of a king or priest, standing in a niche, some portion of which still remains. Unfortunately, the head and the shoulders of the figure are gone, but sufficient remains to show that some of the decoration of the long striped robe was of a very ornamental character.

"About the breast are the remains of bands decorated with alternate rose-like figures, and double or treble squares, one within another, similar to the pattern to be found on the Assyrian monuments. Along the base of the stone, below the feet, runs a single band of the

L

guilloche pattern. The hands of the figure are closed, and pressed against the breast; in the left hand is held a sceptre, somewhat similar to those found in the hands of the figures at Eyuk and Boghaz-Keui.

"The inscription here given in the plate (J. III.) is engraved round the back of the figure, which from this side has the appearance of a circular column. The lines of characters are high up on the stone, and reach about to the level of the waist of the statue; the remainder of the stone is blank. We have, therefore, the last lines of the inscription.

"The surface of the stone seems to have been carefully prepared to receive the carving, which consists of four lines of hieroglyphs at the end, and a portion of another, much chipped away, above these. It is impossible to say how many lines are lost at the commencement, but there cannot be much wanting at the two sides, where the stone appears to have been chipped away for an inch or two.

"This inscription, for which we have waited so long, is of very great interest, being the longest yet known, and containing, as it does, many new characters of quaint and unknown forms, and at the same time repeating characters and combinations of characters known to us from the other inscriptions from the same site.

"On looking at the stone, the question will probably occur to many, as it did to myself—'Does the inscription belong to the statue? or was the statue utilized for the inscription?' I am inclined to believe that the two are separate productions."

PLATE XI.

" J. IV. is also from Jerabis, and now in the British Museum. The figure here represented is peculiarly of Assyrian form, and probably, when complete, would have four wings, otherwise the two lower ones—now the only ones remaining—would not have been represented ; the greatest height is 2 feet 6 inches, and the greatest width 2 feet 2 inches. In the right hand is held a basket or vase, as in the figures of the Assyrian sculptures. The other arm was no doubt raised, and held in the hand a sceptre, or perhaps some sacred object. It may be worth remarking that the turning point of the border of the robe is square, and not rounded, as in Assyrian costume. Bonomi[1] figures one of the few Assyrian ones known with a square border."

PLATE XII.

J. V. stood as Plate IV. in the "Transactions of the Soc. Bib. Arch.," and J. VI. stood as Plate V., and J. IV. was also marked Plate VI. Of these plates Mr. Rylands says, " Plate IV., figs. 1, 2, 3 and 4, and

[1] "Nineveh and its Palaces," 1853, p. 265.

Plate V., fig. 1, include all the fragments in the British Museum.

"There are other stones at Jerabis yet to be sent to England. One is a fragment of a human figure, with an inscription running in lines down the sides in the usual manner. The others are, I believe, without inscriptions. Reduced woodcuts of them have been published,[1] but, being nothing more than illustrations, they cannot, of course, be depended upon as perfectly accurate."

PLATE XIII.

Plate XIII. is made up of an inscribed fragment (J. VI.) from Jerabis, now in the British Museum, and a sketch by Professor Sayce of the Cartouche on the right-hand side of the figure of Niobe on Mount Sipylos. I have also added eight seals discovered in 1851 by Sir A. H. Layard at Kouyunjik, and now in the British Museum.

PLATE XIV.

IBREEZ INSCRIPTION.

The Ibreez plate is reproduced from the "Transactions of the Society of Biblical Archæology,"[2] where it was published in 1876, from a drawing made by the Rev.

[1] The *Graphic*, 11th December, 1880.
[2] Vol. iv. part ii.

E. J. Davis. The inscriptions had been so imperfectly copied, that only a few of the characters were recognizable as Hittite. Through the kindness of Professor Sayce and Mr. Rylands, I am now able to present the inscriptions on the figures thoroughly revised and corrected. Mr. Davis gives a good description of the sculpture, which had been previously copied in 1838, by Major Fisher. The tableau was on a limestone rock of deep red colour, by the base of which flowed the Ibreez river in a deep narrow channel. Ibreez is in the Bulgar Dagh, near the Kulek Boghaz, or Cilician Gates. We here insert Mr. Davis' minute and interesting description.

"June 9th.—I rose at daybreak and proceeded to draw the bas-relief. The rock on which it is carved rises like a wall, from the water of the stream, to a height of about 40 feet. Its colour is of a deep dull red, or yellowish-red, but stained and dyed in lighter and deeper patches, by exposure to the sun and air through so many centuries. The portion on which the bas-relief is carved has been chiselled down and prepared for the work; the rest of the rock surface remains in its natural state.

"The bas-relief consists of two figures (one much larger than the other), cut in considerable but not very high relief, not exceeding, I think, more than 4 or 5 inches. I can, however, only give the various dimensions *by guess*, as I had no means of measuring the figures, which were quite out of reach from the side of the stream on which I stood, and indeed quite inaccessible without a long ladder. But by dint of careful comparison, I think my conjectural measurements are not very far wrong.

"The larger figure is about 20 feet in height, the smaller about 12 feet, and the feet of the larger figure are from 8 to 9 feet above the level of the stream, which flows at the base of the rock. It seems to be a representation of some great personage offering prayers or thanksgiving to a deity, the god as it would seem of corn and wine.

"The design of both figures (though naturally somewhat rough in the outline, owing to the coarseness of the material and natural decay) is very good; the anatomy is extremely well indicated, much after the manner of the Assyrian sculptures. The left hand of the larger figure is especially well executed, the delicate outline of the thumb articulations being very well rendered, not in the conventional style of the Egyptian sculptures, but as if copied directly from Nature.

"The limbs of the larger figure are massy and bulky; in this point also the work resembles Assyrian rather than Egyptian work. The god is represented with a high conical hat or helmet, from which project four horns, two in front, two behind. The rim is formed by a flat band, and a similar band or ribbon runs round the hat-work. A snake seems to be attached to the hat.

"I was for some time in doubt whether this was

meant to represent a snake, or only another ribbon, but the peculiar shape renders it more probable that this was meant for a snake; and after long examination with the glass under various lights, I came to the conclusion that it must be so.

"The beard is very thick and close curled, and runs quite up to the temples. The hair is of a similar character, disposed in rows of thick curls, but without ornament. Neither of the figures appear to have earrings. The god is clad in a close-fitting tunic, reaching half-way down the thigh, and turned up both in front and behind, in a species of 'volute' ornament. The lower part of the arms from above the elbow is bare, but while the fold of the tunic sleeve is represented on the left arm, it is quite omitted on the right arm.

"On the wrists are massy but plain bracelets; round the waist is a broad girdle, ornamented with carved parallel lines *like* arrow-heads, but obviously not *intended* to represent arrow-heads. The legs from the middle of the thigh downwards are bare, the muscles of the calf and the knees being well rendered. He wears boots turned up in front, and bound round the leg above the ankle by thongs, and a piece of leather reaching half-way up the shin, exactly as it is worn to this day by the peasants of the plain of Cilicia round Adana.

"In his outstretched left hand he holds a large handful of ears of wheat—bearded wheat, the wheat of the country—the stalks reaching the ground behind his left foot, which is stepping forward, and between his feet is represented a vine stock. In his right hand he holds a cluster of grapes, two other larger clusters hang from the branch he is grasping, and behind him hangs a fourth cluster.

"The expression of the face is jovial and benevolent, the features well indicated, especially the highly aquiline nose. The lips are small and not projecting, and the moustache is short, allowing the mouth to be seen. The inscription is carved on the space between the face and the line of the arm, hand, and ears of wheat.

" In front of him stands the other figure. The expression and character of feature in this is very different. The eye seems more prominent, the nose more curved and flattened upon the face, the lips more projecting, the hair and beard equally or even more crisped and thickly curled. On the head is a tall rounded cap, with flat bands round it, on which seems to be sewn square plates (of gold, perhaps). In front of the cap is an ornament of precious stones, such as is still worn by Oriental princes.

" The figure is clad in a loose long robe covered with squares, and heavily fringed at the bottom : compare Deuteronomy,[1] also the dress of Aaron as it is described in Leviticus.[2]

" A mantle, embroidered below, and secured at the breast by a clasp of precious stones, covers the robe ;

[1] Deut. xxii. 12, and Numbers xv. 38.　　[2] Lev. ii. 7, 8, 9.

round the waist is a massy girdle, from which hangs a heavy tassel or fringe. On the right leg, just below the fringe of the under robe, appears to be the lower part of the trousers, and the feet are shod with shoes curved up in front. One hand, with the forefinger erect, is extended in front of the face, as if in the attitude of prayer or praise.

"After long and close examination, I could not decide whether this was the right or left hand. On the whole, I concluded it was the left hand, especially as I thought I could detect the indication of the nail of the forefinger. On the other hand, the position of the arm rather resembles what would be the position of the *right*, the left arm being in that case wrapped up in and hidden by the mantle.

"A heavy collar or necklace surrounds the neck; it appears to be of rings or bands of gold, surrounding some other material. The end of the necklace hangs upon the shoulder. As in the Assyrian figures, perspective is only in part observed in the drawing of both these figures.

"Behind the smaller figure there is also an inscription carved upon the smooth portion of the rocks. Some of the characters are similar to those of the upper inscription; some appear to be heads of animals; one represents unmistakably the head of a man, the eye, beard, nose and conical cap being very distinct. In my drawing I have not sufficiently rendered the conical cap.

"But this inscription is much obliterated, and I was not able to decipher the first letter of the upper line.

"There is another inscription below the bas-relief, and just above the present level of the stream. This also seems to consist in great part of the heads of animals. A portion of the rock surface has been smoothed for it; but it is so very much obliterated that it is utterly impossible to make out a considerable part of it, the outlines even of that I have represented are very faint and indistinct. The villagers said that there were yet other inscriptions, but below the present water level, and only visible when the stream is at its lowest at the end of summer."[1]

PLATE XV.

TYANA INSCRIPTION.

This inscription is published from a copy made by Mr. W. M. Ramsay, at Tyana in Cappadocia. It was referred to by Professor Sayce in a letter to the "Academy," Aug. 5, 1882. The copy is not so perfect as could be desired, but it is clearly Hittite, and its publication here for the first time may help in the decipherment of other inscriptions. Col. Sir Charles Wilson informs me that this inscription is incised and not in relief, like all the other inscriptions except the Babylon Bowl (Plate XXV.).

[1] "Transactions of Soc. Bib. Arch.," vol. iv. part ii.

PLATES XVI. XVII.

HITTITE SEALS.

In 1851, Sir Henry Layard discovered eight seals in the Record Chamber of Sennacherib's palace at Konyunjik. These are now in the British Museum, and Mr. Rylands has published facsimiles of them in the "Transactions of the Society of Biblical Archæology;"[1] and they are reproduced on Plate XIII.

Besides these, M. G. Perrot published, in the "Revue Archéologique,"[2] eighteen seals belonging to M. Schlumberger, who had acquired them three years before at Constantinople from a merchant, who assured him that he had brought them from the interior of Asia Minor.

The seals have been re-drawn by Mr. Rylands for the "Transactions of the Society of Biblical Archæology," and by his kindness are reproduced here, and with the exception of that with the griffin, all appear to be of the same character. The material is clay.

PLATE XVIII.

THE PSEUDO-SESOSTRIS.

We are indebted to Mr. Hyde Clarke for the photograph of the Pseudo-Sesostris here reproduced, and to Professor Sayce for the restoration of the characters on the panel. Mr. Hyde Clarke declared in the

[1] Vol. viii. part ii.   [2] December 1882.

"Journal of the American Oriental Society," in 1865 (vol. viii. p. 380, 1866), that the monument "distinctly resembles the sculptures of Pterium (*i.e.*, Boghaz-Keui) and others of that type;" and Professor Sayce has shown that this monument, as well as those of Boghaz-Keui, is distinctly Hittite. It is impossible to compare this picture with the sculptures in Perrot's great work on Asia Minor without being convinced that they are all of the same character.

Herodotus, on his return from Egypt, saw two sculptured figures in the Karabel Pass, and he declared them to be images of the great Sesostris. One of the figures, the Pseudo-Sesostris, was discovered on the face of the rock, about 140 feet from the ground, by Renouard in 1839. It was afterwards copied by Texier; and Canon Rawlinson published it in his "Herodotus" in 1875 (vol. ii. p. 174).

The second Pseudo-Sesostris (see Plate XX.) was discovered by Dr. Beddoe in 1856; and twenty years afterwards M. K. Humann, a Prussian engineer, made imperfect drawings of it, which were published by Professor E. Curtius, in 1876, in the "Archäologische Zeitung."

In September 1879 Professor Sayce visited the Karabel Pass. He found the second Pseudo-Sesostris close to the ground, not far from the other Sesostris, and he considers it "the particular figure described by Herodotus."[1]

[1] "Trans. Soc. Bib. Arch.," vii. 265.

PLATE XIX.

This plate consists of fragments of sculptures and inscriptions from Jerabis, now in the British Museum. They have been carefully drawn by Mr. Rylands, and are here published with a view to making all available material accessible to the general public. Some details as to the dimensions of the fragments will be found in Appendix No. 4.

PLATE XX.

Figure 1 is the reproduction of a sketch made by Professor Sayce of the second Pseudo-Sesostris (see Plate XVIII.).

Figure 2 is on the flat side of a large column brought from Jerabis, and now in the British Museum. The inscription J. III. (Plate X.) is on the circular side of the column. The figure is fully described by Mr. Rylands on pages 145, 146.

Figure 3 is an inscribed fragment from Jerabis, now in the British Museum.

Figure 4 is a grey limestone seal, found by Sir A. H. Layard at Nineveh,-and published in the "Proceedings of the Society of Biblical Archæology." It may, as Mr. Rylands suggests, be compared with a combination of characters on the Babylon Bowl (Plate XXV.).

Figure 5 is taken from Lajard's "Culte de Mithra" (Plate XXIII. figure 1).

PLATE XXI.

This plate consists of nine fragments of inscribed stones from Jerabis.

PLATE XXII.

J. V. and VI. are also broken pieces of basaltic stones with mutilated inscriptions. The fragments may be seen in the British Museum.

The Cartouches of Rameses II. may be compared with the inscriptions on the Niobe published by Ed. Gollob.

PLATE XXIII.

The double-headed eagle of Eyuk, is reproduced from Perrot's "Galatie et Bithynie." It resembles the double-headed eagle in the procession at Boghaz-Keui (Plate XXIV. figure 3). Each talon of the eagle rests upon a hare or rabbit, and the two heads support a figure of which only the flowing skirt and the Hittite shoe are visible. There are other important sculptures at Eyuk of distinctly Hittite character (see p. 68).

PLATE XXIV.

The pictures on this plate are copied from M. Perrot's "Exploration Archéologique de la Galatie et de Bithynie," Paris, 1862. Texier had given drawings of them in his "Description de l'Asie Mineure," but these M.Perrot found "were far from rendering faithfully the expression of the figures cut in the rock,"[1] but by the aid of M. Delbet's photographs and M. Guillaume's drawings he has reproduced the sculptures in a manner which makes his work of the greatest value.

Figures 1, 2 and 3 form a double procession, sculptured in low relief round the three sides of a great natural chamber in the massive rocks of Boghaz-Keui. The chamber, open to the sky, is of irregular quadrilateral form, and is not shut in towards the south. Figure 1 is the cortège on the left side. Figure 2 is on the right side; and figure 3 shows the two parts of the procession meeting at the further end of the grand *salle*. Starting from the entrance on the right and left sides, the two sets of figures seem to march until they meet at the bottom. The figures increase in size in the procession from $0^{m.}75$ at the point of starting, to 2 metres at the point of meeting. The figures on the left with the tall pointed hats and short tunics are supposed, by M. Perrot, to be men. Those on the left with the mural crowns, plaited skirts, and hair falling on the shoulders, he considers women.[2] The figure immediately behind the leader of the procession on the right differs from the others.

For the various opinions held regarding the procession by Texier, Lajard, Raoul-Rochette, Kiepert,

---

[1] "Galatie et Bithynie," p. 324. [2] *Idem*, p. 331.

Hamilton, and Barth, see Perrot's "Galatie et Bithynie." Professor Sayce recognized in the sculptures a series of divinities, and draws attention to the various details which mark them as Hittite.[1]

Figure 4 is also from Boghaz-Keui. It is sculptured on a projection of a rock near the entrance of the grand *salle*, towards the lower end of which it is looking. The figure is about $2\frac{1}{2}$ metres high, and is thus larger than any of the figures in the procession. The feet are shod with the distinctive Hittite shoes, which rest on the summits of two mountains. Its right hand supports a winged solar disk, in the centre of which is a bearded figure, which has the arms lifted up as if in the act of dancing. On each side of the figure stand two objects which are supposed to be bulls, and at the extremities are primitive Ionic columns. On the same wall of rock is figure 6. This consists of a large figure, like those on the left side of the great procession (figure 1), with the left arm round the neck of a smaller figure, which in many respects resembles figure 4. M. Perrot advances curious speculations, founded on peculiarities supposed to exist in the winged disk, but I am inclined to think that the disks are the same, and that the difference of appearance arises from defects in the stone.

Figure 7 is carved on the same rock as figure 6, a little to the left of it. It seems to be a gigantic sword hilt. The head, which is adorned with the pointed

[1] "Transactions of Soc. Bib. Arch.," vii. 254–257.

hat jewelled, and with earrings, is that of a man. The shoulders consist of the fore-quarters of two lions. Two couchant lions extend towards what would be the blade of the sword. Boghaz Keui, where these and other Hittite sculptures exist, was doubtless the ancient Pteria. Herodotus narrates the arrival of Cresus in the part of Cappadocia called Pteria, where he ravaged and enslaved the Syrians, though they had done him no harm. Cresus was here attacked by Cyrus, and after several indecisive engagements, withdrew. The Leuco-Syrians of Herodotus appear to have been the Hittites, who often traversed Syria in their border warfare.

PLATE XXV.

This plate is the picture of an inscribed bowl or vase found at Babylon, and also of the inscription reproduced in circular form. The bowl or vase resembles an Oriental mortar. It stands $8\frac{3}{8}$ inches high, and is 13 inches in diameter. The bason, in which spices may have been pounded, is $4\frac{3}{4}$ inches in depth. The base is $7\frac{1}{2}$ inches across and $2\frac{1}{4}$ inches in height. The inscription, like that of Tyana (Plate XV.), is incised. The material of the bowl is basalt, not very close grained, or, as the Arabs would say, not well cooked. It was offered for sale to the British Museum, but has been since taken away. Mr. Rylands has drawn attention to three characters in combination on the bowl, resembling those on the seal in Plate XX. figure 4.

I have received from Professor Sayce a note with reference to the inscription which appears at the end of his chapter on Decipherment, p. 177.

PLATES XXVI., XXVII.

In the first edition of this book I gave on Plate III. the picture of a lion, on the Castle of Marash, said to be covered with Hittite characters. The picture referred to on page 141 was made from a photograph taken by Dr. Gwyther, who also brought to this country squeezes which, though not perfect, showed clearly that the inscription was Hittite.

The stone has been taken to the Museum at Constantinople, but excellent duplicate casts have been made and sent to the British Museum and to the Society of Biblical Archæology by Mr. F. D. Mocatta, a member of the Council of the Society of Biblical Archæology.

The inscriptions are on the breast and left side of the lion, and there is one line on the left side of the back which is a part of the side inscription. The characters, as Professor Sayce has pointed out to me, closely resemble in many respects the Hamath. Some of the figures are sufficiently distinct to settle controversy on other points. The well-formed horse's head on the breast of the lion shows that Mr. Rylands was right in stating that the head on the Boss of Tarkondêmos was that of a goat. On the side and left fore-leg there are excellent pictures of a hare in different attitudes, much less conventional than those of the Egyptian hieroglyphics. On the left shoulder there is what seems to be the remains of a defaced image. It may be that of one figure standing on another, resembling some of those on Plate XXIV. The engravings are made from a photograph.

HITTITE AND CUNEIFORM INSCRIPTION ON THE SILVER BOSS OF TARKÒNDÉMOS.

About twenty years ago a convex silver plate, something like the skin of half a small orange, was offered to the British Museum for sale. The plate, which looked like the knob of a staff or dagger, had in the centre the figure of a standing warrior with certain unknown hieroglyphics on each side of him. The standing figure and the hieroglyphics were enclosed within a circle, and outside this circle round the rim of the boss there ran a cuneiform inscription. This curious and unique antiquity was looked upon as a forgery at the British Museum, and rejected; but an electrotype facsimile was made by Mr. Ready, and preserved in the Museum.

About three years ago Professor Sayce was engaged in an examination of the Vannic inscriptions, and came across an account of this silver boss by Dr. Mordtmann, who had seen it in the possession of M. Alexander Jovanoff, of Constantinople, who had procured it from

Smyrna. Professor Sayce concluded from Dr. Mordtmann's description that the hieroglyphics might be Hittite, and that the cuneiform inscription, which Dr. Mordtmann ascribed to the syllabary in use in Van, might prove to be a key to the hieroglyphics. In this view he was confirmed by the character and form of the boss.

In the "Transactions of the Society of Biblical Archæology" he gives an interesting account of his hunt for the boss. He first discovered a facsimile published by Dr. Mordtmann in 1862.[1] In this facsimile he saw, as he anticipated, the undoubted Hittite hieroglyphics. He next discovered, in that most wonderful of all treasure houses, the British Museum, the electrotype facsimile, made so many years before, of the boss itself.

As Mr. Ready had forgotten the circumstances under which the electrotype was made, Prof. Sayce feared it might have been a cast manufactured at Constantinople. His fears on this point were, however, set at rest when M. F. Lenormant, who had seen the original at Constantinople twenty years before, forwarded to him a cast taken by himself. M. Lenormant's cast and the electrotype in the British Museum were found to agree perfectly, and there was no further reason to doubt the correctness of the transcript.

It must be confessed that there are some who still doubt the genuineness of the silver boss, which it is feared is now lost. Scepticism is a virtue in the

[1] Münzstudien (iii. 7, 8, 9): Leipzig.

archæologjuist, st as faith is an essential to the divine. But the inscription before us leaves no ground for reasonable doubt. True, there are centres of forgery at Athens, Smyrna, Aleppo, Damascus, and Jerusalem. Jewish shekels and Phœnician gems have been forged; Moabite pottery with Moabite and Himyaritic characters have been equal to the requirements of the market; and other more audacious attempts have recently brought fame or infamy to a practised hand in the art of deceit.

SILVER BOSS OF TARKONDĒMOS WITH HITTITE AND CUNEIFORM INSCRIPTION.

All these forgeries, however, were imitations of things known to the forgers. Any common handbook of alphabets supplied all the requisites for the literary part of the work. The forgeries are simply imitations or adaptations. Imitative skill alone was required.

The boss with the bilingual inscription comes under quite a different category. If forged, the forger must have performed a miracle. The boss was seen and copied by M. Lenormant twenty-four years ago. A facsimile of it was published by Dr. Mordtmann in

1862, ten years before I first suggested that the Hamah inscriptions were Hittite remains.

If the boss is forged the forger must have invented a new language in a new syllabary. In addition to this, he must have invented a new art, for the art is the same as that which has been recognized during the past few years as characteristically Hittite.

In the silver plate, in the raised characters, in the dress, posture and form, of the central figure, we see all the evidences of recently recognized Hittite art, just as clearly as we recognize the Hittite hand in their own peculiar hieroglyphics. The forging of the silver boss would have been the greatest miracle on record, and few will have sufficient faith to believe in the performance of such a miracle at Smyrna only a quarter of a century ago.

I now add Professor Sayce's reading and analysis of this interesting inscription in his own words, as an introduction to the general chapter on decipherment which he has written for this book.[1]

"Once satisfied of the correctness of the copy, we have little difficulty in reading the cuneiform legend. This runs:—

D.P. Tar - rik - tim - me šar mat Er - me - e

Tarrik-timme, king of the country of Ermé.

"The forms of the characters refer us to the age of

[1] "Transactions of Soc. Bib. Arch.," vol. vii. part ii. (1881), p. 297.

Sargon. The last character has the archaizing form found, for instance, on the stêlê of that monarch discovered in Kypros, the ideograph used to denote 'king' belongs to the same period, and the third character (which ought to be ⟦⟧) has been slightly changed in form, either through the unskilfulness of the engraver, or out of that affectation of antiquity and love of variety which caused the cuneiform characters in the so-called hieratic writing of Nineveh to be modified at the pleasure of the scribe.

"The age of Sargon would agree well with historical probabilities. It was in his time that Assyrian culture first gained a permanent footing in the west, while the overthrow of Carchemish and the last relics of Hittite power in B.C. 717 would naturally lead to the disuse of the Hittite mode of writing and the spread of the cuneiform characters employed by the Assyrian conquerors. At this period, and at this period only, can we expect to find the two systems of writing used side by side.

"It must be remembered, too, that Kypros and Kilikia were in close connection with each other; and that it is on the Kyprian stêlê of Sargon that the peculiar form of the last character found on the boss recurs, while the owner of the boss was probably a Kilikian prince. His name is aptly compared by Dr. Mordtmann with that of the Kilikian king Ταρκονδίμοτος and his son of the same name, mentioned by Dio Cassius and Tacitus as living in the time of Augustus.

"The name, which is also found on coins, is made Ταρκόνδημος by Plutarch ('in Anton.' 61), and a Tarkodimatos, Bishop of Ægæ, in Kilikia, is found in Theodoret ('Hist. Eccles.,' p. 539).

"Tarkondêmos would exactly represent the Tarriktimme of the inscription. As I stated in my paper on 'The Monuments of the Hittites,' Tarkon or Tarku is probably identical with the first element in the names of Tarkhu-lara and Tarkhu-nazi, kings of the Gamgumai and of Melitene in the eighth century B.C. The nasal of the Greek form of the name probably means only that the dental following it was pronounced hard.

"The localization of the country over which Tarkondêmos ruled, is a matter of greater difficulty. It is tempting to identify it with the land of Urume, mentioned in the Assyrian inscriptions, since Tiglath-Pileser I. (B.C. 1130) says that in his time '4,000 Kaskayans or Kolkhians and Urumayans, as soldiers of the Hittites,' garrisoned the conquered country of Subarti or Semitic Aram, which had previously been subject to 'Assur.' However, the inscription of Assurnatsir-pal [1] shows that Urume lay to the south-west of Lake Van, and therefore too far to the east for a king who bears a distinctively Kilikian name.

"It may be the Urme of the Vannic inscriptions [2] which Mordtmann identifies with the modern Urumiyeh. Moreover, had Urume been the country named

[1] W. A. I. I., 20, 13.   [2] Schulz, xii. 22.

on the boss, we should have expected 𝍢 *ur*, and not ►⊨𝍞 *er*. The same objection lies against identifying the kingdom of Tarkondêmos with Urima, the modern Urum, on the Euphrates, north of Carchemish. I would therefore place it in the neighbourhood of the Kilikian range of mountains called Arima by the classical geographers. It is here that Kallisthenês placed the semi-mythical Arimi of Homer (Strab., xiii. 4, 6), near the river Kalykadnos and the cave of Korykos.

"It is now time to analyse the twice-repeated Hittite transcript of the cuneiform legend. It is clear that the scribe or engraver first wrote the characters on the right side, then those on the left, since the Hittite characters always read contrary to the direction towards which the animals' heads look, and in this particular inscription the animal's head at the commencement looks towards the right.

" A comparison of the characters with those accompanying the figure of the Pseudo-Sesostris at Karabel shows that he must have begun with the two upper ones—between the spear and the shoulder of the central figure ; next, he must have made the obelisk-like character between the spear and the lower part of the figure ; and then, in accordance with the boustrophedon manner of writing which distinguishes all the known Hittite inscriptions, have recommenced outside the spear, from the bottom of the boss, working upwards from below. Consequently, the ' four vertical lines,' as Mordtmann called them, will be the last character in the legend.

"We should further expect that the royal name would be included in the space between the spear and the shoulder, where the characters come, as it were, out of the mouth of the figure, while the character enclosed between the legs ⧊ and the lower part of the spear would denote the kingly title. In this case, what Mordtmann termed an obelisk would be the ideograph for 'king,' the double obelisk ⧊⧊ signifying 'country.'

"Now, a study of the Carchemish inscriptions had already led me to the same conclusion. In these inscriptions (J. II. 1, 1) we find the double obelisk in a position which made me fancy that it denoted a country, while it seems to interchange with a triple obelisk, (J. I.) △△△ the form of which exactly resembles that of the primitive hieroglyphic from which the ideograph of 'country' and 'mountain' (⩓) was derived in the cuneiform system of writing. Dr. Mordtmann's comparison of it with the peculiar shape assumed by the rocks in the neighbourhood of Cæsarea confirms this identification, and suggests the possibility that Kappadokia was the locality in which the Hittite hieroglyphics were originally invented.

"However this may be, the double obelisk, wherever it occurred, was, I found, preceded by what looked like a single obelisk, which if the double obelisk meant 'country' must signify 'king.' The boss of

Tarkondêmos confirms both conclusions, and the matter is raised above doubt by the further fact that the ideograph of 'king' really represents the royal head-dress. We have only to compare its form on the boss and in the Carchemish inscriptions with the head-dress of the chief figures at Boghaz Keui[1] to perceive at once that this is the case. Just as the rocky district of the north, from which the Hittites had come, suggested to them their ideograph of country, so the pointed cap worn by the kings suggested to them the mode of representing the royal title.

"Further confirmation of this identification is afforded by the inscriptions of Hamath. Here the published copies had given the pictures of a palm-branch, where a comparison with the monuments of Carchemish would have led us to expect the royal cap. Before the discovery of the Carchemish inscriptions, the position of this palm-branch had more than once induced me to believe that it must denote the idea of 'king,' but I could not in any way associate this idea with the object supposed to be depicted by the hieroglyph. A careful examination, however, of the casts of the Hamath inscriptions has shown Mr. Rylands that the hieroglyph in question is not the picture of a palm-branch at all, but probably a reproduction of the royal cap as represented at Boghaz Keui. At Hamath, therefore, as well as at Carchemish and Kilikia, the idea of 'king' was represented in the same way.

[1] See Plate XXIV.

"Now that we have identified the Hittite representatives of 'king' and 'country,' there is little difficulty in determining the two groups of characters between which they come. The two hieroglyphs which precede the ideograph of 'king' must contain the royal name read from top to bottom; the two which follow the ideograph of 'country,' that of the territory of Tarkondêmos, read from bottom to top. Consequently ⟨glyph⟩ is 'tarku' or 'tarrik,' ⟨glyph⟩ 'timme,' ⟨glyph⟩ 'er,' and ⟨glyph⟩, or ⟨glyph⟩ 'me.'

"The last character, without the little side-stroke, is of frequent occurrence in the Hittite inscriptions, and we find the side-stroke itself added to characters in several cases where the end of a sentence or paragraph seems to be noted (see J. I., Col. A. 4, Col. C. 1, D. 2; J. II., 3, 4; H. i. I. 2; ii. 2, I. 2; iii. 2; iv. I. 2; v. 3, 4; and 'Karabel,' I.). Since \\ // (also written ⟨glyph⟩) is attached as a phonetic complement to the ideograph which I have conjectured to mean 'he says,' the third person singular of the verb which bore this significance would have ended in 'me.'

"The first character in the name of Tarkondêmos is called a goat's head by Dr. Mordtmann in the 'Journal of the German Oriental Society,' and the Rev. B. H. Cooper reminds us that the valley of the Kalykadnos was famous for its breed of goats. The inscription shows us that, as in the cuneiform inscriptions of ancient Babylonia, the name of an individual was not marked by any determinative. We cannot, therefore, expect to find such a determinative either in the monumental inscriptions or in the seal impressions found at Kouyunjik. These seal impressions, I may observe, do not appear to have belonged to royal personages, since the ideograph of 'king' does not occur on them, but to Hittite merchants who traded in Nineveh. The same is the case with the Phœnician seal impressions found along with them.[1] One of the seal impressions contains the character ⊪ ⊪, 'me'; another has ⌶, which I fancy must be the ⚹ of Hamath, or ⌇ of Carchemish, the ⚶ of our Kilikian boss. Mr. Rylands believes that the sign ⌇ represents the bent leg and foot of a doe, or wild goat.[2]

"Armed with the key afforded to us by the bilingual inscription of Tarkondêmos, we can now attack the Hittite inscriptions with a fair chance of success. The first result obtained from the determination of the two important characters for 'king' and 'country,' is that the two long inscriptions from Carchemish both belong to the same monarch, whose name is written ⌸ ▨ ⚶ ⌁ ; that the first six characters of the other inscription from Carchemish contain the name of another sovereign; that a royal name is hidden among the characters attached to the Pseudo-Sesostris; and

[1] The name which occurs on the Phœnician seal impressions is ꜥ𐤎𐤏𐤊𐤓𐤀 (Akar-ezer, עברי𐤅ר), not Attur-asar, as it has been read.
[2] On one of the seals we find ⌇ ⌇, which also occurs in the Carchemish inscriptions. It may be a picture of the girdle of the priestess of the Asiatic goddess which is thus represented in a sculpture copied at Carchemish by Mr. Boscawen.

that royal names also occur in the inscriptions from Hamath. With the help of the Assyrian records we ought in time to be able to make them out.

"By the side of the royal cap (🏛), the Phrygian cap (🏛) is also met with in the inscriptions used as an ideograph. It seems to have the same meaning of 'king' or 'lord,' though the one hieroglyph may have denoted a 'rex' (Assyr., 'sarru;' Heb., 'melech'), the other a 'regulus' (Assyr., 'malicu;' Heb., 'sar').

"In Mr. Boscawen's copy of the Aleppo inscription 🏛 occurs three times where we ⊅ ⊄ should have expected 🏛, and in one case we have 🏛 🏛, which seems to mean 'king of kings.' If so, ⊅ ⊄ will be the ideograph of plurality. The single crescent (⊅) is used in the Hamath inscriptions before the ideograph of 'king,' in such a way as to make me suspect that it here denotes the name of an individual.[1]

"A character, which I believe to signify 'above,' is sometimes associated with the royal cap. This has the shape of a basket-handle (⌒); but Mr. Boscawen has pointed out to me that it represents the eyebrow on one of the figures at Boghaz Keui. To this day the Georgian women paint their eyebrows black in such a manner as to draw a continuous line or bar from one side of the forehead to the other. This black bar would have exactly the appearance of the character now under notice.

[1] It is similarly used in the Carchemish inscriptions (J. I., Col. D. I. 5, Col. II., 3, 4). In J. III., line 3, it is followed by the picture of a man, and that again by the ideograph of "king."

"Mr. Rylands has been the first to observe that the peculiar shape given to the picture of the arm in the inscriptions, is similar to the hand and arm of a figure in the sculptures at Boghaz Keui ;[1] it is plainly due to the fact that the picture is really one of a long-sleeved glove, which has a thumb but no fingers. The use of gloves, like that of boots, is one more proof of the northern origin of the Hittites, who must have descended from the mountains of Armenia and Kappadokia at an early date. After establishing themselves at Carchemish, they subdued the Semitic population, and planted themselves in Kadesh on the Orontes, and even in Hamath—one branch of them settling west of the Afrin, where they were known to the Assyrians as the Patinai, and another branch penetrating as far as the southern part of Palestine.

"We have only to glance at the costume and arms of the natives of Van, as depicted on the Balawat bronzes, to see that they were cousins of the Hittites, and the striking resemblance between the helmets worn by the latter and those of the early Greeks probably results from the fact that the Greek helmet was really of Hittite origin.

"Herodotus (i. 171) expressly states that the Greeks had borrowed their helmets as well as the 'emblems' on their shields from the Karians, and the Karians, as we now know, were once subject to Hittite influence. I am tempted to see in the emblems or symbols on the

[1] c. f. p. 85.

shields a reminiscence of the Hittite hieroglyphics. The Egyptian text of the treaty between Rameses II. and the Hittites states that a silver plate was attached to the Hittite copy, in the centre of which was a figure of the god Sutekh, like the figure of the warrior in the centre of the boss of Tarkondêmos, round which ran the Hittite inscription—'This is the (figure) of the god Sutekh, the king of heaven and (earth).' Such a device might well have suggested the ornamentation of the shield. As for the helmet, it was disused by the Hittites under the burning sun of the south. In their wars with the Egyptians they contented themselves with a close-fitting cap like that worn by the figure on the Kilikian boss."

CHAPTER XI.

DECIPHERMENT OF THE HITTITE INSCRIPTIONS.

LIST OF CHARACTERS.

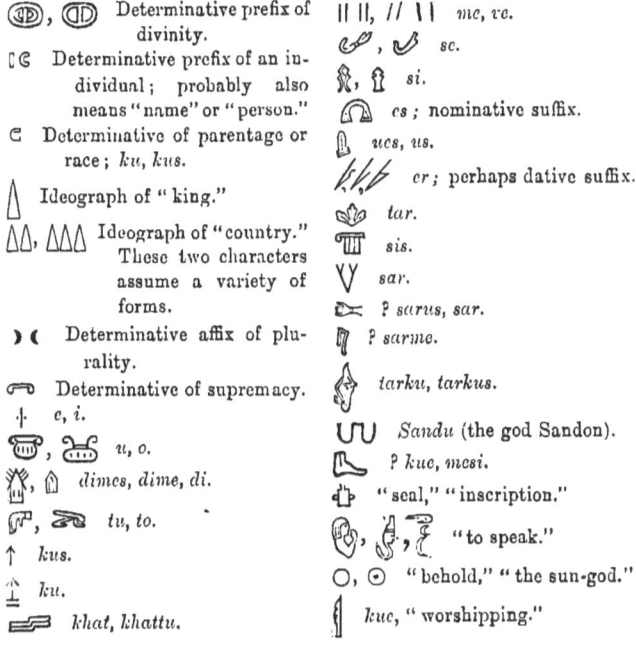

In Dr. Taylor's recently published work on "The Alphabet," the following comparative table of eight

Cypriote and Hittite characters is given, and certain phonetic values assigned to the Hittite characters upon my authority.[1]

HITTITE.		CYPRIOTE.	
o◌o ▫◌▫	i, e	)'(	yi
🯄	ka, ku	⇧	ka
𓐍 𓊽	te, to	六 入 F	to
▫▫	me, mo	[] ⊕	mo
🍃	se	Y 님	se
🯅	si	⇧	si
◌ 🯅	ti, di	↑	ti, di
▣	u	≋ ⩔	o

The history of the table is the following. About two years ago I presented a memoir to the Society of Biblical Archæology, in which I endeavoured to determine the powers of some of the Hittite hieroglyphics with the help of the bilingual inscription of Tarkondēmos (for which see the "Transactions of the Society of Biblical Archæology," vii. 2). Among the hieroglyphics were eight which I concluded denoted either simple vowels or single consonants, followed by single vowels. A few months afterwards, Dr. Taylor suggested

[1] Inserted by permission of Dr. Isaac Taylor and Messrs. Kegan Paul, Trench and Co.

to me that if I wished to test the truth of my theory of the origin of the Asianic or Cypriote syllabary from the Hittite system of writing, I ought to compare together those Cypriote and Hittite characters which, according to my conclusions, had the same phonetic values. I did so, and the results were most unexpected. In each of the eight cases, as will be seen from a glance at the table, the resemblance was almost perfect.

Now it will be asked by what process I had managed to assign values to these eight characters? In order to answer this question, however briefly, I must give in detail the several stages in the history of my attempt to decipher the Hittite texts. They do not, it is true, carry us very far; but this is not to be wondered at when we consider the small number and mutilated condition of the inscriptions at present at our disposal. And even a beginning in decipherment is better than no decipherment at all.

The bilingual inscription of Tarkondêmos in cuneiform and Hittite, gives us the values of two ideographs—the royal cap denoting "king," and the double mountain (which also appears as a triple mountain) denoting "country"—as well as the phonetic values of four characters. These are *tarku*, represented by the head of a goat; *timme* or *dime*, which I prefer to read *dime* on account of the Greek—δημος, *er* and *me*. Unfortunately, the Assyrian character expressing *me* has also the value of *ve*, though *me* is here its most probable value.

Now the three inscriptions from Carchemish contain a group of characters which occurs somewhat often in all of them, and, in the two of which the beginning is preserved, comes almost at the commencement of the first line. The group is also followed by the two ideographs of "king" and "country." It must therefore denote a proper name which, for the moment, we will write X. At the beginning of the inscriptions it would naturally be in the nominative case, and that this is actually the fact is rendered probable by the characters which precede it.

J. I. begins with a picture of a human head and arm with the hand pointing to the mouth, followed by the character —*me*, like four of the Hamath inscriptions which begin in the same way. This is evidently an ideographic representation of "speaking" or "saying," —*me* being the phonetic complement or final syllable of the word. In J. II. the place of the ideograph is taken by what, as Mr. Rylands pointed out to me, is a "hieratic" form of the character, more carefully drawn in J. III., lines 2, 4, 5, where it represents a face with a word, in the shape of a lozenge, proceeding out of it. The place of —*me* is also taken by a vase-shaped character which I conjecture to have a phonetic value, expressing the pronunciation of the word "he says." That —*me* was the suffix of the third person singular, may be gathered from the proper names Tarku-dí-me, Sanda-sar-me (King of Kilikia, B.C. 660), and Uas-sur-me (King of Tubal, B.C. 738).

THE HITTITE INSCRIPTIONS.

The Assyrian inscriptions show that Tarku or Tarkhu was the name of a god, and Sanda (also written Sandu) is plainly the sun-god Sandon, who, as Ed. Meyer has proved, was not the chief deity of Lydia, as is sometimes supposed, but of Kilikia. Hence the three proper names enumerated above will mean the gods Tarku(s), Sandon and Uas "do" or "are" so-and-so.

Let us now return to our proper name X. This is written with four characters in J. II. 1 and III. 2—the last character being the head of an ibex in the first instance, and of a goat in the second—with five characters in J. III. 3, and with six characters in J. I. 1, 2 and 4, 5. The first three characters are always the same; the last of them being the verbal suffix —*me*, and where the name is written with five or six characters, the fourth character is also the same.

In J. I. 1, where the name appears with six characters, its position at the beginning of the inscription and after the word "he says," indicates that it must be in the nominative case, and since the last character is one which occurs very frequently at the ends of groups of characters or words, the obvious inference is that it denotes the suffix of the nominative case. This inference is confirmed by the fact that it interchanges with two or three other characters of similarly frequent occurrence at the ends of words, as well as by the fact that two or more words occasionally follow one another, like noun and adjective, with this character attached to each of them.

What the termination of the nominative in Hittite proper names was, seems to be told us by the Assyrian and Egyptian texts, in which they constantly end in *s*. We may therefore provisionally assume that this character, which looks like a yoke, 🝆, had the value of *es*.

Now the bilingual inscription of Tarkondêmos has taught us that the goat's head had the value of *tarku*, which in the the nominative would be *tarkus*. Consequently, where it is replaced by two, or three, other characters (the word being in the nominative), we must give to these the values of *tar-ku-es* (J. I. 1, 2), *tar-ku-** (J. I. 4–5), and *tar-ku(s?)* (J. III. 3), the flower having the value of *tar*, the shadûf and cord, ◠̑, the value of *ku*, and the shadûf alone the value of *ku(s?)*, while the arm or glove found in J. I. 5, and used like *es* as a suffix, must, for the present, remain undetermined. This conclusion is verified by a coin of Tarsus, on which we find not only *t-r-z* in Aramaic letters and ΤΕΡΣΙ in Greek, but also the flower of the Hittite inscriptions.[1] The flower also symbolizes the name of a god at Boghaz Keui, who stands on the heads of two priests and *has a goat at his side*. A cuneiform inscription copied by Mr. W. M. Ramsay at Kaisarieh informs us that Tar was the name of a Kappadokian deity.

[1] Barclay V. Head: "The Coinage of Lydia and Persia," p. 45, and Plate III. 11.

That the shadûf without the cords, which I have provisionally transcribed *ku(s* ?), really had the value of *kus*, may be inferred in the following way. Three of the inscriptions from Hamath (H. I., II. and IV.) present the same text with only one or two variations. One of these variations comes at the end of the text, where the last character, the ideograph of king, is preceded in one instance by a group of characters, the last of which is the nominatival *es*, and in the other instance by a group which terminates with the cordless shadûf. The ideograph which follows them makes it probable that the two groups represent proper names, and we shall see presently that this probability is raised to a certainty by the fact that they are both compounds, the first elements of which are the names of Sandon and another god. I believe that I have found both names on the squeeze of the inscription taken by Dr. Gwyther at Merash.

The first explanation that strikes us of the interchange of these two proper names is that one is the actual name and the other a patronymic; and several facts go to show that *ku-s* is really a patronymic suffix. Thus in J. I. 2-3, the royal name X, with the nominative suffix (after the insertion of a title or two, the first of which is "king"), is followed by what must be a proper name, since it is preceded, as we shall see, by the determinative of an individual. This name terminates in *kus*, followed by *er* (as determined by the bilingual inscription; this *er* is shown by a comparison of passages to be a suffix). What is apparently another proper name comes after it, also terminating in *kus* and *er*. This name, which we will call Z, the second name being Y, is formed by a character which seems to be the same as that which is read *dime* on the boss of Tarkondêmos.

At all events, the same character, followed by the phonetic complement *me* and the nominative suffix -*es*, in the first line of an inscription copied by Mr. Boscawen at Carchemish, is defined by the words "the king of the country of . . . .," the word preceding it, which is unfortunately broken, being apparently the one I have shown to mean "he says." I see therefore no way of avoiding the conclusion that in J. I. the king Ta(?)-*-me-Tarkus gives the names of his father and grandfather, and that the inscription copied by Mr. Boscawen belongs to the grandfather, Z or Dimes.

The Hamath texts afford a further proof that -*kus* represents the patronymic suffix. Three of them begin with the word "he says ; " then comes a bar which must denote supremacy, since it is thrice (J. I. 2, 5 ; III. 3) placed over a man's head clad in the royal cap and followed by the ideograph of "king." Next we have what, as we shall see, is the determinative of an individual ; then a character which, for reasons to be given below, I read *tu* or *to*, then *me* (or *ve*), and lastly the nominatival *es*. This gives us the name Tumes or Tuves, with which it is tempting to compare that of Tou or Toi, the king of Hamath in the time of David.

Tumes is followed by another word also in the nominative, and that again by a group composed of an arm between two curious objects and the suffixes *ku* and *es*. This latter group occurs in a list of proper names in the inscription discovered by Mr. Ramsay at Bor (Tyana), line 2. It will be noticed that the suffix *kus-* or *ku-es* is usually accompanied by the small semicircle ☾, which I therefore conclude is the ideographic representative of sonship or origin. Sometimes this semicircle stands by itself without its phonetic exponent (as in the name first quoted from the inscription of Bor); in this case we must read it *ku* or *kus*.

The patronymic suffix, as might be expected, not only signified a man's parentage, but also the race from which he was sprung. In J. I. 1, and II. 1, the king of Carchemish is called king of a country, the name of which is represented by three lines to which I conjecturally give the value of *khattu*. As this character is followed by the nominatival suffix, it is clear that the Hittites often substituted an adjective for a genitive, saying, for example, "Carchemishian king" instead of "king of Carchemish." Now in J. III. 3, the king is called *khattu* (?)-*kus*, the ideograph of country being omitted, and this is immediately preceded by another word, which I conjecture to read "Carchemish," to which the suffix -*us* is also attached. The mark, ⊕, which comes between them, may express the conjunction "and."[1]

I have just noticed that the determinative prefix of "country" may be sometimes omitted. This is also the case with the determinative prefix of divinity. The meaning of this ideograph—which seems to be a degenerated form of the winged solar disk—is given us by the sculptures of Boghaz Keui, where it is prefixed to the names and symbols of the various deities whose figures are carved upon the rock. It is similarly prefixed to the name of a goddess at Eyuk.[2] But it is wanting before the name of the god Tarkus in the name of Tarku-dimes, and in J. III. 3, we have the names of three divinities placed side by side, each with the nominative suffix, but all without the determinative, though the third name represents a god at Boghaz Keui, who has the winged solar disk above his head and a curved staff in his right hand, while the first name is found with the determinative in the very next line of the inscription from Carchemish (J. III. 4).

So, again, the names of three divinities come together in J. III. 5, none of which have the determinative, though this is attached to the middle name in H. III. 1,

[1] The patronymic *kus* throws light on the name of the god Tarkus, which will be a patronymic of Tar, the name of another god, as we have seen above. It also explains the name of Sandakos whom Apollodòros makes a Kilikian hero. Sandakos will be "the son of Sandou" the Sungod.

[2] See "Trans. Soc. Bib. Arch.," vii. part 2, p. 258.

and the Aleppo text (see also J. V. 1). In the same way the determinative precedes the name of the god whose image is sculptured at Ibreez—as also in H. V. 3—but is omitted where this name forms the first element in that of the Hamathite king mentioned above (H. I. 3), as well as upon the Kouyunjik seals. From these facts we may conclude (1) that the determinative prefix of divinity was usually, if not always, omitted when a divine name entered into the composition of a proper name, and (2) that it might also be omitted when the divine name stood alone.

There is another determinative prefix which I think can be made out with certainty, and which can similarly be inserted or dropped at the pleasure of the scribe. This is the determinative of an individual, ꟼꓛ, the use of which is clearly indicated by the inscription of Tyana. Here it is not only prefixed to the two royal names of son and father, with which the inscription begins, but also to what is evidently a series of proper names, since some of them have the patronymic suffix, while one of them, as I have already observed, is a name that occurs in the Hamathite texts (H. I. 1, II. 1, IV. 1). It is represented by the arm between two objects, followed by the patronymic. In J. I. the name of king X is once written with the determinative (line 4), and the name of king Y twice (lines 2, 3). Elsewhere the names appear without it, like the name of king Z (Dimes), which, however, is written with it in the inscription copied by Mr.

Boscawen. The ideograph bears a most remarkable resemblance to the Egyptian hieroglyphic which denotes the "half" of a royal cartouche, and I believe I have found cases in which it stands by itself in the sense of " person " or name."

The ideograph of plurality is, I think, the double semicircle)(, which is attached as a determinative affix to the sign for "country," in H. I. 2, II. 2, IV. 2 (where it is followed by a phonetic complement; cf. III. 2). In J. III. 3 the ideograph is attached to the verb " to speak," and here it is preceded both by the name of king X, and also by another name which occurs again in line 5, but this time without the determinative prefix. From J. II. 1, where the *mutual* action of shaking hands is represented, it would appear that *me* was the suffix of the third person plural as well as of the third person singular.

I must now turn to the name of a deity which is mentioned both at Ibreez (line 1) and at Hamath (H. V. 3). At Ibreez a king is represented in the act of adoring a god, and since the inscription accompanying the sculpture contains the name of only one divinity —that is, only once exhibits the determinative prefix of a deity—it is plain that this name must represent the god. This is rendered still more plain by the fact that the snake-like ideograph of which the name consists is really the ornament of the god's head-dress. Now we know what the name of this god was. He is figured with the same attributes on the coins of Tarsus, and was in fact the Kilikian Baal, whose native name has been shown by Ed. Meyer to have been Sandôn or Sandan.[1] The name of the god, though without the determinative, forms the first part of the royal name which occurs on the Kouyunjik seals. In one example the name ends with the nominative suffix, preceded by *me*, between which and the name of Sandon comes a character of unknown sound. It is not difficult to determine who this prince Sandon-*-me-es must have been. The seals were deposited in the record chamber of Assur-bani-pal, and seem to have once been attached to documents in the shape of contracts.

Now there were two princes of eastern Asia Minor, and two princes only, so far as we know, with whom Assur-bani-pal came into contact. These were Mugallu king of Tubal, and Sanda-sarme king of Kilikia. Sanda-sarme not only came to Nineveh himself, but his daughter was added to Assur-bani-pal's harem.

As we know from a monument discovered by Langlois that the Hittite mode of writing was used in Kilikia, it is difficult not to conjecture that some at least of the Kouyunjik seals belong to the marriage-contract of Sanda-sarme's daughter. It is equally difficult not to conclude that the Sanda-*-me(s) of the seals is the Sanda-sarme of the Assyrian inscriptions. This will

---

[1] I feel uncertain whether the name was pronounced Sanda or Sandu in Kilikian. In the inscriptions of Assur-bani-pal mention is made, not only of Sanda-sarme, but also of Sandu-arri, and the Greek writers have Sandan and Sanda-kos as well as Sandon.

give us the phonetic value of the character which follows the name of Sandon, and it is interesting to observe that the same proper name is found in the inscription of Tyana (line 3).

A similar name occurs on one of M. Schlumberger's seals, the character *sar* being here replaced by the arm, which may have the same value. I believe that the name of Sanda-sarme also occurs in the genitive case on certain of the Kouyunjik seals, where it is preceded by what is evidently a picture of a writing-tablet, with the two strings by which it was suspended. The character seems therefore to mean "seal;" it is followed by the name of Sandon, and that again by two characters, one of which looks like a basket, while the other is a shepherd's crook.

The basket is of very common occurrence in the inscriptions, so common, indeed, as to suggest that it represents a vowel. This is confirmed by our finding it sometimes omitted and sometimes inserted in the same word. Thus a word which from its position appears to signify "worshipping" begins simply with *ku* in the Ibreez inscription, but with *ku* followed by the basket in H. V. 2, 3. I therefore assign to the basket the value of *u* or *o*. Hence on the Kouyunjik seals *u* will be the phonetic complement of *Sand-u*, the Greek Sandôn.

Equally common, and frequently associated with *u*, is another character, ▫╟▫, to which I give the value of *e* or *i*, for the following reasons. If we compare two forms of the word just mentioned, which are found in H. III. 1, and V. 3, we shall see that *ku-me* (or *ku-ve*) takes the place of *ku-u-e*. In H. V. 1, again, the patronymic suffix, which is written *ku-es* in H. I. 1, is written *ku-e-es*. Like *u*, too, *e* is sometimes inserted and sometimes omitted in the same word. Consequently the word which I render "worshipping" must be read *kûe, kumeku* or rather *kuveku* being, I believe, the first person singular.

There are two other characters of which, I think, we may determine the phonetic values. The name of king Y is written with the horizontal arm (? *sar* or *sarus*) in J. I. 2, with the uplifted arm followed by *u-es* in J. I. 3, with the uplifted arm followed by the knotted cord, 🪢, in J. I. 3, and by the sacred tree (a god's symbol, apparently) followed by the knotted cord in J. I. 5. It follows from this that the knotted cord was pronounced *ues* or *us*. In J. I. 3, moreover, the name of king Z is once written Dime(s)-kus-er (where *er* is perhaps the suffix of the dative), and once Dime(s)-ku-*-er, the glove which I have denoted by an asterisk intervening between *ku* and *er*. It must therefore have the value of *se*.

I now pass on to one or two characters for which I would propose phonetic values with greater hesitation. I have already noticed that the kings of Carchemish call themselves kings of "the country III.," the numeral III. being apparently the ideographic representative of "Hittites."

In J. III. 2, however, this ideographic mode of representing the name of the country is replaced by two characters, which seem to be phonetic, followed by the suffix *se-e-se*, or *-sese*. Now at Hamath the territorial name is always expressed in this phonetic fashion. Here we have (H. I. 2) *x-y-si-es*, (H. II. 2) *x-y-sis*, and (H. IV. 2) *x-sis*. Comparing these three ways of writing the name, we should have *khattu* or *khat* for *x* and *tu* or *to* for *y*. I make the vowel of the second character *u*, on account of the proper name Khattu-khi found on the Assyrian monuments. Since the people of Carchemish were called Hittites by all their neighbours, whether Egyptian, Assyrian, Hebrew or Vannic, it is probable that this was also the name by which they called themselves.[1]

Two of M. Schlumberger's seals contain a name which consists of two characters, the first of which is the hieratic form of the ideograph of "speaking," while the second is *er*. Then comes the title "king of the country III." I am inclined to compare the name with that of Sangara, the king of Carchemish, who is mentioned by Shalmaneser II. If this comparison is right, the word "to speak" will have been pronounced *sanga*. But the comparison is of course very doubtful,

---

[1] An ideograph, the meaning of which is pretty clear, though I can suggest no phonetic reading for it, is the solar disk. This stands at the beginning of the inscription of Merash, and is followed by the ideograph of " king " and a proper name. It can hardly, therefore, have any other signification than "behold." In J. III. 5, it is preceded by the determinative of divinity and must here, accordingly, denote the Sun-god.

and the Egyptian monuments mention other Hittite princes—Mauthaner, Sapzar—whose names terminated in *er* or *ar*.

The end of a paragraph was indicated by a small oblique line, as I pointed out, in 1882, in the "Transactions of the Society of Biblical Archæology" (vii. 1, p. 301). Good examples of its use occur in J. III., as well as in the first line of H. I. and II., and it is attached to the final *e* of one of M. Schlumberger's seals and to the final *me* of the boss of Tarkondêmos. A similar line indicates the end of a Kappadokian cuneiform inscription, copied at Kaisariyeh by Mr. Ramsay.

As will have been seen from the foregoing investigation, the Hittite system of writing resembled that of the Egyptians or of the Assyrians; or, in fact, of any people which employed hieroglyphics. The writing was partly ideographic, partly phonetic, and made use of determinatives. The phonetic characters, as in Egyptian or Assyrian, sometimes represented a monosyllable, sometimes a dissyllable, sometimes both. Thus ◊ may be ideographically read *Dimes* with the nominative suffix, but more usually it would represent the dissyllabic *dime*. At times, however, the phonetic complement *me* might be added, and in this case it would read *di*. The ideographs seem to be attached to the phonetic characters which represent the sound of the word they express almost as often as in Egyptian, though of course they may also stand alone without

o

any phonetic complement, or with only the grammatical suffixes expressed.

Thus at Ibreez and in H. V. 2, the word *kue* is written without any determinative; in H, III. 1 and V. 3, the ideograph of a man's profile and neck is added; and in H. IV. 4 this ideograph stands alone without the phonetic *ku*. These determinative ideographs must be distinguished from those which, as in Egyptian, may be added to a phonetically written word, because they have the same sound (though not the same meaning) as the latter.

Thus in J. III. 4, the double boot is evidently the determinative of a word signifying "to go," of which *tar* (or with its suffixes *tar-kue*) is the phonetic equivalent. On the other hand, the single boot must be appended to the word *kue* in J. III. 4, merely because it had the same pronunciation.[1]

The phonetic and determinative ideographs may be expected to occur together, and I fancy that we have an example of this at Ibreez. Here the figure of a musical instrument is attached to the phonetic characters *se-tu*, the signification of which is defined by the addition of an arm in the attitude of offering. As in other hieroglyphic scripts, moreover, the Hittite characters ought to be polyphonous, but I have as yet met with only one possible case of this. We have just

---

[1] (*Note, Second Edition.*) I now see, however, that the two words in this line must be different ways of writing the same word, the animal's head being that of a goat not of an ox. Hence they will be *tarku-ku-u-e* and *tar-*KU*-u-e*, with the double boot attached to both (1885).—A. H. S.

seen that the boot seems to have the value of *kûe*. But a comparison of a proper name in J. II. 3, 8, with its patronymic in J. II. 7 and IV. 4, goes to show that it had also the value of *mesi*.

The Hittite writing is always boustrophedon, and the first line reads from right to left except in the case of the first inscription at Ibreez, which is made to proceed from the head of the deity, and accordingly runs from left to right. A word does not end with a line, and the lines read from the direction towards which the characters look. All known Hittite inscriptions, with the exception of those of Tyana (Bor) and a bowl from Babylon, are in relief.

The forms of the characters vary very much, not only on monuments coming from different localities, but even on those of the same locality and the same age. We have only to compare the three monuments of king Ta(?)-me-Tarkus from Carchemish to discover this. Hence the resemblance of the forms of the characters in the cartouche near the image of "Niobê" on Mount Sipylos in Lydia to those found at Carchemish is very striking, and makes it probable that those who sculptured the "Niobê" were conquerors from Carchemish.

The inscriptions of Hamath show us in several instances what may be termed hieratic forms. Thus the character *tu*, which has the form of a hand in J. I. 4, J. II. 6, 7, and J. III. 2, 4, has become unrecognizable in H. I. 2, 3, 4, &c.; and the form of *si* presents a similar difference in J. III. 5 and H, I. 3.

The same character may vary in shape, however, even in the same inscription; in J. I. 4, for instance, the bird resembles an eagle (as in J. III. 1, 5), whereas in line 2 it is more like a dove, and in J. II. 3 it looks like a duck. A good deal of latitude, in fact, was left to the taste or skill of the engraver; thus the character *er*, which Mr. Rylands believes to represent the bent leg of a doe, is depicted on the boss of Tarkondêmos with hair upon it, like the hair on the leg of Tarkondêmos himself; everywhere else this detail is omitted.

By way of conclusion I will give tentative renderings of one or two of the inscriptions, in so far, at least, as the method of decipherment I have been explaining will enable us to make them out. The historical inferences to be derived from these translations must be left for others to draw. The inscription copied at Ibreez by Mr. Ramsay between the head and arm of the principal figure is as follows :—

"Worshipper of the god Sandon, the great (god), the twice-mighty (prince) Eu .. es offers vegetable offerings of grapes."

The name of the king, which occurs again in the first and second lines of the second inscription of Ibreez, is also the name of the king to whom the inscription of Tyana belongs. Here the name is preceded by the determinative prefix, and he is called "the son of Setueses (or Sedu-eses) the king of the Kuans." The word *tar-e* at Ibreez seems to mean "vegetables," *tar* being the picture of a flower, and we may gather from the sculpture that *es* here signifies " a bunch of grapes."

The three short inscriptions of Hamath (II. I., II. and III.) may be rendered thus :—" Says the prince : Tuves (? Tou) .... *erses*, the son of .... king of the country of Ereku . . (?) the supreme (?) king of countries : .... the king of the land of the Hittites, the powerful, ... ruler, ... (the son of Sandusetue (?)) the king." In H. V. the name of Tuves is omitted.

J. II. commences with the words : " Says Ta (?) . . . me-Tarkus the king of the bull country, the king of the land of the Hittites : the goddess of Carchemish has caused an alliance," between himself and Mesi and another person, whose son E .... is mentioned in lines 5 and 8.

Such attempts at translation are no doubt very meagre and unsatisfactory : but if the method pursued in the preceding pages is a sound one, they stand at all events on a firm foundation, and with the help of fresh materials may lead on to more important results. It must not be forgotten that the inscriptions we possess at present are but few and mutilated, and we must not, therefore, expect our endeavours to decipher them to be more than a beginning. But in this, as in so many things else, the beginning is half the whole.

A. H. SAYCE.

THE BABYLON BOWL.

The inscription on the bowl found at Babylon is interesting not only on account of the fact that it is incised but also because of the hieratic forms of the characters occurring on it. Thus ∩ can scarcely be anything else than the yoke, which I read *es*; while the eagle has the exceedingly degenerated form discovered by Mr. Rylands on a gem from Kouyunjik, and published by him in the "Proceedings of the Soc. of Biblical Archæology," May 6, 1884 (p. 228). The line-divider (see p. 184) indicates that the inscription ends just after the two ideographs ᴅᛁ ᴅᛁ (*ni*), which I interpret "persons," and it is again used to mark off what I believe to be a territorial title, since it consists of four characters, the last of which is the cypher III, which elsewhere seems to denote "Hittite." As three deities are mentioned, one of them being the deity whose name appears on the monuments of Carchemish, and whom I believe to be Atys, as well as certain individuals whose names are preceded by the determinative, the inscription appears to record the dedication of the bowl to the gods Sandon, Atys, and another divinity. The second character of the inscription is probably a picture of a bowl. The dedicators, like the deities, are three in number; hence, perhaps the cypher III to which I have drawn attention.

A. H. SAYCE.

APPENDIX I.

(See pp. 7, 126.)

THE following is the passage in the Odyssey referred to by Mr. Gladstone :—

Πάντας δ' οὐκ ἂν ἐγὼ μυθήσομαι οὐδ' ὀνομήνω,
ὅσσον λαὸν ἔπεφνεν ἀμύνων Ἀργείοισιν,
ἀλλ' οἷον τὸν Τηλεφίδην κατενήρατο χαλκῷ,
ἥρω' Εὐρύπυλον· πολλοὶ δ' ἀμφ' οὐτὸν ἑταῖροι
Κήτειοι κτείνοντο γυναίων εἵνεκα δώρων·
κεῖνον δὴ κάλλιστον ἴδον, μετὰ Μέμνονα δῖον.
Od. xi. 516–521.

"The time would fail should I in order tell
What foes were vanquished, and what numbers fell;
How lost through love, Eurypylus was slain,
And round him bled his bold Cetaen[1] train.
To Troy no hero came of nobler line,
Or if of nobler, Memnon, it was thine."—POPE.

I was gratified by receiving Mr. Gladstone's permission to publish the following letter not only because of his general agreement with my conclusions, but also on account of the fresh light which he had shed on

[1] Κήτειοι or Hittite.

the subject. Besides, it is only fair that every explorer should have credit for his discoveries.

LETTER FROM THE RIGHT HON. W. E. GLADSTONE.

"REV. AND DEAR SIR,—I thank you very much for your kind gift. The first announcement of the work you have produced filled me with a lively interest, for it belonged to a region on the borders of which I have long, though but intermittently, laboured. Your account of the local extension of Hittite influence is in complete conformity with the idea which conceives them as within the circle of possible Trojan alliances. I may add to the suggestion which I first published, in fear and trembling, that the manner of the mention in Homer is completely in acccord with your doctrines as to the greatness of the Hittites. (1) Because the slaughter of their chief seems to be the crowning exploit that had been performed by the son of Achilles. 'I will not,' says Odusseus, 'name all that he slew, but only the hero Eurupulos.' (2) Because the Keteioi are named without epithet, description, or indication, which accords with the idea of their being a famous and well-known race.

"The gradual building up of primitive history is, in my eyes, to the full as interesting and as fruitful a process as the extension of physical sciences, which attracts a thousand-fold more attention.

"I remain, Rev. and dear sir, faithfully yours,

"W. E. GLADSTONE."

Soon after the publication of this letter, a writer in the *St. James's Gazette*, Oct. 21, 1884, impugned Mr. Gladstone's conclusion on philological grounds. He asserted that the identification of the Keteioi of Homer with the Hittites of the Bible was a blunder, because, he said, "the Greek *Kappa* is the Semitic *Koph*, and not the *Cheth* which is the first letter of the word Heth." The same argument has since been advanced in the *Church Quarterly*, for July, in an Article for which the Rev. C. J. Ball, of Lincoln's Inn, takes credit.

The following reply, which appeared in the *St. James's Gazette*, Oct. 27, 1884, effectually disposes, I think, of this philological objection:—

"SIR,—My attention has just been called to a paragraph in your issue of the 21st, in which your correspondent criticises a suggestion made by Mr. Gladstone with reference to my book 'The Empire of the Hittites.'

"Your correspondent says:—

"'Mr. Gladstone now patronizes the Hittites, and identifies them with the Homeric Keteioi. Many Englishmen will conclude that since Mr. Gladstone says so, it must be true. But what is the evidence? The Greek *Kappa* is the Semitic *Koph*, and not the *Cheth* which is the first letter of the word Heth.'

"This is only true as regards what I may call Semiticized Greek. It is not true as regards

Hellenized Greek. For example, the word Haran, the first letter of which is *Cheth*, is rendered Charran in the Septuagint, the New Testament, and in Josephus (Semiticized Greek). It is rendered, however, Karrai, first letter *Kappa* by Dion Cass., xxxvii. 5, Strabo, xvi. 747, and other Greek writers beyond Semitic influence; and I have before me an Imperial Greek coin on which the name is spelled in the same manner.

"It would thus appear that Mr. Gladstone's suggestion is in perfect accordance with the analogy of Greek usage outside the range of Semitic influence.

"I am, sir, your obedient servant,

"W. WRIGHT.

APPENDIX II.

(See p. 80.)

PERHAPS the part of my book around which controversy has been keenest is that which relates to the language of the Hittites. When I wrote, the balance of opinion was in favour of the non-Semitic character of the language, and that view continues to gain acceptance. Mr. Poole tells me he no longer adheres to the opinion to which I referred on p. 80. There are scholars, however, whose views are deserving of respectful consideration, who still believe that the language of the Hittites was Semitic. M. Halévy, for instance, writes me, " Pour ma part, je tiendrai les Hittites pour des Semites, jusque ce qu'on m'ait donné la preuve du contraire."

The Karnak list of " the allied Kings of Kheta " in the time of Thothmes III. has been re-examined by the late M. Lenormant, M. Golenischeff, M. Wiedemann and other Egyptologists, and the conclusion arrived at is that a very small proportion of the names are Semitic.

The Rev. Henry George Tomkins presented to the

Society of Biblical Archæology, at the meeting in June last, the result of a very painstaking examination of the same list with the view of throwing "Some light on the topography of Hittite land." Mr. Tomkins ventures to add a few more names to those in the list considered Semitic, but he comes to the conclusion that " more than four-fifths of the entire list of names" are "to be classed as non-Semitic." With this concensus of opinion I agree. At the same time it is well, I think, to remember that the Egyptian dress may conceal the real character of some of the Hittite names, and it may happen that further discovery may lead to further light. It is also possible that a map of the land of the Hittites may yet be discovered which will lead to the certain identification of many places with respect to which we can only now guess vaguely. All the names of Hittites in the Hebrew Scriptures appear in Semitic guise. Hittites with unpronounceable names on joining the Semites would assume or receive Semitic names. Others might have their names Semiticised. Both processes go on side by side in Damascus to-day. Troublesome foreign names are replaced by such names as Abdulla, servant of Allah, or Abu Hanna, father of John, or if they are at all of Semitic cast they are shaped and fashioned to pass current as genuine Semitic names.

On meeting you for the first time an Arab commences the process of kneading your name into his own mould. If the name is unmanageable he finds out your son's name, and calls you Abu Yakoub,—"father of James," or "father of a red beard." But if your name can be Semiticised he will Semiticise it. This leads sometimes to awkward results. An eminent American friend of mine called Bliss had his name sometimes Semiticised into *Iblis*, and another gentleman called Dennis had his name sometimes Semiticised into Danas, which means *dirt.* The same process goes on throughout Western Asia, and I have just been obliged to change the spelling of a Leipsic printer's name on a Persian Testament, because it was capable of being Persianized so as to express a vile meaning. Such instances are too common to require enumeration, and the process of acclimatizing foreign words and restamping them so as to fit them for common currency,[1] is not confined to modern times. I content myself with these general remarks, simply adding that confident dogmatism as to the language is not warranted by the present state of our knowledge. Egyptologists, after a hundred years' study of the hieroglyphics, are not yet agreed as to the family of languages to which the Egyptian belongs.

[1] Good illustrations are the well-known Abu Simbel, the "Father of a Sickle," from Psam-polis, the "City of Psam," or the English word Beefeater, which is generally supposed to be from "Beauffetier," or such places as Shotover, in Oxfordshire, from *Chateau Vert.* Such instances of *Volks Etymologie* are common to all languages.

APPENDIX III.

(See p. 90.)

(*The Academy*, March 28, 1885.)

EMPIRE OF THE HITTITES.

TENDRING RECTORY, COLCHESTER,
March 21, 1885.

"WITH some reluctance I ask leave to register a protest in the *Academy* against the unprovoked aggressions of which I have been the victim in Mr. Wright's 'Empire of the Hittites.' I had hoped that a reputation for caution and general accuracy would have neutralized the effect of these aggressive remarks from a new writer; but I find that Mr. Wright's attacks have in some quarters been cited to my disadvantage. Reviewers to whom the Hittites are strange folk greedily seize on personalities like these to fill up their space. I have just received from America a number of critico-theological magazines, in which one of the damaging sentences is quoted with (it is true) a very full context and no comments. As I learn that a new edition of 'The Empire of the Hittites' is expected, may I publicly express the hope that all the author's references to my article 'Hittites' in the ' Encyclopædia Britannica' (which is by no means diametrically opposed to his own views) may be omitted ? Mr. Wright's opinions on Old Testament criticism differ very widely from my own; but this gives him no just cause for stigmatizing the critical views expressed in my article as a 'survival,' or for the repeated slurs cast upon my character as a scholar.

"No other course than that which I now adopt is open to me, since a friendly expostulation after a similar attack in the *British Quarterly Review* produced no satisfactory result.

" May I add, as a contribution to the general subject, that I am not aware of any material point which I have to retract in my article. That Mr. Wright will have to recall some of his statements and hypotheses, seems at present more probable than that I shall have to change my own view of the Hittites in Genesis.

" T. K. CHEYNE."

(*The Academy*, April 18, 1885.)

LONDON, *April* 3, 1885.

" Dr. Cheyne's note calls for a reply from me. He has several times recently referred publicly to what he calls his 'friendly expostulation' with reference to my article in the *British Quarterly*. That 'friendly expostulation' was a private contemptuous letter to the editor, in which he professed to speak of me, *leniently*, as an aged American missionary living at a distance from centres of thought and study. And he added—

'All American scholars still think the Bible is equally accurate in a full historical sense throughout.'

" He admitted that his own information was not up to date, but he added—

"'A fair and generous writer would, I think, have added to his reference a remark that Mr. Cheyne could not have been acquainted with the latest discoveries, vol. xii. of the *Encyclopædia Britannica* having been issued in March 15th, 1881, with a notice that it had been somewhat delayed. He would also have mentioned that the article 'Hittites' came forth in the list of articles, and was therefore necessarily written long before publication (in fact, upwards of a year).'

"This 'friendly expostulation,' which was certainly not intended for my eyes, reached me through the generous kindness of the editor. By the same medium, my reply, a portion of which was as follows, reached Mr. Cheyne:

"'Mr. Cheyne thinks that had I been fair and generous I would have given a long account of how his article appeared in the *Encyclopædia Britannica* to account for his ignorance. I had no right to assume that he was ignorant. I thought that when Mr. Cheyne, as a clergyman and commentator, assailed the accuracy of a Bible statement, he must have come to his conclusions with care. And I could only assume that when he published his views in the *Encyclopædia Britannica* he would have courage to stand by his statements. But is Mr. Cheyne now prepared to give this explanation on his own behalf? He would not give Moses and the prophets the benefit of the doubt, where he did not know. Will he recant and rectify his rash statements now that I have drawn his attention to a stone? Will he publish a note in a future volume of the *Encyclopædia Britannica*, stating that he has changed his mind as to the accuracy of the Bible with reference to the Hittites? I shall be happy to add Mr. Cheyne's explanations in the reprint of my article.

"'I know you will excuse me if I take little notice of Mr. Cheyne's personalities. It is not a very high style of argument to state, as *major prem.*—'*All American scholars still think that the Bible is equally accurate in a full historical sense throughout*,' and then to assume [incorrectly] that I am an ancient American missionary living in some benighted place. It is curious that notwithstanding my disadvantages he does not challenge a single fact which I have stated.

"'Surely it would be an equally fair and generous method for Mr. Cheyne to treat his statements and mine on their merits without these suppositions. And let me also add that it would be both fair and generous to admit that the Bible is true until it is proved false. It is not fair and it is not scientific to scatter doubts where you are simply ignorant.

"'Need I say that I have not the shadow of ill-feeling towards Mr. Cheyne. I shall be glad to meet him, or to correspond with him, but I shall always defend an assailed Bible when I can do so.'

"I trust Dr. Cheyne will excuse me for quoting somewhat extensively from a correspondence to which he is in the habit of referring, especially as the quotations meet pretty fully the assertions and assumptions in his present letter.

"He is good enough to say my views are 'by no means diametrically opposed to his own,' but he thinks his 'reputation for caution and general accuracy,' should in some *à priori* way neutralize my views when they have the misfortune to differ from his.

"His 'contribution to the general subject' consists of a boast and a prediction. The boast is 'I am not aware of any material point which I have to retract in my article.' How, then, was I *unfair* and *ungenerous* for not apologizing for the defects of his article? The prediction is that it seems more probable that I shall have to withdraw my statements than that he will have to change his views of the 'Hittites of Genesis.' Now, unless this question is settled in Dr. Cheyne's *à priori* way, it seems that probabilities point the other way. And, indeed, as appears above, Dr. Cheyne saw reason more than two years ago to modify his views with regard to the 'Hittites of Genesis.'

"Dr. Cheyne is pleased to contrast his principles of Old Testament criticism with mine, of course without knowing what mine are. But on this point there need be no mystery. For the purposes of my book it is enough to assume that the Bible is a venerable old document which professes to deal with certain facts. These facts I assume to be true until I have reason to doubt them, and on this principle I welcome every discovery and scrap of genuine evidence which add to the reasonable probability of the statements in the Bible.

"The *Saturday Review*, referring to the point at issue

between Dr. Cheyne and me, fitly sums up the case thus:

"'Granting that the sacred writers were unscrupulous, it would still be impossible to imagine why they should fill their early records with the most matter-of-fact references to a purely imaginary people. There is no nonsense that the professors of the Higher Criticism will not talk.'

"I have nothing to do with Dr. Cheyne personally. But Dr. Cheyne's articles in the *Encyclopædia Britannica* are public property, and he has no right to demand that I shall omit all references to his assertions. I venture to say that such a demand was never made before by an author. Why should he make such a request, seeing he has nothing to alter? It has been my aim not to misrepresent Dr. Cheyne's statements, and in the second edition of my book, now in the press, I have softened a few phrases which I feared might give pain; but until he formally withdraws certain assertions discrediting Bible narratives I shall consider it my duty to confront his assertions by the ascertained facts of modern research.

"WILLIAM WRIGHT."

(*The Academy*, April 25, 1885.)

TENDRING RECTORY, COLCHESTER,
April 20, 1885.

"I willingly accept Dr. Wright's concession, which though insufficient, is all, I suppose, that his point of view allows him to make. I wish he would also mention that, though I do not 'recant,' my objection is not, and never has been, to supporting the statements of a Biblical writer by sound archæological evidence, but to the mixing up of statements in the Book of Genesis with statements in the Book of Kings. I am very sorry that he commits himself in his reply to a most inaccurate sentence from another weekly paper. No one would guess from Dr. Wright's letter that the Book (not Books) of Kings was quite distinct from the Book of Genesis, and I have fully ratified the agreement of the former with recent archæological discoveries. He has quite unintentionally done me (as well as my cause) an injury against which I have protested and still do protest. If I have been unfair or even uncharitable to him I apologize. There were certainly, however, charitable things in that 'expostulation' (the substance of which was, of course, meant for Dr. Wright); one pathetic appeal I well remember; and was it really uncharitable to acccount for the vehement tone of the article referred to on the assumption of the author's different nationality? It was quite otherwise meant. If Dr. Wright is not an enemy of that many-sided criticism of Old Testament writings, which I have, without many helpers, most inadequately tried to promote, I can only rejoice. But he still tells us that he has written on the assumption that 'the Bible is a venerable old document which professes to deal with certain facts.' To me this seems a bold historical heresy. Would it not promote a better understanding between writers of different schools if we all agreed to give up the expressions 'Hittites' (in the present connexion) and 'Bible,' substituting (with Mr. Hyde Clarke) 'Kheta' for the one and 'Scriptures' for the other? Too great a readiness to adopt Anglo-Biblical forms of names is most inconvenient; and as for 'Bible,' the linguistic misconception involved in the word has long since been pointed out. And here I beg leave to drop the subject. "T. K. CHEYNE."

"P.S.—I much wish that Dr. Wright had not printed one particular sentence from my 'expostulation,' that relative to '*all* American scholars.' Three years ago I had only heard of American scholars who held opinions similar to Dr. Wright's; now I know that trained American scholars—friendly if not actually committed to historical criticism—were already on their way back from Germany, and that a sense is growing up in America of the reconcileableness of critical freedom with a warm love for the contents of the Christian revelation. This growing variety of opinion in America, had I known of it, would have forbidden me to offer that excuse for Dr. Wright, which he, much to my regret, has viewed as an insult."

(*The Academy*, May 2, 1885.)

LONDON, *April* 27, 1885.

"In the midst of much that is incoherent in Dr. Cheyne's letter he has not made very clear his attitude *pro tem.* to the Bible. My assumption that 'the Bible is a venerable old document which professes to deal with facts' he declares to be 'a bold historical heresy.' The assumption is one which no scientific man, whether he believed in the Bible or not, would challenge. For the purposes of my book it was unnecessary to assume any higher authority for the Bible than that accorded to any other venerable book. I thought I should be here on common ground with Dr. Cheyne. I did not even assume that the Bible *deals* with facts, but only that it *professes* to deal with facts. Is it this lowly and self-evident assumption that Dr. Cheyne stigmatizes as 'bold historical heresy?' Or is it simply the word 'document' instead of documents that Dr. Cheyne makes so much of? He speaks of the 'seventy tablets' of Sargon as a 'venerable document,' and he would hardly call it heresy to speak in the same convenient way of the collection of books which make up the Bible. If this should be his meaning I am quite willing to use 'collection of documents,' or any similar phrase, but without changing my position in any other way.

"A few secondary matters in Dr. Cheyne's letter require correction. He begins by accepting my 'concession.' I am not aware that I have made any concession, or that I can make any concession consistently with loyalty to facts.

"He says: 'No one would guess from Dr. Wright's letter that the Book (not Books) of Kings was quite distinct from the Book of Genesis.' I have made no reference in my letter to either Book or Books of Kings. Does Dr. Cheyne's theory permit him to annotate without consulting his text?

"I am not sure if Dr. Cheyne still labours under the impression that I am an American. He thinks it was not uncharitable to account for my criticism 'on the assumption of the author's different nationality.' It is my privilege to know a number of American scholars who, with firm loyalty to the Bible, advocate as I do the fullest critical freedom; and I think Dr. Cheyne would act more charitably if he conceded ordinary morality to scholars of every nationality.

"I notice with pleasure the increase of courtesy in Dr. Cheyne's style, and I think it is to be regretted that he considered it necessary to import personal matters into this controversy, or to raise the absurd cry of 'heresy.'

"Having said so much, I think the time has come for closing this controversy. Dr. Cheyne admits that the references to the Hittites in the Book of Kings are in accordance with 'recent archæological discoveries.' He wishes me to mention that he does not object to support 'the statements of a Biblical writer by sound archæological evidence.' He admits that the Kheta of the Egyptian inscriptions, the Khatti of the Assyrian, and the Hittites of the Bible are the same people. He admits that Hittite influence 'extended even into Asia Minor.' He considers it proved 'that the Hittites penetrated through the Eastern barrier formed by the Taurus range,' and he recognises evidence of the extension of their power to the shores of the Ægean. He is favourable to the hypothesis that the Hittites were the early civilizers of Asia Minor, and he considers them non-Semitic, and the authors of the Hittite inscriptions.

"It would thus seem that we are agreed on all points but one, namely, the accuracy of the account of the Hittites in the Book of Genesis. On this point there should no longer be any difference between us. Dr. Cheyne admits *publicly*, 'that a branch of the Kheta may once have existed in Palestine;' but he adds, 'unfortunately there is no historical evidence that it did so.' Since he wrote these words, as I have already pointed out, Dr. Cheyne admitted *privately*, that he had reconsidered the question, and I cannot understand why his full recognition should be any longer withheld from a cause which his own industry has done so much to promote.

"The new edition of my book is delayed by the preparation of additional plates of new inscriptions and sculptures, but I shall not regret the delay if thereby I may be able to add Dr. Cheyne's maturer conclusions.

"WILLIAM WRIGHT."

The correspondence ends here, and Dr. Cheyne has not, as far as I am aware, publicly withdrawn or modified any of his statements regarding the Hittites of the Book of Genesis. In one of his letters he wishes me to state his view on a certain point, but as a passage generally suffers in being detached from its context, I have judged it safest to reproduce the entire correspondence, and I sincerely hope that Dr. Cheyne will not complain of injury to himself and his cause by the reproduction of his own words.

APPENDIX IV.

WIDTH BETWEEN THE LINES OF THE INSCRIPTIONS FROM HAMATH, JERABIS, ETC.

By W. H. RYLANDS.

N.B.—Where fragments are given the widest existing portion of a line has been measured.

H. I. (Pl. I.) $4\frac{1}{4}$ and $4\frac{1}{2}$ inches.
H. II. (Pl. I.) $4\frac{1}{2}$ and $4\frac{3}{4}$,,
H. III. (Pl. II.) $4\frac{1}{4}$ inches.
H. IV. (Pl. III.) $4\frac{1}{2}$ and $4\frac{3}{4}$ inches.
H. V. (Pl. IV.) $4\frac{1}{4}$ inches.
J. I. (Pl. IX.) 5 to $5\frac{1}{4}$ inches.
J. II. (Pl. X.) 4 to $4\frac{1}{2}$,,
J. III. (Pl. XI.) 4 to $4\frac{1}{2}$,,
J. IV. (Pl. XII.) Fig. 4, 4 to $4\frac{1}{2}$ inches.
J. V. (Pl. XIII.) Figs. 1 and 2, 5 and $5\frac{1}{4}$ inches.
,, ,, Fig. 3, $5\frac{1}{4}$ inches.
,, ,, Fig. 4, 5 inches.
J. VI. (Pl. XIV.) Fig. 4, $4\frac{1}{4}$ inches.
,, (Pl. XIX.) Fig. 1, 23 in. high, and about 18 in. wide.

APPENDIX IV.

J. VI. (Pl.   XIX.) Fig. 4, 10 inches by 4 inches.
"   "   Fig. 5, lowest line, 2½ in., what remains of line.
"   "   Fig. 6, 5¾ in., what remains of line.
"   "   Fig. 8, 6 in., what remains of line.
"   "   Fig. 9, 5½ in., what remains of line.
"   (Pl.   XX.) Fig. 3, 6 inches.
"   (Pl.   XXI.) Fig. 1, 3¾ inches, what remains.
"   "   Fig. 2, 4 inches.
"   "   Fig. 3, 4½ inches.
"   "   Fig. 4, 3 inches.
"   "   Fig. 5, 4¾ inches.
"   "   Fig. 6, 2 inches.
"   "   Fig. 7, 2 inches.
"   "   Fig. 8, 3 inches.
"   "   Fig. 9, 4½ inches.

I have inserted the above measurements, prepared by Mr. Rylands, as certain theories have been based on the supposed uniformity of lines and spaces.

APPENDIX V.

(See p. 166.)

The following communication was read by Mr. Theo. G. Pinches, at the Soc. Bib. Arch., on March 3, 1885.

"THE NAME OF THE CITY AND COUNTRY OVER WHICH TARḲÛ-TIMME RULED.

"It will be remembered that the now well-known boss of Tarḳû-timme bears an inscription in Hittite and Assyrian or Babylonian which may prove, ultimately, of great value in enabling scholars to find out how to translate the strange hieroglyphs from Aleppo and Jerabis. Now as the name of the city or country over which Tarḳû-timme reigned is the most doubtful part of the inscription, some scholars reading the name *mât Ermê*, 'land of Ermê,' others *mât Zumê*, 'land of Zumê,' a few remarks upon this subject may not be quite useless. As I purpose speaking only of the wedge-inscription on this boss, I reproduce it here :—

D.P. Tar - ḳu - u - tim - me   šar   mât   Er - me - e.
    Tarḳû - timme,   *king of the land of Ermê.*

APPENDIX V.

"Prof. Sayce is of opinion that these forms must be referred to the time of Sargon of Assyria, and this is not by any means unlikely, for they bear a close likeness to the half archaic, half Babylonian style adopted during his reign,[1] though it must be confessed that the forms are not quite archaic enough. Transcribed into pure late Assyrian, the inscription would be as follows:—

𒁹 𒌓 𒋺 𒀭 𒁹 𒃲 𒀸 𒁹 𒁹

and in pure late Babylonian, as follows:—

𒁹 𒀸 𒋺 𒀭 𒁹 𒃲 𒀸 𒁹 𒁹

"It seems best, therefore, to regard these forms as pure Babylonian, possibly slightly modified by Assyrian influence. If the inscription be regarded as being connected with the Babylonian wedge-writing, the number of characters correctly given is seven, the incorrect ones being the second (*Tar*), the third (*ḳu*), the fifth (*tim*, which might equally well be ⋈ *mu*), and the eleventh (*e*).[2]

"The reading of all the characters, therefore, stands, except in the case of the last but two (⊨𐏑), and for this, the character for 'city,' I would propose the more usual reading of *ál* (*álu*), 'city,' instead of *er* or *zu*, and translate the whole,

"Tarḳû-timme, king of the land of the city of water."

---

[1] Compare Lyon's "Keilschrifttexte Sargon's," pp. 20-26.

[2] It must also be noted that the forms are equally incorrect from an Assyrian point of view.

"Can this 'watertown' be Kadesh, on the Lake of Hums? If so, this inscription makes it almost certain that the people who used these hieroglyphs were really the Kheta or Hittites, with whom they have been identified.

"Whether the Kheta or Hittites are to be identified with the people of Ḫatti of the Assyrians, is doubtful (see Schrader, 'Keilinschriften und des Alte Testament,' pp. 107-111). It may here be noted that besides the well-known *mât Ḫatti*, hitherto identified with the Kheta or Hittites, a similar name, with a single *t* and long *a*, occurs; and that these are distinct countries may be gathered from the following passages, taken from an omen-tablet in W.A.I., vol. iii. pl. 60, col. 1, lines 37-38 and 45-47 :—

Ûmu   XVI   KAM   atalû   išakkan,   šar   Akkadi D.S.
Day   16th   an eclipse   happens,   the king   of Akkad

imât, D.P.   Nergal   ina mâti   ikkal.
will die,   Nergal in the land will eat up.

Ûmu   ešrû   atalû   išakkan, šar   mât Ḫa - at - ti
Day   20th   an eclipse happens, the king   of Ḫatti

šûma,   šar   mât Ḫa - a - ti   itebbi - ma   kussâ   iṣab - bat.
the same, the king   of Ḫâti   will come and the throne will take.

That is :—

"If, on the sixteenth day (of the month Ab), an

APPENDIX V.

eclipse happen, the king of Akkad will die, Nergal[1] will destroy in the land."

"If, on the twentieth day, an eclipse happen, the king of Hatti will die, the king of Ḥâti will come and take the throne."

Ûmu	XV KAM	atalû	išakkan,	mâr šarri	abi - šu
Day	15th	an eclipse	happens,	the son of the king	his father

idâk - ma	kussâ	iṣab - bat	û	nakru	itebbî - ma
will kill and	the throne	will take,	and	an enemy	will come and

mâta	îkkal.
the country	will eat up.

Ûmu	XVI KAM	atalû	išakkan,	šar mâti a - ḫi - ti
Day	16th	an eclipse	happens,	the king of a foreign land

šuma,	šar mât Ḥa - a - ti	itebbî - ma	kussâ	iṣab - bat
the same,	the king of Ḥâti	comes and	the throne	takes.

zunnu	ina	šam - ê	melû	ina nakbi	ibattaku
Rain	in	heaven,	flood	in the channel	will overflow.

That is :—

"If, on the fifteenth day (of the month Elul), an eclipse happen, the son of the king will kill his father and will take the throne; and an enemy will come and destroy the country."

[1] The pestilence.

"If, on the sixteenth day, an eclipse happen, (the son of) the king of a foreign land will kill his father, and the king of Ḥati will come and take the throne. Rain from heaven, and flood in the channel will overflow."

"From this it may be inferred that besides the land of Ḥatti there was also another country called Ḥâti, strong enough, and, seemingly, ever ready, in those very ancient times, to take advantage of any circumstance to conquer the land of Ḥatti, or, indeed, any other country whose internal dissensions made it likely that it would fall an easy prey to an invading army. These two localities, Ḥâti and Ḥatti, probably lay very close together, and (it is not unlikely) got confused, in the course of time, in the minds of the nations around. It is to be noted that, though the Hebrew חֵת, חִתִּים correspond very well with the Assyrian Ḥatti (better Ḥattê), yet the Egyptian form Kheta, with its single dental, agrees better with the land Ḥâti mentioned above. Certain it is, that the Ḥatti of the Assyrian inscriptions lay on the sea coast, so that it is probable that, at least in early times, Ḥâti was the name of the country farther inland—perhaps to be identified with the Egyptian Kheta."

Reply of Prof. Sayce to the above, communicated in the "Trans. Soc. Bib. Arch.," May 5th, 1885 :—

THE INSCRIPTION OF TARKONDÊMOS.

"During the last few months so many unwise things have been written about the Hittites and their hieroglyphics, and so many mis-statements about the cuneiform inscriptions have been made in connection with them, that I am very glad to find Mr. Pinches coming forward in the last number of the Proceedings of this Society, to discuss in scholarly manner the now-famous boss of King Tarkondêmos. I had not intended to return to the subject, but his communication induces me to show why I cannot agree with his alternative rendering of the text.

"His first rendering of the title of Tarkondêmos is the same as mine—'king of the country of Erme'—and is, in fact, the rendering which an Assyriologist would naturally give. I need hardly tell those who have had much experience of cuneiform texts that the first character in the proper name is not *zu*, but *er* or *eri*; those who are not Assyrian scholars may refer to the syllabary in my 'Elementary Assyrian Grammar,' Nos. 29 and 104, in order to see the difference between the forms of the two signs. Fortunately, moreover, the character is one which is not polyphonous in proper names; it reads only *er* (or *eri*). But it so happens that when used ideographically it is employed as the determinative of the name of a city. Mr. Pinches, therefore, very ingeniously asks whether we may not translate 'the country of the city of water.' To this question, however, the answer must be 'No;' and for the following reasons:—.

"(1.) It is only in Assyrian that *mê* signifies 'water.' In Hebrew and Phœnician the corresponding word is always the plural מִים (construct מֵי), and the Aramaic form of it is מַיָּא (or מֵי), while the Arabic and Ethiopic forms are equally unlike the Assyrian, and were, moreover, employed by populations which had no contact with Asia Minor. Unless, therefore, we suppose that the subjects of Tarkondêmos the Kilikian spoke Assyrian, we cannot ascribe to them the word *mé* in the sense of 'water.'

"(2.) Tarkondêmos cannot have used the characters ideographically, as the Semitic Babylonians used the old Accadian characters, giving to them a Semitic pronunciation, since in this case 'the phonetic complement' (the vowel *e*) would not have been used and we should have had in place of it the ideograph of plurality 𒈨𒌍.

"(3.) It is difficult to believe that Tarkondêmos would have translated the name of his city into Assyrian, unless his subjects spoke Assyrian, and did not understand the meaning of the name of their own city. An Assyrian lexicographer writing at Nineveh might very conceivably translate into his own language the names of foreign places of which he happened to know the signification: in the case of a Kilikian king such a proceeding would have been senseless.

"So much for the name of the country over which Tarkondêmos ruled. It was called Erme or Erime, reminding us of the Ἄριμοι of the Greeks. That it was in Kilikia results from the fact that the names of Tarkondêmos and Tarkondimatos are Kilikian, and are found only among Kilikians and Pisaurians. This fact, was long ago pointed out by Mordtmann.

"Mr. Pinches' reading of the royal name itself is most ingenious, and I wish I could see my way towards accepting it. But two difficulties present themselves. (1) The character which follows ⟼ *tar* has, it is true, been misformed by the native artist, but it bears a closer resemblance to the Assyrian ⊏⊐⫪, *rik*, than it does to ⊏⊐, *qu*, followed by ⟨, *u*. (2) The Greek transcription of the name shows that the second element in it began with *d*. Now it is a well-known rule of Assyrian phonetics that *d* becomes *t* after a preceding 'hard' consonant, but not after a 'soft' consonant or a vowel. Consequently *timme* with *t* presupposes a preceding *k*.

"Neither of these two difficulties, however, is insurmountable; we *might* read *dim* instead of *tim*, while the vocalization of *qu* would admirably suit the Greek form with *o*.

"However this may be, I am unable to follow Mr. Pinches in distinguishing between the Khatti and the Khâti of the astrological tablets. The passages quoted by Mr. Pinches were translated by me more than eleven years ago in my Paper on the Astronomy and Astrology of the Babylonians (Trans. Soc. Bibl. Arch. vol. iii. part 1), and as a reference to my translation will show, I took the same view as Mr. Pinches when dealing with the first of the two passages. I had subsequently to change my opinion. Not only is a long vowel interchanged with a double consonant in several of the proper names found on the Assyrian monuments, but it actually is so in the case of the Hittites themselves. Thus Tiglath-Pileser I., in the same inscription, writes the name not only *Kha-at-te* with a double *t*, but also *Kha-te-e* with a single *t* (W.A.I., iii. 5, 15), while the evidence of the Vannic inscriptions is decisive upon the point. In these the name is always spelt *Kháte* (and *Khati*) with only one *t* and a long vowel (see my Memoir on the Vannic Inscriptions in the Journal R.A.S. vol. xiv. parts 3 and 4.)

"I much doubt whether the references to the Hittites in the astrological tablets are as early as the time of Sargon of Accad. They seem to belong rather to those interpolations and glosses which were perpetually being added to the old work. Thus in the second passage quoted by Mr. Pinches the original reading appears to have been: 'the king of a foreign land seizes the throne,' the alternative reading, 'the king of the Hittites comes and seizes on the throne,' being a later gloss. At the same time, the contact between Babylonia and the Hittites must have taken place at a sufficiently early time, since the art and legends of Carchemish were indebted to Babylonia and not to Assyria. Assyria, however, did not rise into notice until the sixteenth century B.C., and I see no reason for supposing that the Hittite occupation of Northern Syria took place much before that date.

"I must conclude with a protest against the persistent misrepresentations of my own views and statements regarding the Hittites, which I find have been repeated not only by anonymous amateurs, but even by scholars, who ought to have referred to my 'Memoir on the Hittite Monuments,' published in the Transactions of this Society, and at present the only detailed exposition of my opinions and conclusions, in order to see what it is I really have said. I find myself assumed to be in opposition to the theory which makes the culture of Western Asia Minor emanate from Kappadokia, and traces the prehistoric road-system of Asia Minor to the same locality. I am further told that I maintain that Hittite inscriptions, wherever found, are all in the same language, and that the Hittites themselves were a single homogeneous people. It is evident that those who credit me with such doctrines have never taken the trouble to read my memoir for themselves. Had they done so, they would have found that what I really have maintained is diametrically the opposite to what I am supposed to have maintained. The keystone of my theory is that the Hittites were a Kappadokian people, and that the ruins of Eyuk and Boghaz Keui testify that they remained so up to the last. In my 'Herodotos' I have even gone so far as to suggest that the primitive population of Armenia and the greater part of Asia Minor was allied to them by blood. I have said over and over again that Herodotos and Strabo were wrong in calling the Kappadokians

Syrians, or White Syrians. The Hittites were mountaineers; their boots were snow-shoes, their ideograph for 'country' represents a mountainous region. Their presence in Syria must be explained by conquest; they drove a wedge, as it were, into the territory of the Semites, and their final overthrow by Sargon the Assyrian marked the ultimate success of their Semitic rivals. The Hittite power was a Kappadokian power, though the Vannic inscriptions prove that we must understand Kappadokia in a large sense.

"But I have further tried to show that Hittite culture does not begin until after the Hittite occupation of Northern Syria, and the establishment of Hittite kingdoms at Carchemish, at Hamath, and at Kadesh. This is proved by the character of Hittite art. Hittite art is based on Babylonian models, and therefore presupposes contact with Babylonia. Nay more; the sphinxes of Eyuk, and the image of Niobê in Lydia, indicate acquaintance with Egyptian sculpture, and this again takes us to Kadesh, whose monarchs contended against Egypt, as the Egyptian inscriptions tell us, with the help of subject-allies from Asia Minor. It was not until the Hittite tribes had undergone the influence of Babylonian and Egyptian culture in Syria that it became possible to erect the monuments, which have been almost our sole clue in the reconstruction of what has been termed—for want of a better name—the Hittite empire.

"Some of these monuments were, I believe, the records

of conquest; others were the work of the indigenous inhabitants of the countries in which they are found, who had passed under the influence of Hittite art. The boss of Tarkondêmos is evidently a native Kilikian work, and if the Kilikians belonged to the Hittite family, might be described as the work of the Kilikian tribe of Hittites. On the other hand, the monuments of Karabel and Giaour Kalessi appear to me to be records of conquest. They represent soldiers commanding the entrance of passes, and thus dominating over the countries to which the passes lead. Moreover, the forms of the characters used on the monument of 'the Niobê,' and, so far as they are legible, at Karabel, so closely resemble those found at Carchemish as to admit of no other reasonable hypothesis except that they were carved by the same people, more especially when we remember the differences that exist in the forms of the characters used at Carchemish itself, and above all, between the forms employed at Carchemish and at the comparatively neighbouring town of Hamath. This argument, however, I am fully aware, can be thoroughly appreciated only by those who have spent some years in the study of Hittite hieroglyphs.

"By way of conclusion, let me quote what I have said in the opening pages of my 'Herodotos' (p. 5) : 'The Syrians of Herodotos (i. ch. vi.), were really the Hittites of Carchemish, who did not belong to the Semitic race at all, and had originally descended from the mountainous region of the North. . . . . Herodotos tells us

(i. 72, vii. 72) that the inhabitants of Kappadokia and Kilikia were Syrians, and Hittite remains in the shape of sculptures and inscriptions have been found in these countries. The tribes inhabiting them probably belonged to the same race as the Hittites, and spoke cognate dialects.'

"After this I hope that I shall not again be credited with believing that Syria and not Kappadokia was the centre of Hittite power, or be called to task for forgetting that the Hittite system of writing may have been used by tribes speaking different languages and belonging to different nationalities. It matters little to me what theories about the Hittites others may hold, so long as they do not ascribe to me opinions which I have never expressed. I am indeed prepared for anything after the statement of an anonymous reviewer of Dr. Wright's interesting book, who gravely alleges that the decipherment of the Hittite hieroglyphs would be a more wonderful feat than that of the cuneiform inscriptions. It is clear that he has never heard how the latter were deciphered, and how Grotefend made his famous guesses without the aid of a bilingual text. It is a pity that anonymous reviewers, when they deal with matters of science, do not acquire a little knowledge of the subject about which they write.

"A. H. SAYCE."

April 25, 1885.

INDEX.

Aaron, 152
Abraham, 14, 46, 47, 66, 91, 97
Abrie, 40
Abu el-Fida, 130
Abydos, 21, 106
Academy, 154, 206
Accad, 36
Accadian, 226
Adana, 151
Adonis, 75
Afrin, 175
Ægæ, 167
Ægean, 22, 59, 63, 126
Agane, or Agade I., 37, 122
Ahab, 120
Ahimelech, 80, 89, 115
Ahiramu, 40, 118
Aholibamah, 80
Ai, 112
Aintab, 62, 63
Akar-ezer, 173
Akerith, 106, 108
Akh, 77
Akbarru, 13
Akhkilli, 130
Alarodian speech, 83
Aleppo, 22, 23, 53, 55, 63, 100, 107
   inscription, 8, 55, 63, 141, 142, 171, 187
Alphabets in Asia Minor, 69
Amalekites, 93, 111
Amanus, Mount, 62
Amasia, 61
Amazons, 60, 74
Amenemhat II., 14, 99
Amen of Ramessu Meriamen, 27
   the Sun, 32

American P. E. Soc., 2, 131
Amon, 24, 77, 108
Amon Ra, 20, 27
Amorites, 23, 47, 92, 93, 107, 111
Amu, 13
Anabasis, 116
Anah, 80
Anakim at Hebron, 46, 111
Anatolia, 60
   dress, 61
   monuments of, 60, 86
Anaugas, 106
Angora, 59
Antioch, 83
Aphrodite, 74
Appollodorus, 186
Aram, 168
Aramæans, 38, 110
Aramaic letters, 182
Arathu, 106, 107
Ard el-Huleh, 49
Arima, 169
Arimi of Homer, 169
Ἄριμοι, 226
Armageddon, 16
Armenia, 175
Arnema, 77
Arpad, 63
Artemis, 74
   of Ephesus, 74
Arvad (Aradus), 21, 22, 41, 53
Astoreth, 73
Ashur, 38, 39
Asia Minor, 22, 35, 60, 63, 68, 69, 99, 127, 155
Asianic scripts, 125, 179
Assur, 43, 44

234   INDEX.

Assurbanipal, library of, 36
　harem of, 189
　like Alexander, 15
　record chamber, 189
Assur-Nasir-Pal, 39, 41, 117, 118,
　119, 131, 168
　conquests, 41
　records of, 39, 117
　wars with Hittites, 39
Assyria, 12, 38, 41, 44, 117, 119
Assyrian, 8, 120, 167, 179, 182,
　192
　astronomical tablets, 36
　inscriptions, 45, 52, 189, 193
　monuments, 82, 183, 192
Assyrians, 131, 179, 184, 193
Assyriologists, 37, 132
Astaratu, 31
Astarte, 73, 74, 76
Astartha, 77
Atargatis, 73, 74
Atom, Lord of On, 27
Attar-asar, 173
Attys, 73, 75, 198
Augustus, 167
Azaz, 63
Aztec, 131

Baal, 73, 75, 76, 107, 189
Baal-bek, xviii
Baal-Berith, 76
Baal-Gad, 114
Baal-Melkorth, 76
Baal-Shemaim, 76
Baaltis, 75
Baal Tsephon, 76
Baal-Zebub, 76
Bab-ej-Jisr, 140
Babylon, 68
Babylon Bowl, 154, 157, 161,
　195
　note on, 198
Babylonia, inscriptions of, 172
Babylonian art, 128
　deities, 75
Babylonians, 95, 126

Bagtche Pass, 62
Bahiani, 40, 118
Balaam, 53
Balawat bronzes, 175
Ball, Rev. C. J., 201
Banias, 49
Barth, 160
Bashemath, 80
Bathsheba, 94
Battle scene, 20
Bedawîn, 19, 100, 105
　hostages, 5, 129
Bedawi tribe marks, 129
Beddoe Dr., 156,
Beeri (Foutanus), 80
Beersheba, 47, 103, 111
Beischehr, 61
Benhadad of Damascus, 42, 116, 121
Bethel, 49, 112
Beyrout, 21
Bible and inscriptions, 95
Bible indications of Hittite nation-
　ality, 80, 87, 88
　coincident with Babylonian
　inscriptions, 96
　confirmed by Karnak inscrip-
　tions, 103
　references to the Hittites, 91,
　123
　summary of Hittite references,
　48, 88, 91, 94
Birch, Dr. Samuel, 15, 37, 101, 104
Bisri, 39
Black obelisk, 42, 121
Boghaz-Keui, 57, 59, 60, 75, 146,
　156, 159, 160, 161, 171, 174,
　175, 182, 186
Bonomi, 147
Book Town, 48, 71
Bor, 62
　(Tyana), 185
Boscawen, Mr., 55, 143, 171, 173,
　174, 184, 188
Boss of Tarkondêmos, 163, 165
Boustrophedon, 138, 169, 186, 195
British Museum, 12, 37, 63, 121,
　147, 148, 163, 164

INDEX. 235

Brugsch Bey, 13, 14, 16, 18, 33, 47, 99
  estimate of Hittite power, 52, 72, 102
  his identification, 51
  quotes non-Semitic names, 81
  thinks Mineptah II. the Pharaoh of the Exodus, 114
Bulgar Dagh, 62, 149
Burckhardt, 1
Burton, Capt., 3, 4, 11, 124, 129, 138
Byblus, 122

Cæsarea, 170
  Philippi, 49
Canaan, 87, 102, 105
Canaanite allies, 72, 74
Canaanites, 86, 92
Cappadocia, 57, 63, 75, 86, 161
Cappadocian alphabets, 70, 126
  peasantry, 62, 86
  troglodytes, 86
Carchemish, 17, 22, 35, 38, 40, 43, 44, 63, 74, 96, 118, 120, 122, 132, 143, 167, 169, 175, 185, 192
  finally overthrown (in 717 B.C.), 122
  inscription, 143, 170, 171, 173, 174, 195, 198
  king of, 185, 191, 192
Carian, 70, 126
Catalogue of Egyptian conquests, 102
Caussin, M., 130
Cave of Machpelah, 92, 100
Centres of forgery, 165
Chaldea gave religion to the Hittites, 74
Characters, list of, on Hittite inscription, 177
Chebar, 48
Chensuneferhotep, 27
Cheyne, Rev. T. K., 89, 90, 96, 97, 98, 135
  compares authority of the Bible with Egyptian and Assyrian inscriptions, 97, 98

Cheyne, Rev. T. K., letters from, with rejoinder, 206–217, xi
  on the battle of Kadesh, 109
Chinnereth, 113
Cilician, 69, 151
  gates, 57, 63, 149
Claremont-Ganneau, M., 142
Clarke, Mr. Hyde, 128, 129, 130, 131, 155
Clay books, 36
  seals, 130
Colchians, 53
Comparison of Cypriote and Hittite characters, 178
Conder, Capt., 49, 84, 86, 123, 131
Confederacy in Canaan, 102
  at Kadesh, 106
Constantinople Museum, 7, 142
Cooper, Rev. B. H., 172
Corean, 131
Crawford, General, 55
Cresus, 161
Cromwellian orders, 16
Crusader, 8
Curtius, Prof. E., 156
Cybele, 60
Cypriote and Phœnician inscription, 125, 129
Cypriote syllabary, 70, 125, 126
Cyprus, 16, 53, 69, 74
Cyrus, 161

Dabigu, 42, 121
Damascus, 1, 4, 6, 12, 90, 98, 121
Daphne, 53, 76
Darb Tak et-Tahun, 140
Dardani, 106
Dardanians, 22, 53, 59
David, 50, 175
  census, 49
  his empire, 94, 115
  King, 80, 94, 135
  the King's warriors, 115, 133
Davis, Rev. E. J., on Ibreez monument, 56, 148, 149–154
Debir, 48

INDEX.

Decipherment of Hittite inscriptions, 177–197
Deir-Atiyeh, 5
Delbet, M., 159
Delitzsch, Dr., 114, 122
Deputation to Waly, 10
Derbe, 56, 57
Derwishes, 5
Dimes, 187, 191, 193, xviii
Dio Cassius, 167
Drake, C. F. T., 3, 12, 55, 124, 142
Duncker, 110, 111, 117, 121
Duplicate names, 80, 89

Ebers, Professor, 101
Egypt, 14, 16
  enemies of, 13, 16
  hieroglyphics of, 1, 101, 131, 193
Egyptian records, 13, 26
  art at Karnak, 102
  early foes, 13
  estimate of Hittites, 21, 26, 33, 51
  history, 13
  stones confirm Bible references, 115
Egyptians, 8, 25, 176, 183, 193
Egyptologists, 15, 132
Eisenlohr's discovery, 71
Eleutherus valley, 21
Eliezer, 91
Elisha's prophecy, 116
Elohistic narrator, 97
Elon, 80
Encyclopædia Britannica, 89, 135
Ephesus, 58, 74
Ephron, 89, 92
Eregli, 61, 62
Ereku, 197
Erime, 226
Ermé, 166, 220, 225, 226
Esau's wives, 80, 92
Etham, 111
Euphrates, 16, 39, 42, 50, 51, 117
Euxine, 63

Eyuk, 57, 60, 75, 146, 158, 186, 229
  double-headed eagle of, 158
Ezekiel's statement, 48, 111

Fisher, Major, 56, 149
Forgery, centres of, 165
French Vice-consul, 140

Gamgumai, 83, 168
Ganneau, M. C., 141, viii
Gauzanitis, 22, 77
Gaza, 40, 102
Gebal, 41
Gentiles, 13
Geographical names compared with English, 45
  position of Hittite inscriptions, 54
Georgian women, 174
Germanicus Cæsar, 15
German Oriental Society, 172
Germans, 62, 68
Gesenius, 130
Giaour Dagh, 62
Giaour-Kalessi, 59, 231
Gilead, 50
Girls, Hittite, 75
Gladstone's Homeric Synchronisms, 7, 126
  letter from, 199
  opposed, 201
Golenischeff, M., 203
Gollob, E., 158
Goodwin, C. W., 26, 109
Goshen, 100
Great king of the Hittites, 22, 26
Greek, 8
  alphabet, 70
  helmet, 175, 176
  Sandon, or Sandan, 180
Greeks, early, 166
Green, W. Kirby, Consul, 4, 6, 8, 12
Grotefend, 232
Grove, Mr. G., 79
Growth of opinion, 55
Gühling, 56

Guillaume, M., 159
Gurum inscriptions, 57
Gwyther, Dr., 141, 147, 162, 183

Hadadezer, 94
Halak, Mount, 114
Halévy, M., xiv
Hall of Pillars, 102
Halys, 57, 85
Ham, 87
Hamah inscriptions, 1, 5, 124, 131, 171, 174, 183, 192, 195, 197
  at Aleppo, 141
  casts taken, 11
  declared Hittite remains, 22, 55, 70, 127
  detailed description of stones, 137–141
  discovered, 1
  efforts to secure them, 2
  first copies, 3
  first published, 2
  five inscriptions, 137
  four inscribed stones, 137
  in danger, 8
  may confirm Bible story, 135
  neglected, 1
  neither Assyrian nor Egyptian, 132
  permission to copy, 7
  purchased and removed, 9
  rediscovered, 2
  search for the inscriptions, 6
  stones in Constantinople Museum, 141
  Sultan consulted, 7
Hamath, 175, 188
Hamathites, 7, 9, 43
Hamathite texts, 184, 187
Hamilton, 160
Hamites, 92
Hammia, xviii
Harat-ed-Duhan, 139
Harmachu, 27
Husyn, 5
Hâti, 223, 224

Hatta, Hetteh, Hattin, 49, 224
Hatti, 223, 224
Hazael, 120
Hazazi, 118
Head, Mr. Barclay, 67, 182
Hebrew, 80, 192
  monarchy, 88
  Scriptures, 12
Hebron, 46, 47, 91, 100, 103
Hellenic characters, 70
Henderson, Consul, 143
Hermon, 50, 113
Hermus valley, 59
Herodotus, 58, 156, 161, 175
Heth, 53, 87, 89, 91, 100
Hierapolis, 63
Himyar, 130
Himyaritic, 129, 130, 131, 165
Hissarlik, 67, 69, 127
History of the Hebrew monarchy, 88
Hittites, 7, 12, 13, 14, 15, 16, 19
  Alarodian, 82
  allies, 20, 23, 53, 84, 106
  and Accad, 36
  and cuneiform inscriptions, 164
  and Cypriote characters, 127
  and Hyksos dynasty, 46, 99
  armies, 113
  art, 56, 65, 68
  as colonists, 97, 98, 100, 101
  as merchants, 97, 98, 100, 101, 133
  as warriors, 71
  at Hebron, 46, 97
  at Jerusalem, 48
  at Kirjath-seper, 47
  at the battle of Merom, 49
  at Zoan, 46
  before Nineveh or Babylon, 52
  Bible account, 88
  Bible references, 48, 49, 91, 94, 123
  borne captive to Assyria, 44, 122
  characters, list of, 177, 178
  chariots, 17, 24, 41, 71, 113, 118, 119, 120

Hittites—*continued.*
confederation, 20, 35
copy of treaty of peace, 71, 109
culture, 70, 128, 134
defeat at Megiddo, 104
defeated, 16, 105
deities, 74, 75, 77
destruction of empire, 43
disappear from history, 44, 123
dynastic alliance, 33, 110, 133
endurance, 35, 41, 43
geographical extent of empire, 45, 59, 63, 117
girls, 75
importance, 18, 20, 37, 51, 104, 117
in Ard-el-Huleh, 49
in Asia Minor, 41
in Egyptian pictures, 84
inscriptions and Bible, 45, 95
   at Hamah, 124
   declared Hittite remains, 127
   described, 139, 177
   measurements by Mr. Rylands, 218
   raised, 67, 137
in Syria and Asia Minor, 53
in the Book of Exodus, 101
in the Book of Judges, 112
in the hieroglyphics, 85, 101
in the mountains, 111
Karnak list, 52, 102
king of, 22, 24, 25
Kadesh, 16
land of, 49, 51
language not Semitic, 79, 82, 203
learning, 65, 70, 71
library, 48
linguistic connection with Georgians, 82, 83
literature, 70, 71, 133, 134
monuments, 127
monuments on border of Egypt, 14
names, 82
name significates, 80, 89

Hittites—*continued.*
names in Palestine, 49
nationality, 79
nineteenth cent. B.C., 88, 96
not Semitic, 79, 82, 85, 87
origin, 85
overthrown finally by Sargon, 43, 122
physical type of, 84, 85
priestesses, 74
princes, 183
princess, 34
Queen-mother of the princess who saved Moses, 34
religion, 73, 75
sculptures, 54, 58, 61, 62, 84
seals, 155
silver plates, 65, 66, 67, 71
standard weights, 67
three hundred geographical names, 45, 52
treaties, 19, 21, 22, 26, 65, 109, 176
tribute, 18
war with Assyria, 38, 39, 42
wealth and empire, 35
wives, 110, 115
women, 75
writing boustrophedon, 138, 186, 195
Hivites, 92
Hommell, xv
Horeb, 92
Hornets, 92, 110
Hor the Smiter, 104
Horus, 27
Huleh, 50, 113, 114
Humann Herr, 59, 60, 156
Hums, 5
Hurunaya, 38
Hyksos dynasty Hittite, 47, 48, 99

Ibrahim Pasha, 9
Ibreez, 56, 57, 148-154, 187, 188, 194, 195
   deity, 187

INDEX.   239

Ibreez, inscription, 56, 148, 187, 194, 196
Ibsamboul, 21, 34, 83, 84, 106, 110
Iconium, 56, 57
Idalion, 125
Ideograph of king, 170–176, 180
  of country, 170–172, 180
Iflatûn Bûnar, 61
Ihem, 16, 103
Ilion, 53
Inscriptions, Aleppo, 8, 55
  are they Hittite remains? 12, 124
  Boghaz Keui, 57
    decipherment of, 177
  Eyuk, 57
  Giaour-Kalessi, 59
  Gurum in Cappadocia, 57
  Hamah, 54
  healing powers of one stone, 140, 143
  Ibreez in Cilicia, 56, 148–154
  Jerabis (Carchemish), 55
  Karabel Pass, 58
  measured by Mr. Rylands, 218
  on silver plate, type of inscriptions on stones, 67
  on the Niobe, 158
  Tyana, 57, 154, 187, 196
Ionia, 58
Irkhulina of Hamath, 42
Isaac, 92
Ishmael, 92
Israelites, 92, 103
Israelitish influence, 131
Issus, 62
Istar, 75
Ivriz, 61

Jabbour, 4
Jablonski, 56
Jabin, King, 93, 113
Jacob, 101
Jamnia, 19
Japanese, 131
Jebel Kalamoun, 5

Jebusites, 92, 93
Jehoram, 116
Jehu, 120
Jerabis, 55, 96, 139, 143, 147, 157, 158
  inscriptions, detailed description of, 143–148, 218
Jerablus, 61, 63
Jericho, 112
Jerusalem built by Hittites, 48, 111
Jessup, Rev. S., 2
Jews, 13
Joab, 50
Johnson, Consul U.S.A., 2, 131
Joppa, 21
Jordan, 93, 113
Joseph, 49, 101
Joshua, 50, 93, 111, 112
  by Lake Merom, 93, 114, 135
Joshua's promised land of the Hittites, 53, 103
Jovanoff, Mr. A., 163
Juda, South of, 48
Judith, 80

Ka, 31, 77
Kadesh, 16, 17, 18, 48, 50, 75, 96, 104, 108, 175, 230
  battle of, 20, 21, 83
  destroyed, 17, 19
  mixed races still in, 86
Kafirs, 13
Kaisariyeh, 61, 182, 193
Kallas, M., 139
Kallisthenês, 169
Kalykadnos, 169
Kamaiz, 72
Kamru or Kamlu, xviii
Kanaan stormed, 19, 111
Kanulua, 40, 118
Kappadokia, 170, 175, 182, 229, 230
Karabel, 58, 59, 156, 169, 231
Karians, 175
Karkish (Keshkesh), 106, 107
Karnak inscriptions, 15, 20, 21, 52, 102, 106

Karnak list of Hittite towns, 52, 102
Kaskayans, 38, 168
Kati, 106
Kefr Hatta, 49
Keith Johnston's Geography, 45
Kelah Shergat, 37
Kemi, 26, 33, 109, 134
Κήτειοι, 7, 70, 126, 199
Khar, 13
Khattai, 70
Khatte, 39
Khattu, 185
Khattu-khi, 192
Khazaz, 63
Khâti, 227, 228
Kher, 77
Kheta (Khatti), 13, 19, 26, 27, 33, 51, 65, 70, 107, 118, 119, 120, 126, 134, 222, 224, 227
Khetam, 111
Kheta-sira, 27, 33, 82
Khethites (Hittites), 14, 51
Khilibu (Aleppo), 77, 107
   his ambassadors, 65
   his daughter, 33, 110
   his copy of treaty, 65, 109
   his generals, servants, &c., 72
   in Egypt, 133
Khira(bu), 31
Khirpasar, 72
Khisasap, 31
Khissap, 77
Khita, 31
   Peruvian, 131
   Baal, 189
Kiepert, 159
Kilikia, 167, 171, 189
Kilikian king, 167
   boss, 176, 231
Kilikians, 83, 168
King of the Hittites, 25, 121
   beautiful daughter of, 34, 110
   great, 22
   miserable, 22
   of Kadesh, 18
   vile, 22
Kings of the Hittites, 42, 116

Kings of the Kheta, 19, 51
Kirjath-sêpher (City of Books) 48, 71
Kirkamish (Carchemish), 106
Kishon, 16
Kodeshoth, 79
Kolkhians, 168
Komagenê, xvii
Komagenians, 83
Komana, 75, xviii
Korykos, 169
Kostatin-el-Khuri, 3
Kouyunjik, 148, 155, 173, 198
   seals, 187, 189, 190, xvii
Kuai, 83
Kuans, 82, 196, xvii
Kuas, xviii
Kulek Boghaz, 149
Kume-Kues, xvii
Kummukh, xvii
Kumukus, xvii
Kurds, 61, 81
Kurkh, 120
   monolith, 42, 120
Kurt Dagh, 62
Kyme, 74
Kypros, 167

Lajard, 157, 159
Lake Van, 163, 164, 168, 175
Land and the Book, 100
   of Goshen, 100
   of the Hittites, 49, 51
Lang, Mr. H., 69, 125
Langlois, 189
Layard, Sir H., 121, 148, 153, 155, 157
Lebanon, 18, 37, 50, 103, 112, 113, 119
Leka, 106, 107, 108
Lenormant, M., 82, 163, 164, 165, 203, xviii
Leuco-Syrians, 161
Library of Sargon, 95
Libyan, 129, 131
Literary people (Hittites), 54, 70, 134

INDEX. 241

Louvre inscription of 12th dynasty, 14, 47, 99
Lubarna, 40, 118, 119
Lûeizeh (Luz), 49
Luksor, 21, 106
Luz (Bethel), 49, 112
Lycaonia, 128
 speech of, 56
Lycian, 70, 126
Lydda, 49
Lydia, 59, 63, 66, 68, 128, 181
Lydian, 69
Lyon, 221
Lysians, 106
Lystra, 56, 57

Ma, 75
Maacah, 41
Mabug, xviii
Machpelah, 91
Magian religion, 39
Malik Salah Mahmoud, 68
M'alûla, 5
Malunna, 106, 107
Mamre, 47
Manetho's statement, 48, 111
Marasara, 28
Marash, 57, 63, 173, 183
 inscription, 141, 147, 162
Ma'rib dyke, 130
Mariette Bey's view, 14, 47, 64, 71, 99, 101
Maspero, Prof., ix, x, xviii
Masu, 106, 107
Mautenara, 28, 29
Mauthaner, 193
Maut Lady of Asheru, 27
Max Duncker, 110, 111, 117
Mazor, 81
Medinet Abou, 35, 115
Megiddo, 16, 49
 battle of, 16, 103
 siege of, 17
Melitene, 168
Membij, 63
Meneptah I., 28

Merash, 183, 192, xvii
Merom, 49, 93, 112
 battle of, 114, 135
Mesi, 197
Mesopotamia, 16, 18, 21, 37
Meyer, Ed., 181, 189, ix
Migdol battle, 35
Mina of Curchemish, 67
Mineptah II. the Pharaoh of the Exodus, 34, 114
Miserable king of the Hittites, 22
Mita the Moschian, 44
Moabite pottery, 165
 stone, 8
Mocatta, Mr. F. D., 162
Mœsius, 22
Mohammed, 140
 Ali, 141
Mohammedans, 13
Mongolian, 84
Monolith of Kurkh, 42, 120
Month, 107
Mordtmann, Dr., 163, 164, 165, 170, 227
Moschi, 83; Moskhi, xvii
Moses, 93, 113
Mount of Beatitudes, 49
Mozambique, 90
Mugallu, 189
Murray's Handbook, 1
Mushanath, 106
Myers, Mr. W., xxiv
Myrina, 74
Mysia, 21
Mysian, 69
Mysians, 53

Nabonidus, 122
Naharaim (Mesopotamia), 103, 106
Nana of Babylon, 73
Nasara, 140
Nationality, 79
Nebk, 5
Negeb, 111
Newman, Prof. F. W., 88, 90, 116, 119
Newton, Mr. C. T., 69

R

Nigdeh, 62, 86
Nilaai, 40
Nimroud, black obelisk of, 42, 121
  Pyramid, 40, 117
Nineveh, 157, 164, 167, 189
Niobê, on Mount Sipylos, 148, 158, 195
Nut, son of, 27

Oppert, Dr. Julius, 44, 122
Oriental name significates, 90
Orontes, 83, 108

Pairaka, 31
Palestine E. Fund, 3, 12, 112
Palmer, E. H., 3
Pamphylian, 69
Panic at Samaria, 116
Paphos, 74
Parthians, 15
Paschal Chronicle, 53, 59
Patiani, 83, 175
Paucker, M., 55, 142
Paul and Barnabas, 56
Peace between Egypt and the Hittites, 19, 21, 22, 34
Pedasus, 53
Pentaur, 21 (Prize Poem), 22, 106
Pergamos, 59
Perizzites, 92
Perrot, M. G., 65, 155, 156, 158, xvi
Persian hosts, 116
Pethor, 42, 53, 120
Pharaoh of the Oppression, 20, 113
  of the Exodus, 34, 114
Pharaoh's army, 16, 17
  chariots, 20
Philistines, 89
Phœnicia, 41, 100
Phœnicians, 13, 16, 19, 53, 73, 105
Phœnician seals, 68, 164
  work, 17
Phrygian, 69, 165
  cap, 174
Pidasa, 106, 107
Pilqua, 77

Pinches, Mr., 37, 122, 220-232
Pisaurians, 227
Pisiri of Carchemish, 44, 122
Pitane, 74
Pitra, 121
Plutarch, 167
Pontus, 61
Poole, Mr. R. S., on dynasty, 14
  on language, 80
Porter, 1
Pra, 77
Pra-Hormakhu, 23
Priene, 74
Pseudo-Sesostris, 155, 156, 157, 169
Ptah, 27, 34
Pteria (Boghaz-Keui), 161
Pterium, 156

Qazuadana, 106, 107

Ra, 34
Ramen-ma (Seti Meneptah I.), 28
Ra-men-pehu (Ramessu I.), 28
Rames, Hittite Ambassador, 27, 66
Ramses, 33
Rameses I. (Hittite treaty), 19, 104, 105
Rameses II. (Sesostris), 20, 105
  cartouches of, 158
  in heroic poem, 22
  march to Kadesh, 21, 105
  marries Hittite princess, 34
  Pharaoh of the Oppression, 20
  temples, 20, 65, 105
  treaty with Kheta-sira, 26
  wars with the Hittites, 53, 72, 106, 113
Rameses III., defeats new confederacy, 35, 114
Rameses Miamun, 26
Ramessu-Meriamen, 27, 28, 29, 30, 32, 33
Ramessu-Miamun, 66, 107
Rammesseum at Ibsamboul, 106
Ramsay, Mr., 62, 154, 182, 193, 196

Raoul-Rochette, 159
Ra-user-ma, 27, 28, 31, 32
Rawlinson, Prof., 38, 39, 102, 121, 156
Ready, Mr., 163
Red Sea, 130
Rehoboth, 111
Religion, 73
Renan, M., 130
Renouard, 156
Revue Archéologique, 153
Rimmon Idri (Benhadad), 42, 43, 121
Ritual not Morality, 75
Rodwell, Rev. J. M., 40, 118
Roman, 8
Rome, 15
Rosellini, xxiv
Rougé, M. de, 101, 106
Royal cap, 174
History of England, 45
Ruten, 13
Rylands, Mr. W. H., 55, 56, 138, 139, 142, 143, 144, 147, 155, 157, 161, 162, 164, 166, 171, 175, 180, 187, 196, 198, 218

Saba, 130
Subarta, 38
Sagurni, 121
Saidnâya, 5
Samahlai, 83
Samaria, siege of, 115, 117, 120
captured, 122
Sanda, 181, 189
Sandakos, 186, 189
Sanda-sar-me, 180, 181, 189, 190
Sandon or Sandan, 181, 183, 186, 189, 190, 198
Sandon-me-es, 189
Sandu, 181, 189, 190
Sandu-arri, 189
Sandu-setue, 197
Sangara, 43, 192
Sapalala, 28, 29
Saplel, Hittite king, 19, 105

Sapzar, 193
Sar, 80
Saracen, 8
Sarah, 91
Sarapaina, 31
Sarasu, 31
Sardis, 58, 59
Sargon, 167
Sargon of Agané, 37, 58, 95, 96, 122, 167, 221
overthrows the Hittites, 43, 122
transplants them to Assyria, 44
Sarpina, 77
Sarsu, 77
Sathekh-beg, xvii
Sayce, Prof. A. H., on early Assyrian tablets, 36, 37, 42, 95, xv
comparison of Cypriote and Hittite characters, 169, 178
decipherment of Hittite inscriptions, 177, 198, xvi
declares the Hittite language non-Semitic, 81, 82
identification of inscriptions as Hittite, 124, 127
Kirjath-sepher, 47
list of Hittite characters, 168
towns, 52
notes on turned-up boots, xxiv
on decipherment, 127
on inscriptions at Boghaz-Keui, Eyuk, and Tyana, 57, 154, 160
proves Herodotus' Sesostris to be Hittite, 58, 156
reads the bilingual inscription on the silver boss, 163, 166–176, 224
shows Hittite power from 17th to 12th century, 110
the empire of Naharaim occupied by Hittites, 117
traces Hittite art to Babylon, 58, 66, 67

Sayce, Prof. A. H.—*continued*.
  traces Hittite monuments throughout Asia Minor, 127
  traces the worship of Atargatis, 74
  translates monolith of Kurkh, 120
Sayyid 'Amr, 140
Schliemann's discoveries, 64, 67, 69, 99, 127
Schlumberger's seals, 155, 190, 192, 193
Schrader, 222, ix
Schulz, 168
Scripts of Asia Minor, 69
Sculptures, 58, 61, 62
Selindy, xviii
Seljukian Sultans, 68
Selucidæ, 8
Semitic-Aram, 168
Semitic language, 82
  names, 80
  Syrians, 81
Sennacherib, 130, 155
Serai, 7, 9
Sesostris, 20, 58, 59, 105, 156, 165
Seti I., 19, 28, 104, 111
Setu-eses, 196
Shalmaneser, 42, 120, 192
  thirty campaigns of, 43
Shasu, 111
Sheikh Hassan, 139
Sidon, 21, 39, 41, 89, 122
Silver boss, 163-176
  plate with Hittite copy of treaty, 66, 71
Sipylos, Mount, 148
Sivrihissar, 59
Smith, Mr. George, 123, 125, 142, 143, 144, 145
  sketches of 55, 143
Smyrna, 58, 64, 74, 99
Solomon, 50, 94, 115, 131, 331, 135
Sons of Heth, 91
Star shower, 10
St. George, 140, 141
St. James's Gazette, 201

Subarti, 168
Subhi Pasha, 4, 6, 7, 142
Sublime Porte, 4
Suki-beki, xviii
Suliman el-Kallas, 6
Sultan, 7
Sutech, 27, 28, 31, 32, 33
Sutekh, 66, 75, 76, 77, 108, 176
  on silver plate, 66, 176
Symbols on shields, 166
Syria, 18, 20, 47, 122
Syriac, 5
Syrians, 19, 53, 81, 116

Taaranta, 31
Tablet with treaty, 65
Tacitus, 15, 167
Tahtim-hodshi = Hittite Kadesh, 50, 94
Tain, 32
Taitatkherri, 31
Tak et-Tahun, 140
Tanais (Zoan), 46, 99
Tammuz, 75
Tar, 182, 186
Taranda, 77
Tarkhu, 181
Tarkhu-lara, 168
Tarku, 168, 181
Tarku-nazi, 168
Tarkû-timme, 220
Tarkodimatos, 168, 226
Tarkondêmos, 162, 163, 168, 178, 179, 182, 196
  boss, 162, 163-176, 193, 196, 225
Ταρκόνδημος, 168
Ταρκόνδιμοτος, 167
Tarkon, or Tarku, 168
Tarku-di-me, 180, 186
Tarkus, 186
Tar-me-Tarkus, 184, 195, 197
Tarrik-timme, 166, 168
Tarsus, 56
  coins, 182, 188
Tartar, 84
Tarthisebu, 27, 65, 81

Taurus, 63
Tawataun, 32
Taylor, Dr. Isaac, *re* Hittite empire, 63, 70, 99
   comparative table of Cypriote and Hittite characters, 127, 169, 177, 178
   identifies inscriptions as Hittite, 124
   identifies Kheta with Hittites, 70
   noticed non-Hellenic characters in certain scripts for which he sought a common source, 69, 70
Taylor, Rev. Canon, viii
Tayyarah bridge, 141
Tell Erfad, 63
Tell es-Salahiyeh, 55, 63
Tell Hetteh, 49
Tell Neby Mendeh, 52, 96
Texier, 156, 158, 159
Thargathazas, 81
Theban people, 15
   poet, 106
Theodoret, 168
Thermodon, 74
Thomson, Rev. Dr., 100
Thothmes I., 14
Thothmes III. (1600 B.C.), 14, 15, 18, 51, 57, 101
   at Megiddo, 103
Tibareni, 83
Tiglath-Pileser, 37, 117, 168, 228
   conquest, 39
   war with Hittites, 38
Tigris, 120
Toi or Tou, king of Hamath, 94, 135, 185
Tomkins, Rev. H. G., 203, xviii
Tôrah of Moses, 96
Treaties—Rameses I. and Saplel, 19
   Rameses II. and Kheta-sira, 21, 26, 176
Tristram, Rev. Canon, viii
Troad, 70, 125
Troglodytes, 86

Trojans, 53, 59
Troy, 64, 99
Tsukha, 38
Tubal, king of, 180, 189
Tum, 109
Tumes, 184, 185
Tunep (Daphne), 76
Turk, 8
Turned-up shoes, 61, 85, xxiv
Tuves, 184, 197
Tyana (Bor), 57, 137, 185, 186, 187
   inscription, 57, 154, 161, 178, 181, 187, 190, 195, xvii
Tyre, 21, 39, 41, 122

Uas, 181
Uas-sur-me, 180
Ulema, 5
Unexplored Syria, 3, 4, 129, 141
Uriah, 89, 94, 115
Urima, 169
Urma Nofirura (Hittite princess), 34
Urme, 168
Ur of the Chaldees, 123
Urum, 169
Urumayans, 168
Urume, 168
Urumiyeh, 168
Usher's Chronology, 91, 96, 101
Uyuk, 60, 62

Van, 164, 163, 175
Vannic inscriptions, 82, 163, 168, 192
Vile king of the Hittites, 21
Virgin Mary, 140

Ward, Dr. Hayes, vii
Weights, standard, 67
Western Asia, kings of, 52
Whitehouse, xi
Wiedemann, M., 203
Wilkinson, ix

Wilson, Col. Sir Charles, 57, 59, 154
   discoveries, 57, 86
   recognizes Hittite type in Cappadocian sculptures, 86
   summary of inscriptions, 59-63
   view as to origin of Hittites, 62, 85
Winged solar disk, 160, 186, 192
Woman's position among the Hittites, 75
Wusum (Bedawi marks), 129

Xenophon, 116

Yabrûd, 5
Yahiru, 40, 118
Yemen, 130
Yuzgat, 59

Zab river, 39
Zaiath Khirri, 77
Zaina, 77
Zulu, 111
Zauazas, 81
Zoan (Tanuis), 46, 47, 99
Zohar the Hittite, 92
Zumê, 220

THE END.

PRINTED BY BALLANTYNE, HANSON AND CO.
LONDON AND EDINBURGH

HAMATH INSCRIPTIONS.

H.I.

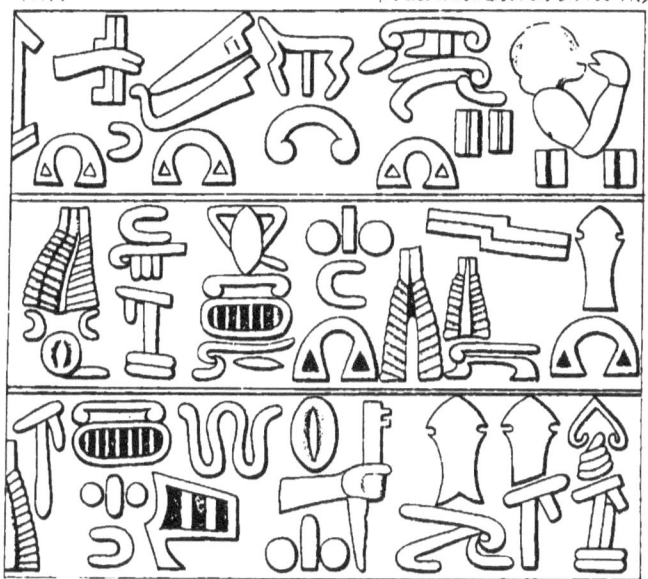

H.II.

Plate 11.
The Empire of the Hittites

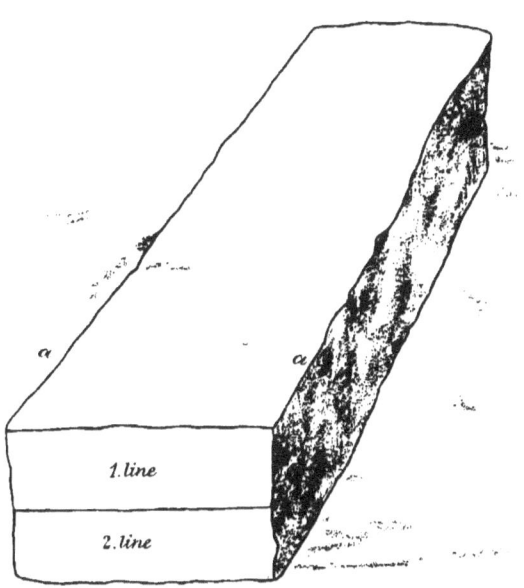

1. line
2. line

The stone on which was inscription
H.III. This is the stone which was
supposed to possess healing power, and
on which thousands of people were in
the habit of stretching themselves. The inscribed
portion from α to α was cut off.

H.III.

The Empire of the Hittites
HAMATH INSCRIPTIONS
H.IV.

CARVED LION ON MARASH CASTLE
WITH HITTITE INSCRIPTION

HAMATH I

Plate V The Empire of the Hittites
ALEPPO INSCRIPTION
(Trans. Soc. Bibl. Arch. Vol VII)

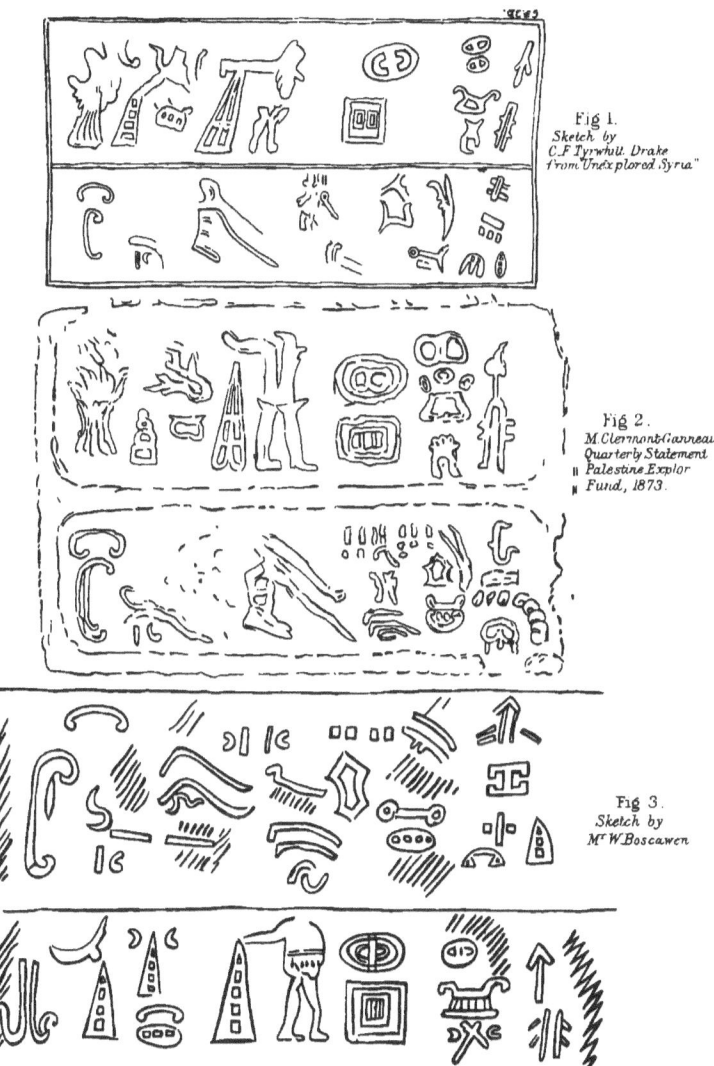

Fig 1.
Sketch by
C.F Tyrwhitt Drake
from "Unexplored Syria"

Fig 2.
M. Clermont-Ganneau
Quarterly Statement
Palestine Explor
Fund, 1873.

Fig 3.
Sketch by
M' W. Boscawen

W.H R   Hanhart imp.

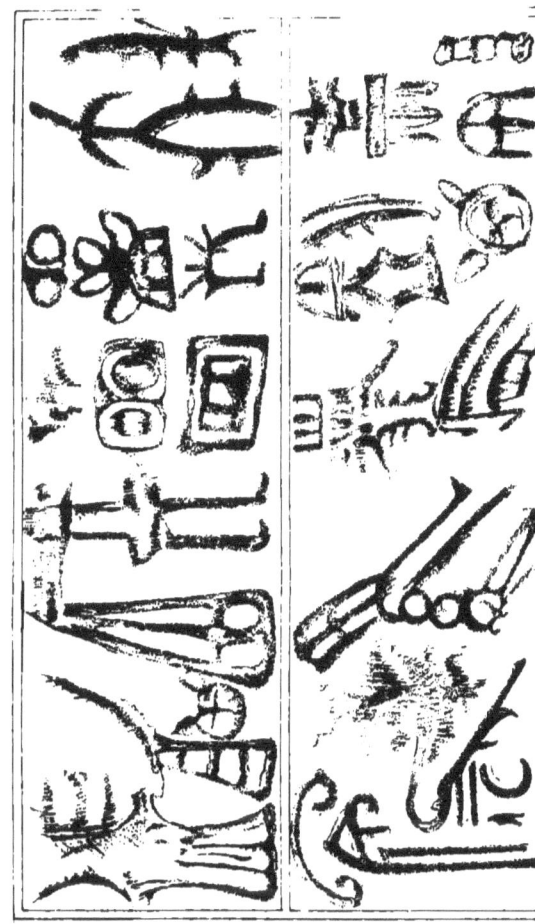

Fig 5 GENERAL CRAWFORD'S COPY OF THE ALEPPO INSCRIPTION

ALEPPO INSCRIPTION.

Fig 4. *From George Smith's Note Book, British Museum Add. Mss. 30423. p. 29*

The Empire of the Hittites

INSCRIPTION FROM JERABIS.

J.II. *Trans. Soc. Bibl. Arch. Vol. VII.*

Hanhart imp

J.III. INSCRIPTION ON THE B
FROM
Now in the

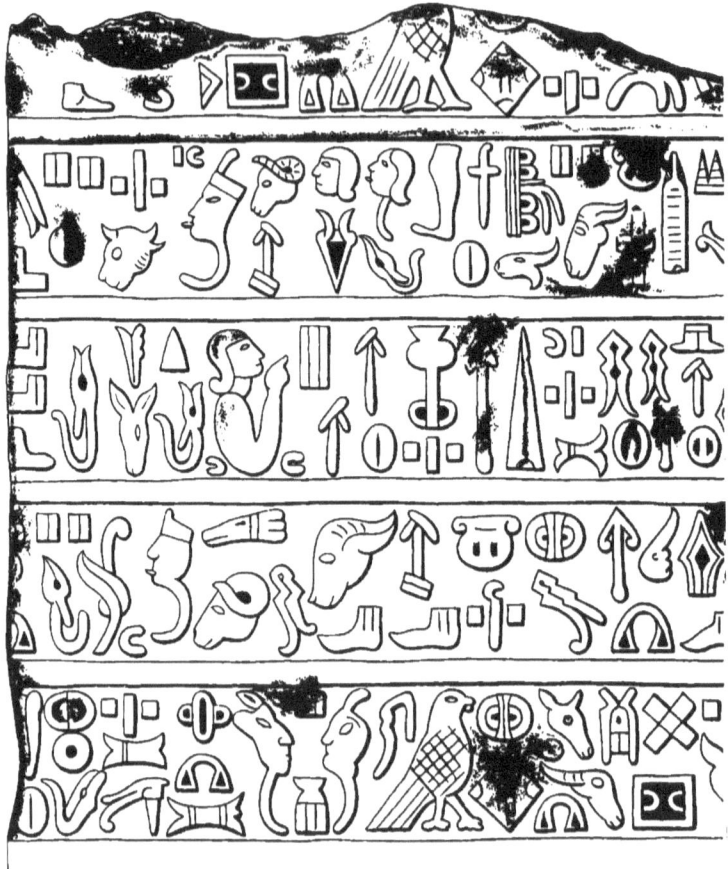

CK OF A BASALT FIGURE.
ERABIS.
ritish Museum.

Hanhart imp

Plate XI

INSCRIBED STONES FROM JERABIS.
J.IV. (Trans. Soc. Bibl. Arch. Vol. VI. Plate VI)

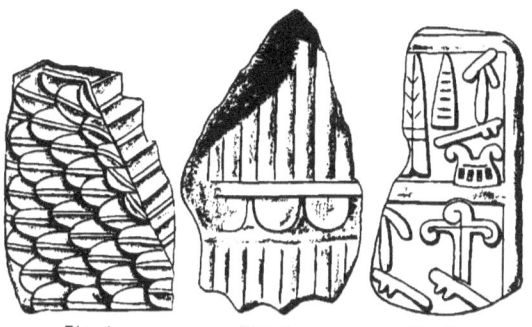

Fig. 1.   Fig. 2.   Fig. 3.

Fig. 4.

Plate XII.
The Empire of the Hittites

INSCRIBED STONES FROM JERABIS.
NOW IN THE BRITISH MUSEUM.

J.V. (Trans. Soc. Bibl. Arch. Vol. VII Plate IV.)

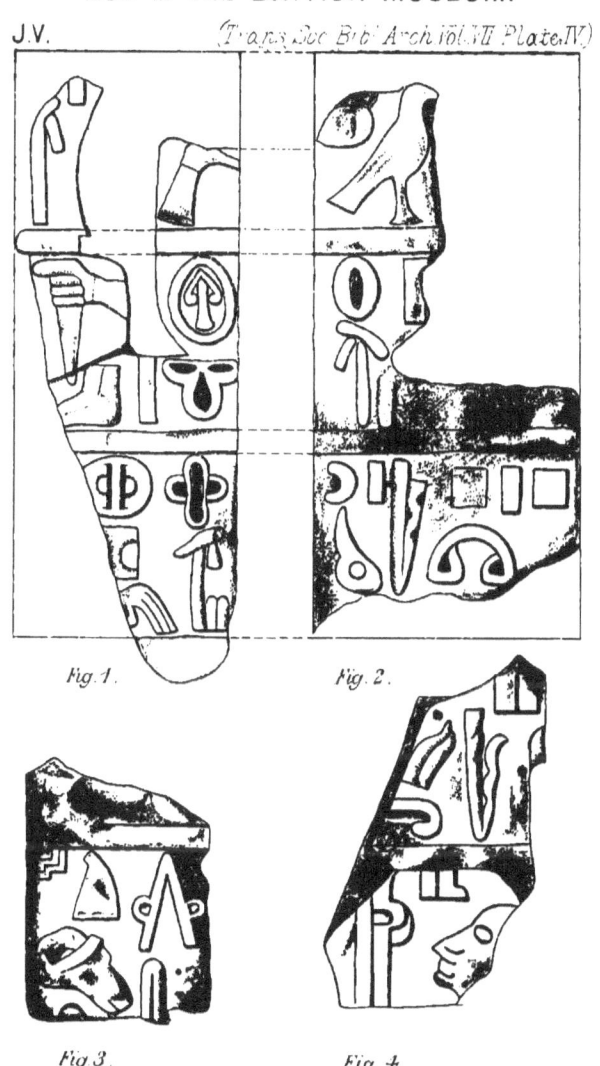

Fig. 1.   Fig. 2.

Fig. 3.   Fig. 4.

Hanhart imp.

Plate XIII.
The Empire of the Hittites

J.VI.   (Trans. Soc. Bibl. Arch. Vol. VII. Plate V)

Inscribed fragment
from Jerabis.
Now in the
British Museum.

Cartouche
on the Right-hand side
of the figure of
Niobe on Mount Sipylos
parallel with the head.
From a sketch by
A. H. Sayce.

SEALS DISCOVERED BY SIR A. H. LAYARD AT KOUYUNJIK, SEP., 1851.
Now in the British Museum.

1

2

3   4

5

6

7

8

W. H. Rylands, del.   Hanhart imp

The Empire of the Hittites

FIGURES FROM DRAWING BY Mʀ DAVIS IN TRANS. SOC. BIBL. ARCH.
SOME OF THE CHARACTERS IN THE INSCRIPTIONS
HAVE BEEN CORRECTED FROM SKETCHES BY Mʀ RAMSAY.

The Empire of the Hittites.

TYANA INSCRIPTION COPIED BY
Mʀ W M. RAMSAY.

TERRA-COTTA SEALS IN THE POSSESSION OF M SCHLUMBERGER PARIS ETC

THE PSEUDO SESOSTRIS.
CARVED ON THE ROCK IN THE PASS OF KARABEL,
FROM A PHOTOGRAPH.

Plate XIX
INSCRIBED STONES FROM JERABIS.

Plate XX.
INSCRIBED STONES FROM JERABIS, Etc.

THE SECOND PSEUDO-SESOSTRIS.
From a Sketch by A.H. Sayce.
Trans. Soc. Bibl. Arch. Vol. VII.

MONUMENT FROM JERABIS.
With Inscription J.III.
on the reverse side.

FROM JERABIS.
NOW IN THE BRITISH MUSEUM.

GREY LIMESTONE SEAL.
Found by Sir. A.H. Layard
at NINEVEH.
Proc. Soc. Bibl. Arch Vol. VI

CYLINDER from
Lajard, Culte de Mithra
Pl. XXIIJ. fig. 1.

Plate XXI.
INSCRIBED STONES FROM JERABIS.

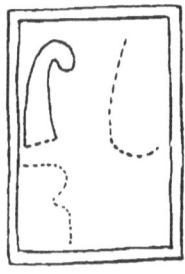  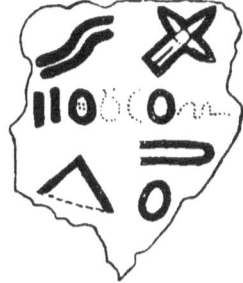

INSCRIPTIONS ON THE NIOBÊ, PUBLISHED BY ED. COLLOB. 1882.

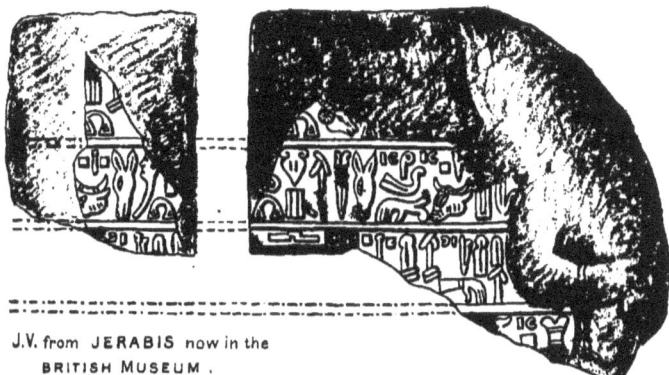

J.V. from JERABIS now in the BRITISH MUSEUM.

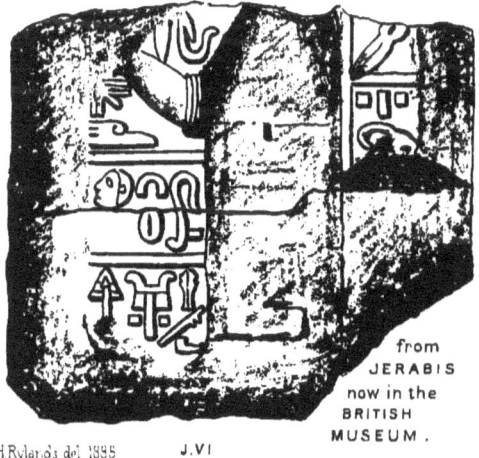

from JERABIS now in the BRITISH MUSEUM.

CARTOUCHES of RAMESES. II.

PLATE XXIII

TWO HEADED EAGLE OF EYUK.

(Galatie et Bithynie by Perrot & Guillaume Pl 68)

Plate XXVI
MARASH INSCRIBED LION - SIDE VIEW.

Plate XXVII
BACK & BREAST OF MARASH LION.

Expositions and Illustrations of Holy Scripture

Published by JAMES NISBET & CO.

AN EXPOSITION OF THE OLD AND NEW TESTAMENTS, wherein each Chapter is summed up in its Contents; the Sacred Text inserted at large in Distinct Paragraphs, each Paragraph reduced to its proper Heads; the Sense given, and largely Illustrated; with Practical Remarks and Observations. By MATTHEW HENRY. Nine Vols., Imp. 8vo, £2 2s.

THE HOLY BIBLE, CONTAINING THE OLD AND NEW TESTAMENTS. With Explanatory Notes, Practical Observations, and Copious Marginal References. By the Rev. THOMAS SCOTT, formerly Rector of Aston, Sandford, Bucks. A New Edition, with the Author's last Corrections and Improvements and 84 Illustrative Maps and Engravings. Six Vols., 4to. Reduced from Six Guineas to Thirty Shillings.

ANNOTATIONS ON THE BOOKS OF HOLY SCRIPTURE, wherein the Sacred Text is inserted, and various Readings annexed, together with the parallel Scripture; the most difficult Terms in each Verse are explained—seeming Contradictions reconciled—Questions and Doubts resolved—and the whole Text opened. By MATTHEW POOL. New Edition, Three Vols., Imp. 8vo, 31s. 6d.

AN EXPOSITORY AND PRACTICAL COMMENTARY ON THE BOOKS OF SCRIPTURE, arranged in Chronological Order. Being a BIBLE MANUAL. Translated from the German Work edited by the late Dr. C. G. BARTH, of Calw, Wurtemberg. Imp. 8vo, 12s.

AN EXPOSITORY COMMENTARY ON THE BOOK OF JUDGES. By the Rev. A. R. FAUSSET, M.A., Canon of York, Editor of Bengel's "Gnomon" in English, &c. Demy 8vo, 10s. 6d.

HORÆ PSALMICÆ. STUDIES IN THE CL. PSALMS: Their undesigned Coincidence with the Independent Scripture Histories Confirming and Illustrating Both. By the Rev. Canon FAUSSET. Second Edition. Demy 8vo, 10s. 6d.

SYNOPTICAL LECTURES ON THE BOOKS OF HOLY SCRIPTURE. By the Rev. DONALD FRASER, D.D. New and thoroughly Revised Edition. Two Vols., crown 8vo, 15s.

METAPHORS IN THE GOSPELS. A Series of Short Studies. By the Rev. DONALD FRASER, D.D. Crown 8vo, 6s.

A COMMENTARY ON LEVITICUS, Expository and Practical. With Critical Notes. By ANDREW A. BONAR, D.D. 8vo, 8s. 6d.

THE LAW OF THE OFFERINGS IN LEVITICUS. Considered as the Appointed Figure of the Various Aspects of the Offering of the Body of Jesus Christ. By ANDREW JUKES. Crown 8vo, 3s.

THE CHARACTERISTIC DIFFERENCES OF THE FOUR GOSPELS CONSIDERED, as Revealing Various Relations of the Lord Jesus Christ. By ANDREW JUKES. Crown 8vo, 2s. 6d.

THE TABERNACLE, PRIESTHOOD, AND OFFERINGS OF ISRAEL. By the Rev. F. WHITFIELD, M.A., Vicar of St. Mary's, Hastings. New Edition. With 22 Illustrations. Crown 8vo, 5s.

ZECHARIAH: His Visions and His Warnings. By W. LINDSAY ALEXANDER, D.D., late of Edinburgh. Crown 8vo, 6s.

Expositions and Illustrations of Holy Scripture—*Continued.*

THE GOSPEL PROMISES SHOWN IN ISAIAH 1–6. By Comparing Spiritual Things with Spiritual. By AGNES E. JONES. 16mo, 1s.

THE SONG OF SONGS. A Practical Exposition of the Song of Solomon. By the Rev. A. MOODY STUART, D.D. Crown 8vo, 6s.

THE SONG OF SOLOMON COMPARED WITH OTHER PARTS OF SCRIPTURE. By ADELAIDE NEWTON. Crown 8vo, 3s. 6d.

THE EPISTLE TO THE HEBREWS COMPARED WITH THE OLD TESTAMENT. By ADELAIDE NEWTON. Crown 8vo, 3s. 6d.

LIGHT AND TRUTH—BIBLE THOUGHTS AND THEMES. By HORATIUS BONAR, D.D. In Five Vols., Crown 8vo, 5s. each.

VOL 1. THE OLD TESTAMENT.	VOL. 4. THE LESSER EPISTLES.
" 2. THE GOSPELS.	
" 3. THE ACTS AND LARGER EPISTLES.	" 5. THE REVELATION OF ST. JOHN.

"Valuable work, well suited for private use or for family reading."—*Record.*

CHURCH AND HOME LESSONS from the Book of Hosea. For Family Reading. By the Rev. A. C. THISLETON. Crown 8vo, 5s.

WITH THE PROPHETS, JOEL, AMOS, AND JONAH. Being Church and Home Lessons from Three Minor Prophets. By the Rev. A. C. THISLETON. Crown 8vo, 4s.

AN EXPLANATORY AND PRACTICAL COMMENTARY ON THE NEW TESTAMENT. Intended Chiefly as a Help to Family Devotion. Edited by the late Rev. W. DALTON, B.D. Two Vols., demy 8vo, 24s.

THE APOCALYPSE: The Voice of Jesus Christ from the Throne of Glory. With an Exegetical and Practical Commentary. By the Rev. J. BAYLEE, D.D. Post 8vo, 9s.

THE APOCALYPSE. A Series of Special Lectures on the Revelation of Jesus Christ. With Revised Text. Three Vols., 8vo, 12s.

NIGHT SCENES OF THE BIBLE AND THEIR TEACHINGS. By the Rev. CHARLES D. BELL, D.D., Rector of Cheltenham, and Canon of Carlisle. Two Vols., crown 8vo, each 5s.

DAYS AND NIGHTS IN THE EAST; or, Illustrations of Bible Scenes. By HORATIUS BONAR, D.D. With Illustrations. Crown 8vo, 3s. 6d.

SCRIPTURE ITSELF THE ILLUSTRATOR: A Manual of Illustrations Gathered from Scriptural Figures, Phrases, Types, Derivations, Chronology, Texts, &c. By the Rev. G. S. BOWES, B.A. Small crown 8vo, 3s. 6d.

ILLUSTRATIVE TEXTS AND TEXTS ILLUSTRATED. By the Rev. J. W. BARDSLEY, D.D. Crown 8vo, 5s.

GLIMPSES THROUGH THE VEIL; or, Some Natural Analogies and Bible Types. By the Rev. J. W. BARDSLEY, D.D. Crown 8vo, 5s.

SCRIPTURAL STUDIES. By the Rev. CHARLES BRIDGES, M.A., Author of "Exposition of Psalm cxix.," &c. With Preface by the Right Rev. E. H. BICKERSTETH, D.D., Bishop of Exeter. Tenth Edition, crown 8vo, 2s. 6d.

London: JAMES NISBET & CO., 21 Berners Street.

www.ingramcontent.com/pod-product-compliance
Lightning Source LLC
Chambersburg PA
CBHW031433230426
43668CB00007B/521